DARK NOON

DARK NOON

THE FINAL VOYAGE
OF THE FISHING BOAT "PELICAN"

Tom Clavin

INTERNATIONAL MARINE / MCGRAW-HILL

Camden, Maine • New York • Chicago • San Francisco • Lisbon
London • Madrid • Mexico City • Milan • New Delhi • San Juan
Seoul • Singapore • Sydney • Toronto

The **McGraw·Hill** Companies

Visit us at: www.internationalmarine.com

1 2 3 4 5 6 7 8 9 DOC DOC 0 9 8 7 6 5

Library of Congress Cataloging-in-Publication Data
Clavin, Thomas.
 Dark noon : the final voyage of the fishing boat
 Pelican / Tom Clavin.
   p.   cm.
 ISBN 0-07-142300-1 (hardcover : alk. paper)
 1. Pelican (Fishing boat) 2. Charter boat fishing—
New York (State)—Montauk Point. 3. Shipwrecks—
New York (State)—Montauk Point.
I. Title.
G530.P415C53 2005
910'.9163'46—dc22   2005015439

Maps by International Mapping Associates

To the "Pacers":
Friends from fourth
grade on . . . and on.

AUTHOR'S NOTE

Events portrayed in this book are based on archival research, the report of the U.S. Coast Guard court of inquiry, over three dozen interviews, oral histories on audiotape, and contemporary and historical print accounts. I was especially fortunate to locate and interview, over a half century later, three of the nineteen surviving *Pelican* passengers. Their vivid recollections were invaluable.

No character in the book was invented, nor are there any composite characters. Neither is any scene "manufactured." In writing the book after two years of research, however, I drew upon the common practices and concerns of 1951 together with interviewees' impressions and observations to bridge a few small narrative gaps and to add texture to selected scenes. In particular, I augmented eyewitness accounts of survivors and rescuers with speculations of family members and other Montauk captains to provide more insight into Captain Eddie Carroll's words and thoughts as the *Pelican* plunged into trouble that day in 1951.

ACKNOWLEDGMENTS

The idea for this book was born on the fiftieth anniversary of the *Pelican* tragedy when I read an interview with Irene Stein in the September 1, 2001, edition of *Newsday,* a Long Island daily. Since then I have spoken to her and other people affected by what happened on the Saturday of Labor Day weekend in 1951. I must first thank those people who shared with me their painful memories, especially Irene Stein and her son John Stein Jr., Martin Berger, Angelo Testa Jr., Seymour Gabbin, and Rita Carroll.

This book is also the result of extensive research and interviews with members of the Montauk fishing fleet, onshore witnesses, family members, and others who had details to contribute. I am grateful to Bill Akin, John Badkin, Howard Barnes, John Behan, John Blindenhofer, Frank Borth, Chris Brown, Bob Byrnes, Henry Clemenz, Sonja Connors, Renee Carey, Lisa Cowley, Frank Dickinson, Bruce DiPietro, Wally Drobeck, Cynthia Dunwell, Perry Duryea Jr., Julie Evans, Paul Forsberg, Bradley Glass, Roberta and Emmitt Gosman, Vincent Grimes, Jesi Hannold, Raymond Hegner Jr., Patrick Henry, Jim Hewitt, Bob Kaelin, Carey London, Joe Luksic, Joe Marmo, George McTurck, Ed Miller, Jim Miller, Frank Mundus, Paul Pasqualini, Tony Prohaska,

Tom Rock, Frank Tuma Jr., Bob and Sybil Tuma, Stuart Vorpahl, B.J. Wilson, Mark Wysocki, and Ron Ziel.

I'd also like to thank Robin Strong and others at the Montauk Library, and the resources of the *East Hampton Star,* the *New York Times, Newsday,* the archives of other New York City dailies at the New York Public Library, the East Hampton Historical Society, the Montauk Historical Society, and the U.S. Coast Guard.

Thanks go also to my agent, Jennifer Unter of RLR Associates, for believing in this book and always being in my corner, and to my editor, Jonathan Eaton, for his diligent work in guiding it to port. Also chipping in with much-appreciated help were Kate Yeomans, author of *Dead Men Tapping: The End of the Heather Lynne II* and a longtime party fishing boat operator, and Walt Fields, Staff Commander in the U.S. Power Squadrons.

And I want to thank those whose support, encouragement, and help have meant a lot to me personally as well as to the writing of *Dark Noon.* Among them are Jon Bonfiglio, Heather Buchanan, Bob Drury and Denise McDonald, Michael Gambino, Harry Kohlmeyer, Kate Lawton, Kitty Merrill, Danny Peary, Rachel Pine, Allen Richardson, Tony Sales, Harold Shepherd, Hugh Wyatt, the gang at Nichol's, and especially my children, Kathryn and Brendan.

DARK NOON

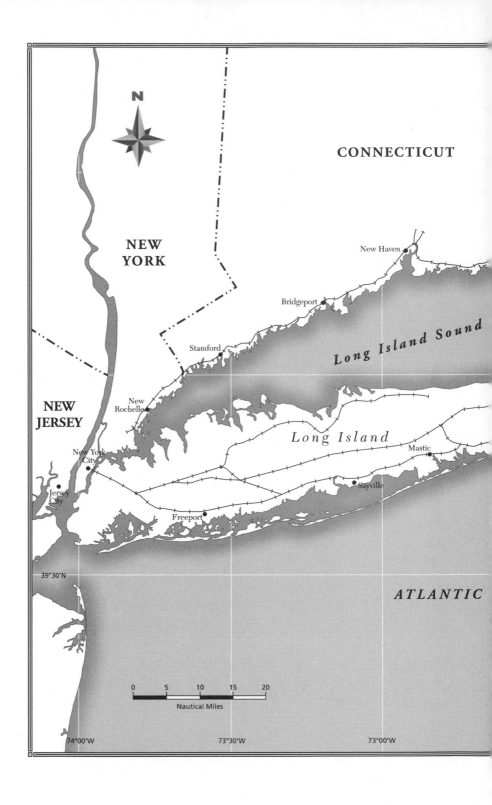

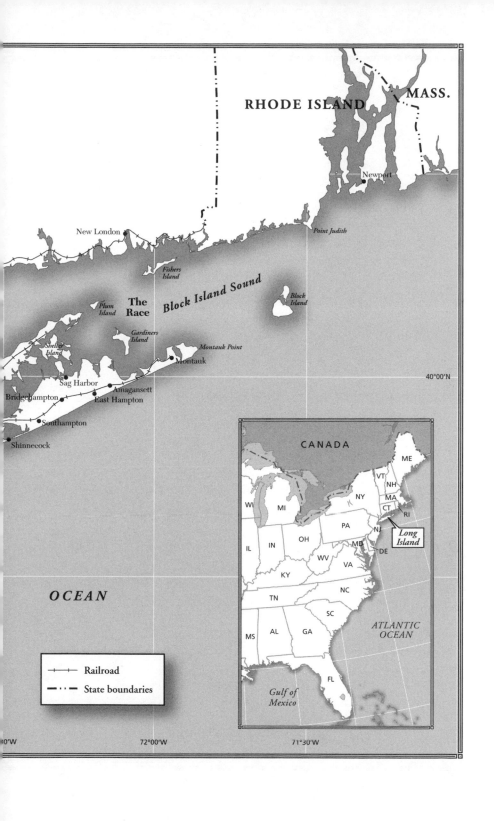

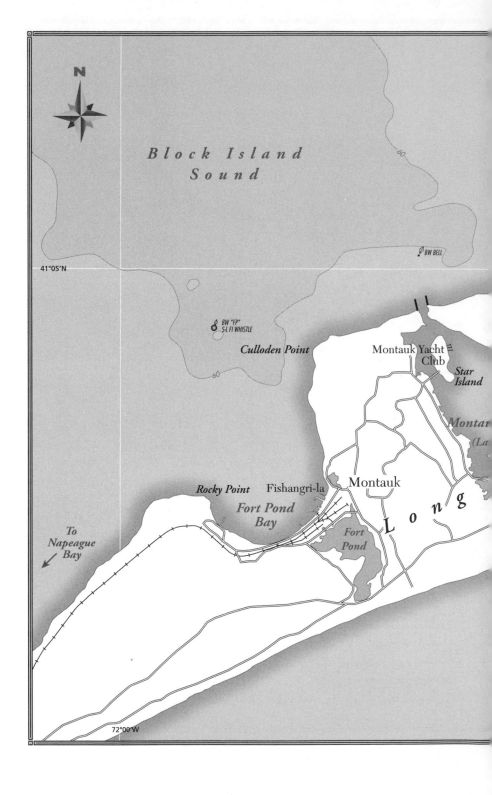

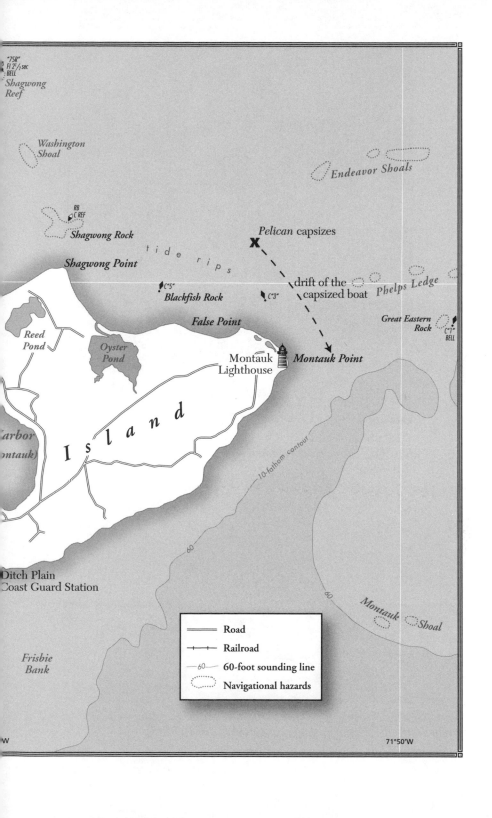

"7SR"
Fl 2¹⁄₂ sec
BELL
Shagwong
Reef

Washington
Shoal

Endeavor Shoals

RB
C REF
Shagwong Rock

Shagwong Point

t i d e   r i p s

Pelican capsizes

✕

drift of the
capsized boat

Phelps Ledge

C"5"
Blackfish Rock

C"3"

False Point

Great Eastern
Rock

C"1"
BELL

Reed
Pond

Oyster
Pond

Montauk
Lighthouse

Montauk Point

I   s   l   a   n   d

arbor
ontauk)

10-fathom contour

Ditch Plain
Coast Guard Station

60

60

Montauk   Shoal

Frisbie
Bank

	Road
┼┼┼	Railroad
—60—	60-foot sounding line
⬚	Navigational hazards

W

71°50'W

A rakish Captain Eddie Carroll aboard the Pelican *the week before the tragedy. He considered many of his passengers his friends.* (NEWS photo)

The Pelican *returning to Montauk from a previous fishing trip, with a manageable number of passengers aboard.* (Corbis)

Captain Eddie (arrow) and passengers before leaving Montauk on September 1. When the Fisherman's Special arrived, the dock filled with potential passengers. (William Morris, *Outdoor Life* magazine)

The heavily loaded Pelican *sets out on its last voyage, with anglers lining the railing.* (William Morris, *Outdoor Life* magazine)

The hull of the capsized Pelican *off the Montauk Lighthouse. Soon, Frank Mundus and Carl Forsberg would arrive to tow it.* (Corbis)

A rescue boat searches for survivors of the Pelican. *This photo was taken by David Edwardes from an airplane.* (David Edwardes/Corbis)

A rescue boat attempts to pick up survivors (hull is shown at lower right). By this time, however, the nineteen rescued would be the only survivors. (AP photo)

The crowd at Duryea's dock watches as the Pelican *is righted by rescue workers. Ten bodies were found inside the boat.* (Corbis)

A locker full of unused life preservers on the Pelican. Only one passenger, John Griffin, put on a life preserver; he survived. (Corbis)

The Pelican's *starboard side, which took the brunt of the waves.* (AP photo)

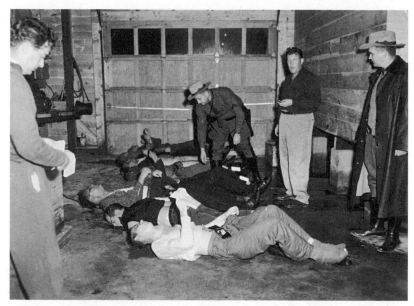

The makeshift morgue at Duryea's icehouse. There were more victims than the local funeral homes could accommodate. (Corbis)

Paul Manko weeps after identifying the body of his son, Wallace Manko, a twenty-three-year-old veteran of World War II. (Yale Joel/Time & Life Pictures/Getty Images)

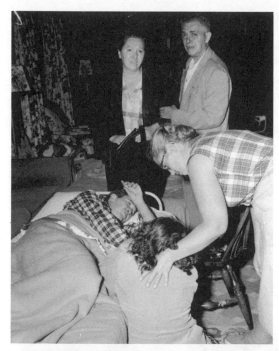

Angelo Testa Jr. is re-united with his mother and fiancée at the Montauk Yacht Club. His father did not sur-vive. (Corbis)

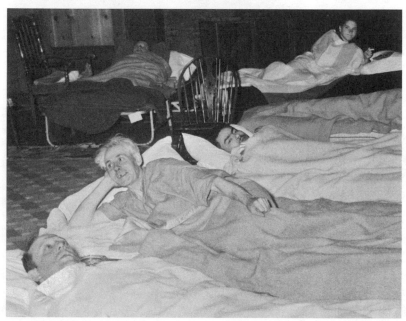

Antonio Borruso (head on hand), the nineteenth and oldest survivor of the disaster, recovers at the Montauk Yacht Club. (Corbis)

John Griffin, who was ridiculed for putting on a life jacket, displays his minor thumb injury. His wife had dreamed of a boat disaster and begged him not to go that day. (New York Daily News)

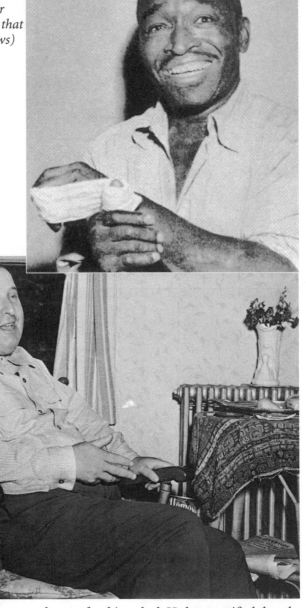

Max Stein relaxes at his summer home after his ordeal. He later testified that the Pelican *was badly overloaded.* (Corbis)

A Good Day for Fishing

The sea is everything. It covers seven tenths of the
terrestrial globe. Its breath is pure and healthy.
It is an immense desert, where man is never lonely,
for he feels life stirring on all sides.

20,000 Leagues Under the Sea,
JULES VERNE

On Tuesday, September 4, 1951, a board of investigation convened at the United States Coast Guard Third District headquarters, 80 Lafayette Street, Manhattan, to seek the causes of a tragic accident. On this sunny late-summer day, the meeting room's blinds were drawn against the glare and the noise of city traffic outside. Already it was stuffy in the crowded room, with all thirty or so chairs filled. Cigarette smoke drifted toward the ceiling. Some people murmured, some shifted impatiently but were quiet. A few, their faces pale and taut, stared straight ahead as if seeing terrifying images on the far wall.

A sudden silence cloaked the room when three men in dress whites entered from a side door. The men sat in straight-backed wooden chairs at a dark wooden table at the front of the room. The expanse of bare white wall behind them was broken by a stand bearing an American flag, only a dozen or so of its forty-eight stars visible.

Rear Admiral Louis B. Olson, commander of the Third District and one of the most experienced officers in the Coast Guard, occupied the middle seat at the table. To his right sat Captain John Roundtree, the district operations officer. To Olson's left was Captain Lewis H. Shackelford, the district marine safety officer. After chatting briefly among themselves, the officers rose, the signal for all present to stand and recite the Pledge of Allegiance.

Seated again, Olson and his colleagues surveyed the room. At the back were reporters and photographers. Every one of New York's dailies had sent someone to cover the inquiry's opening day. Olson disliked having photographers present—grieving family members deserved all the privacy he could afford them—but at least a deal had been worked out so that pictures would be taken only of those who testified.

Neither was he happy that it was already afternoon. The inquiry was to have begun at 10:30 A.M. sharp, but not one of the summoned witnesses had appeared by then. The morning had been wasted—an inauspicious beginning to what promised to be a difficult proceeding.

Between the officers' table and the press sat the survivors of the tragedy and their family members, the victims' family members, and witnesses called in from Montauk to testify. Survivors and victims' family members all wore dazed expressions, as though they were somewhere else.

Olson shuffled a short stack of papers in front of him on the table and cleared his throat. "We are here," he announced, "to conduct an inquiry into the circumstances surrounding the tragedy of the fishing boat *Pelican* this past Saturday."

Olson nodded to Commander Joseph De Carlo, seated on the other side of the table, next to two empty chairs—for the sequence of witnesses and their attorneys. De Carlo looked tired. He had spent much of the past seventy-two hours in Montauk supervising the Coast Guard investigation. "Call your first witness, Commander," Olson told him.

A man stood up. "If we could just wait for that, please," he said.

Olson scowled. "You are . . . ?"

"Joseph Meehan. I'm an attorney representing Captain Edward Carroll and the rest of the Carroll family."

"Mr. Meehan, this is a Coast Guard court of inquiry, not a criminal or civil trial."

"Yes, Admiral, I'm aware of that. I'm here to observe and then advise the Carroll family based on the testimony of others."

Olson looked at Shackelford, then Roundtree. Both shrugged slightly. Captain Carroll's family might, indeed, have reason to fear a deluge of civil suits, and they had a right to have an attorney present. Olson turned back to the lawyer, who had stepped closer to the table.

"Thank you, Mr. Meehan, for introducing yourself. Now we'll continue."

"Admiral Olson, I ask the court to empty the room of any persons representing the press."

"Why, Mr. Meehan?" Shackelford asked, irritation obvious in his voice.

"Sir, we don't know the contents of the testimony that will be given here, and how detailed it will be. Because of the tragic nature of the event being investigated . . ."

"Thank you, Mr. Meehan," Olson said. "We have already made an arrangement with the members of the press, and we're not inclined to change it."

"But Admiral, if I could . . ."

"Please resume your seat, Mr. Meehan."

As Meehan reluctantly stepped back, Olson collected his thoughts. The days of testimony ahead would, the admiral hoped, give them the answer—or answers—to the question of why sixty-four people went out into the Atlantic on the *Pelican*, and only nineteen came back. Olson nodded at De Carlo and repeated, "Call your first witness, Commander."

2

Though it was the easternmost point in New York State, Montauk was still dark at 4:30 A.M. on Saturday, September 1. It would be another half hour before the first tinge of pink began to define the seaward horizon for anyone awake and at the Montauk Lighthouse to see it.

The hamlet was stirring, though. Lights shone here and there at Fishangri-la, the whimsically named sportfishing mecca that included the Union News Dock, the Eat and Run coffee shop, a bar called Liar's Lair, and a tackle shop built into a former airplane hangar. The hangar had been stocked with torpedoes to be tested by the navy in Fort Pond Bay during the war, but the war had been over for six years, and Montauk, like America, had other business to pursue.

At the Eat and Run, cooks heated griddles for the charter boat captains and mates who would start swaying in at five o'clock. By 6 A.M., the coffee shop would be packed, every counter stool and table seat occupied. The air would be filled with the sounds of spitting bacon and percolating coffee, waitresses kidding groggy customers, the striking of matches, and pancake batter and scrambled eggs hitting hot metal griddles.

A brief lull would follow the departure of the charter boat boys at 6:30 to make the two-and-a-half-mile drive to Lake Montauk, from which a dredged channel gave access to Block Island Sound. The captains would board their customers there, then negotiate the channel and head twenty miles or so out into the Atlantic. It wasn't exactly offshore fishing, but it was plenty deep and far enough out for greenhorn and experienced customers alike. Then the lull would end as the open-boat captains filtered in. These men would have until 7:30 to savor breakfast and coffee, because their business wouldn't start until the Fisherman's Special train from New York City pulled in. Then all hell would break loose.

After periodic setbacks, Montauk had finally made it as both a commercial and recreational fishing capital of the country. Its big wooden draggers, eighty to ninety feet long, could pursue herring and groundfish hundreds of miles into the Atlantic, although they often didn't have to go that far. They returned regularly with holds full of fish, which were packed in wooden boxes, as though in ice-lined coffins, and shipped by train to the city. Although Montauk's draggers had always done all right, even during the grinding Depression and the long war that followed it, now—in the summer of 1951—recreational fishing was hot, and anglers from the city could find plenty of it in even half a day at Montauk.

Leisure-time fishing was a lot younger than commercial fishing in Montauk. During the 1920s, people from up-island and New York City had begun arriving by automobile with rods and tackle boxes and brown-paper-bag lunches, asking for the chance to go out on the draggers to catch whatever was running that week. Some of the dragger captains, such as Frank Tuma Sr. on the *Junior*, would let them fish off the stern during one-day trips. Later the Union News Dock, built on Fort Pond Bay in the late 1920s, allowed anglers to put out in small boats or simply fish off the dock.

In the early '30s a few dragger captains, hedging their bets in a plummeting economy, had refitted their boats for charters. Among the pioneers were brothers Frank and Charlie Tuma, Gus Pitts, Harry Conklin, Carl Ericcson, and Henry Sweeting. Not all of New York high society was broke, and with charter prices so low anyway—in 1932, Gus Pitts was charging $18 for his boat for an entire day—the Montauk captains did a steady business. (By the time Pitts retired in the late 1950s, his rate would be $100 a day.)

One by one, captains built houses and brought their wives and children out from the boroughs and Nassau County to live full-time in Montauk. The houses were small wooden structures, not much more than shacks, expanded and improved year by year as cash permitted. Many families built on the south side of Fort Pond Bay, on the two-and-a-half-mile-long spit of land that separated the bay from Fort Pond and carried the Long Island Rail Road (LIRR) tracks and a parallel dirt road. When a couple married, they built their own shack on the next available open lot on the beach.

For a time this settlement was the center of Montauk. Shops sprang up along with icehouses, fish markets, and a post office. There was even a schoolhouse, where the hundred or so families sent their younger children until they were old enough to ship as a mate on a boat or find fishing-related work shoreside to augment the family income. It was, in a way, like homesteading on the prairie 1,500 miles to the west, with fish instead of fields to tend. By 1951, most of the charter captains were sons or grandsons of those firstcomers, berthing their boats next to the Montauk Yacht Club on Lake Montauk.

Whereas the charter captains hired out to small parties by the day or half day, "open" or "head" boat captains charged their passengers individually. Open-boat fishing was a post–World War II development in Montauk, offering—from the Fishangri-la docks on Fort Pond Bay—a less expensive, more informal fishing experience for a blue-collar market than the charter facilities in Lake Montauk, over two miles east. The opening of Fort Pond Bay to Block Island was two miles wide, which made navigation easy for pleasure and fishing boats, and the high bluffs ringing the bay provided shelter from the southerly gales that buffeted Montauk's Atlantic side. It took a few minutes longer for a boat leaving Fort Pond Bay to round the Montauk Lighthouse and venture into the Atlantic, but that was all right with customers if they could enjoy a whole day of fishing for only a few bucks, even on summer weekends.

So at 4:30 A.M. this Labor Day Saturday, the head boats awaited the arrival of the Fisherman's Special, still hours away. The train would pull in at the Union News Dock, and disgorged passengers would have their choice of boats to board—first come, first served, no reservations. There were always at least a dozen open boats tied up at Fishangri-la, sometimes as many as twenty.

Frank Tuma Jr., a second-generation charter captain, maintained gently that the choice between open boat and charter was "whatever the captain preferred to do." But the fact was that the established captains—many of them sailing alongside or having taken over from their fathers—preferred chartering because they didn't want to share their income with Fishangri-la or deal with the mob craziness when the Fisherman's Special arrived. They could afford to be independent, having built up a client list for a quarter century. But a skipper new to the area, having arrived since the end of the war, positioned himself as an open boat at Fishangri-la; it took years to build a good reputation and a steady charter business.

As dawn approached, a few workers carrying lanterns hosed down the Fishangri-la docks. Every few minutes, streaks of headlights piercing the dark signaled the arrival of more charter captains and mates, the bobbing red glows of their cigarettes marking their progress from cars to coffee shop. Later, when the head-boat skippers began their breakfast shift, some would simply stagger up the dock from their boats, where they slept. Houses, money in the bank, community standing—that was what many head-boat skippers hoped to find in the pot at the end of the Montauk rainbow.

3

Word on the docks for Saturday, September 1, was that striped bass would be in good supply for the charter boats and porgies for the open boats, thousands more of them than there would be hooks to snare them. Chances looked good for tuna and cod too. Unfortunately, sharks might also be caught. Sharks were a nuisance: no one wanted to eat them; it was nerve-racking when they came near; and sometimes they cruised along under the boats snapping up bait and snipping off lines and hooks in the process. (One of the head-boat skippers, Frank Mundus, had just begun to think about pursuing sharks with charter customers as a way of graduating from the head-boat business. Eight years later, he would be making a success of that idea.)

The 1951 summer season had been a good one. Just the previous Sunday, Captain Bill Reichert, on the charter boat *Kingfisher*, had sailed into a large school of tuna. The day before, a charter customer on the *Fortenate*, captained by Carl Darenberg, had hooked a blue marlin. The 700-pound monster had fought for four hours. Leaping and diving, it had taken the boat another twenty miles into the Atlantic. Bad luck, though: the fifteen-thread line gave up before the marlin did, and the mighty fish got away. The *Margaret III*, captained by Ralph Pitts, had begun the Montauk Yacht Club Invitational Tournament by catching a 315-pound mako shark. Sure, sharks were a nuisance, but a mako that big was a trophy catch. The next day, the same boat hauled in a 390-pound tuna. And on the third day, an angler on the *El Pescador*, skippered by John Sweeting, fought and landed a 531-pound tuna. Within weeks, a charter customer on the *Scamp II*, captained by Buster Raynor, would set a record with a 961-pound tuna. On the last full weekend in August, all the charter boats in Lake Montauk had been hired out.

There always seemed to be good luck to go around for those fishing aboard the *Pelican* with Eddie Carroll. On Thursday he had hosted a busload of people from Sayville, up-island, one of whom was Mrs. Sadie Schelzo. Off went the *Pelican*, and when the boat hove-to, the anglers dropped their lines. Sadie hooked bottom—or so she thought because of the way her rod bent when she pulled up.

But Eddie knew better. He helped Sadie reel in, and sure enough there was some give, then some more, and the battle was on. The stubborn and inspired Sadie knew she had something, but what a discovery it was when the fish came into view over the side. She was fishing two hooks on one line, and she had a big cod on each.

As Sadie gave a last heave, the line parted, but Eddie and his mate each had a gaff ready, and they snagged both fish. One weighed "only" seventeen pounds, the other twenty-eight. The *East Hampton Star*, the local weekly, predicted that the Schelzo family would be eating cod until Halloween.

All this boded well for anglers and their chosen boats on the first full day of the Labor Day weekend. Six years after the war, people in the New York City area were doing okay—making a living while building modest but comfortable houses in modern subdivisions such as Levittown. The postwar baby boom was still under way, and it seemed as though everyone's neighbor was bringing home a television to watch the Milton Berle comedy show and the Douglas Edwards news reports. There was some worry about the boys getting killed and wounded over in Korea, but the consensus was that the war was going pretty well so far, as long as the Chinese didn't decide to pour over the hills by the millions.

On this Saturday morning ushering in September, the breeze freshened a bit, heralding dawn, but it remained from the southwest, a sign of settled summer weather. The forecast that Gene Goble, owner and dockmaster of Fishangri-la, had tacked to the bulletin board just outside his office the evening before was still there:

> A cold front north of Toronto is moving toward this area and should reach Montauk early Saturday afternoon. We will have increasing south-southwest winds as the front approaches this area, and the maximum will be reached early in the afternoon, at which time we may have south-southwest winds, 25 to 35 miles per hour. We can see possibly, even

storm activity during that period with winds shifting during the early evening to northwest, diminishing, however, to 15 to 20 miles per hour. The winds will continue to shift during Saturday night to the north, bringing a dry cold into this area. Sky conditions during Saturday night and Sunday morning should be overcast, and partly cloudy during Sunday. Winds Sunday are forecast to be north-northeast, 15 to 20 miles per hour. Visibility Sunday will be good.

The forecast was good—not great, but it would allow for a decent day of fishing. The cold front itself wouldn't arrive until late afternoon, and the fresh south-southwest winds ahead of it would probably build slowly, giving boats plenty of time to retreat from the Atlantic to the sheltered waters north of Montauk Point. From there, the four-mile run back to Montauk Harbor (or, for the head-boat captains, the six-mile run back to Fort Pond Bay) would all be in flat water under a lee. A few rough seas south or east of the point might make some passengers queasy, but many of the anglers this Saturday would be regulars, and they had experienced worse. By the time any strong winds out of the northwest arrived behind the cold front, the boats would be back at the dock.

Satisfied with the forecast, the charter captains spat their cigarette butts into the dark, oily water of the harbor and headed for breakfast.

4

New York City subways never slept, and thus were the best way to get to Penn Station to catch a feeder train leaving at 5:15 A.M. Depending on where the anglers lived, heading to Montauk that Saturday meant that they left their homes between 3:30 and 4:30 A.M., groggy with sleep but already imagining heavy fish at the ends of their lines.

Most carried a tackle box in one hand and a rod and reel and a lunchbox or paper bag in the other. Inside the bag might be a thermos of coffee and a homemade egg sandwich, a buttered roll, or a couple of doughnuts for breakfast. You could buy food on the docks in Montauk, but that was a good three hours away. By then, the fishermen would be buying sandwiches for lunch out on the Atlantic, or just beer, or not stopping to buy anything at all so they could get a spot on their favorite boat before it filled up. A few of the travelers carried flasks of whiskey, bourbon, or scotch, but those were tucked inside belts and rear pants pockets.

It was still dark in New York City at 4:30 A.M., and the anglers walking to catch a subway had the streets to themselves except for the occasional drunk staggering home from an all-night binge. The buses were running but sounded far away, offering just a fleeting glimpse as they whined through intersections. A few streetlights, the occasional all-night coffee shop, and milk truck headlights provided the only illumination.

Anglers from the Bronx and New Jersey had the farthest to go, maybe none farther than John Carlson. At fifty, his hair was still black and combed straight back above his lean, square-jawed face. He and his family lived at the Metropolitan Oval in the northern section of the Bronx. His wife, Edith, and his children, Robert and Muriel, were asleep when he slipped out. He liked the streets at night, and as a New York City police captain he had little to fear. Maybe after five more years with the Confidential Squad, he would retire, and then he could fish as much as he wanted. Also traveling from the Bronx this dark Saturday morning was Stanley McKeegan, a police sergeant who was hurrying to meet up with Captain Carlson at Penn Station.

Some of the regulars from Alfie's Tavern, at the corner of St. Raymond and St. Peter streets in the Bronx, half slept through their subway ride down to Penn Station. There was Frank Rubano, William Mellardo, John Vallone, and Vallone's brother-in-law Stanley Olszewski, all young men who just a few hours before had answered last call. At 300 pounds, Stanley was the biggest. All four men were hoping for a spot on the *Pelican*.

Members of the Friedel family took the train to the city from their home in Waldwick, New Jersey. John Friedel, fifty-eight, was a patrolman on the Erie Railroad police force in Jersey City. His wife, Helen, fifty-one, also worked for the railroad, as a payroll clerk. She hated to miss a fishing trip. The couple was going to meet William Friedel, John's younger brother, and William's son, twelve-year-old Richard, in Montauk. Bill was driving out there from his home in Moriches, Long Island.

John and Irene Stein moved quietly about the small, dimly lit kitchen of their third-floor apartment in the Greenpoint section of Brooklyn. Irene wrapped sandwiches for her husband and her father, Andrew Kolesar, and John's brother Rudolph. Though only twenty-five, Irene had been married to John for six years. She'd been immediately impressed by the handsome, charming war hero just returned home in 1945. John had fought in four European campaigns and was wounded on the beach during the Anzio invasion.

When John and Irene first met in Brooklyn, he had read her palm. She was amazed at how detailed and accurate his reading was. Only after they were engaged did he reveal that he had asked her friends about her in advance of that first meeting. She might well have married him anyway, but the icing on the wedding cake for Irene was the long, beautiful letter John wrote to her from a Staten Island hospital, where he was undergoing surgery to remove shrapnel.

Six years later, everything was working out well for them. Their two young children, John Jr. and Judy, were healthy and happy, and that morning were still asleep in their beds. John's two brothers—Adolph was the other one—were like her own brothers, and Rudy and his wife, Lola, and their four children lived right downstairs.

When it was time to go, Irene kissed her husband and wished him good luck, then did the same for her father. He had surprised them the day before, showing up from Passaic, New Jersey, for a weekend visit. When they left, she could hear their footsteps on the stairway. She leaned out the window that overlooked Kingsland Avenue and blew kisses to John when he appeared in a streetlight's yellow glow, accompanied now by Rudy, who had waited downstairs. John turned, waved, and grinned, then hurried off to catch up with his brother and father-in-law.

Irene worried a little about her father, because being on the water made him nervous. She almost wished that John hadn't talked him into this trip. But with John and Rudy there, she thought that nothing bad could happen. Anyway, as her father had said last night, "I'm fifty-six years old, and it's about time I started to live." They would be on the *Pelican*, and the Stein brothers had been on the boat before.

Armas Dolk, a forty-seven-year-old cab driver, probably had the easiest trip to Penn Station. He left his apartment on East 63rd Street, walked a block to Lexington, then four blocks south to 59th Street, caught the express to Grand Central, then took the #7 two stops to Penn Station.

Most of the city had emptied out the day before the holiday weekend, with railroads, airlines, and bus companies reporting capacity traffic. By 7 P.M. on Friday, New Jersey–bound traffic at the Manhattan end of the Holland Tunnel had been backed up in a seven-block-long jam. Authorities reported that the Lincoln Tunnel had experienced its busiest day since opening in 1937. Then the crowds had dwindled, and the subways and train stations had been quiet most of the night. But at Penn Station, the feeder train for the Fisherman's Special was waiting.

5

Even those who had ridden on it before the war didn't know much about how the Fisherman's Special had come to be, or that it was the latest in a line of "cannonball" trains aimed at the eastern end of Long Island.

Austin Corbin had had the cannonball idea first. In 1881 the wealthy New York banker was appointed president of the Long Island Rail Road, a venture that had seemed like a bright idea a few years before but had since gone bankrupt.

To correct that, Corbin was forced to use a lot of his own money, and he almost went broke himself. Then he concocted a dream of Montauk as the port of entry and departure for ships to and from Europe. He pictured placid, open-mouthed Fort Pond Bay accommodating dozens of oceangoing liners, the surrounding hills dotted with custom-built houses. Trains would carry the passengers to and from Manhattan, and there would no longer be a need for the laborious, time-consuming, expensive docking of large passenger ships in New York Harbor.

Corbin poured still more of his money into the dream, including paying $11,000 for a right-of-way to Arthur W. Benson, who had created the Bensonhurst residential neighborhood in Brooklyn and in 1879 bought much of the available land in Montauk. Benson had sensed a good investment, and when Corbin opened his wallet, he was proved right. The rails were extended another twenty-one miles from Bridgehampton to Montauk, and after numerous and expensive difficulties, the first train pulled into the new Montauk station on December 17, 1895.

The dream of a major port never materialized; Corbin died soon after the rails reached Montauk, and his vision sank underground with him. But the "Hamptons," as the South Fork of Long Island was beginning to be called by vacationers and the press, was growing as a summer colony, and people in New York City took to trains—especially express trains—as a reasonably convenient and speedy way of getting there.

Wealthy New York families took root in Southampton first, in the 1870s. They built houses and bathing clubs on the beach. In 1885 the newly opened Southampton Racquet Club became a sports and social center. In 1891, many of these same families founded the Shinnecock Hills Golf Club, the first incorporated golf club in the United States. In 1896, the pattern repeated itself in East Hampton with the opening of the Maidstone Golf Club.

There followed a succession of trains dubbed the "cannonball," all doing basically the same thing, which was to roar past stations that were active during the week but empty on weekends until they reached Southampton, Bridgehampton, and finally the communities of East Hampton Town, strung southwest to northeast like beads along twenty miles of Atlantic beachfront: first East Hampton Village, then the unincorporated hamlets of Amagansett and—last of all—Montauk, the Atlantic outpost. The trains included parlor cars with carpeting and overstuffed chairs, chandeliers dangling from the ceiling, and black porters serving food and beverages.

Then came the Depression.

One of the dozen morning and afternoon papers in New York City at the time, the *Daily Mirror*, a tabloid that claimed to have the city's highest circulation, had the idea of keeping a cannonball service going for a very different clientele. Montauk, after all, was New York's last stop before Ireland or Portugal, and between the two was an ocean teeming with fish.

So the newspaper and the LIRR, which was again at the point of trying anything, this time without Austin Corbin to bail it out, created the Fisherman's Special, a cannonball for the working man who wanted to go after the really big fish—fish you couldn't find off Rockaway, Sheepshead Bay, Coney Island, or the Battery. Well, maybe you could find *some* in those closer waters, but the numbers and sizes off Montauk were much more impressive.

The new train service struggled during the Depression; little except the New Deal could get traction in those years. Then came World War II, and the main object of pursuit off Montauk was German submarines. One of them actually put six Nazis ashore at Amagansett in June 1942 intent on blowing up the airbase and radar station at Montauk. (The six saboteurs were caught, tried, and imprisoned, and their two leaders were executed.) More than sixty years later, the underground recesses of the airbase would rival those at Roswell, New Mexico, as a center of extraterrestrial investigations.

But when the long war was over, and the soldiers and sailors came home, America experienced a postwar economic boom. Plenty of Joes and a few Janes were making a decent buck and enjoying weekends free to boot. It was time for some of them to fish the now-friendly Atlantic Ocean, and to get there fast.

During the war the navy had built a rail spur to the docks at Fort Pond Bay. Whether from courtesy, bureaucratic oversight, or benign neglect, the spur was left intact when the navy left. Now trains could unload passengers only a couple of hundred feet from waiting open boats.

The Fisherman's Special was special, all right. You couldn't beat the price—$2.75 for the three-hour trip to Montauk and return on Fridays, Saturdays, and Sundays during the fishing season. The train originated at the Jamaica station in Queens, where the feeder train from Penn Station stopped and passengers from Manhattan, Queens, Staten Island, Brooklyn, and the Bronx made a mad dash across platforms to secure seats on the Special. The train could seat more than three hundred in comfort, but on holiday weekends it could—and did—take close to four hundred with standing room. Getting a seat on the Special was a merciless exercise; if you weren't alert, or if you stumbled or otherwise found yourself in the back of the stampede, you could wind up taking a lonely train back to Penn Station or standing all the way to Montauk. Fortunately, this was before the electrification of the Jamaica station, because more than one bumbling angler had been known to wind up on the tracks between platforms, rubbing the bump on his head or the knot in his back.

For the ones who made it aboard, though, the Special was part boxcar and part clubhouse. As the train headed east in the cool, breezy darkness of a summer morning, fishing friendships and rivalries were renewed, passengers slept or played cards or read the early editions, and everyone envisioned hooking the biggest fish the waters off Montauk could offer.

6

Eddie Carroll's mate, Robert "Bobby" Scanlon, was the first witness at 80 Lafayette Street on the afternoon of September 4. He was a slight, slim twenty-three-year-old man with a narrow, clean-shaven face and dark, thin hair combed back from a high forehead. He wore a brown shirt buttoned up to the collar, with the sleeves rolled up. He sat down across from the panel members and raised his right hand while Captain Shackelford swore him in.

Scanlon appeared rattled. He was young—though older than many of the Montauk mates. When he spoke, he struggled to complete sentences. The three-member Coast Guard panel took turns questioning him.

COURT: Please state your address.

SCANLON: 1410 Parkchester Road, in the Bronx.

COURT: Not Montauk?

SCANLON: Yes, sir, I live in Montauk now, but not in any one place for long. The Bronx is the last place I lived for a while. Still get some mail there.

COURT: Mr. Scanlon, you were the first mate on the fishing boat *Pelican* on September 1, 1951 . . . this past Saturday.

SCANLON: Yes, sir.

COURT: Is being a first mate your full-time occupation?

SCANLON: No, sir.

COURT: What is your occupation, Mr. Scanlon?

SCANLON: Most of the year, I'm a short-order cook and counter person around Montauk.

COURT: Any particular restaurant?

SCANLON: Not really. Here and there, whatever's open.

COURT: During the fishing season . . . ?

SCANLON: I mate on boats. The captains know me. Captain Eddie always asked for me.

COURT: Do you have a seaman's license, Mr. Scanlon?

SCANLON: No, sir.

COURT: So you do not have a license to operate a fishing craft?

SCANLON: No, sir, I do not.

Commander Joseph De Carlo interrupted to explain for the record that Coast Guard regulations required no such license for a mate on a fishing boat of the *Pelican*'s size. Had he been asked, Scanlon could have explained that few mates were licensed. Who needed a license to bait a hook, gaff a fish, sell beer, mop vomit and fish guts from a deck, or free a clogged toilet? Some mates were as young as sixteen—a few even younger—though admittedly these were mostly sons of the captains they served. If asked, Scanlon might have said that captains complained constantly of how hard it was to find and retain a reliable mate. Young men dropped in and out of the pool of Montauk mates, lured by the prospects, repelled by the work. Those who lasted more than a few trips were considered experienced, and the best of them commanded good money. If pressed, Scanlon might have admitted that he was not one of the top mates—the press would portray him as adequate at best. But Eddie had liked Bobby; maybe, too, Eddie liked paying him less than top dollar.

The questioning continued.

COURT: Mr. Scanlon, what is your experience on boats?

SCANLON: I've fished on small boats and have been around fishing boats for about twelve years.

COURT: Do you have any formal training as a boat operator?

SCANLON: When I was in the army, sir, I attended a mechanics school.

COURT: Did it include marine engines?

SCANLON: No, sir.

COURT: During the last twelve years that you've been around fishing boats, how much of that was in Montauk?

SCANLON: Just this year, sir.

COURT: You have not been a mate on a boat out of Montauk before?

SCANLON: No, sir.

COURT: Is it fair to say that you were a short-order cook until April or May, and then for the first time you were a mate on fishing boats out of Montauk?

SCANLON: Yes, sir.

7

The sky was barely brightening, yet the train platform at the Jamaica station in Queens was full, the smell of cigarettes and hot coffee strong. The more experienced riders had known automatically what platform to catch the Fisherman's Special on, and the first-timers had wandered over to where the crowd carrying tackle boxes and fishing rods was gathering.

Several people had taken the train from Brooklyn to Jamaica. Alvin Brown, a forty-six-year-old driver for the Hartford Transportation Truck Company, was accompanied by his nephew, George Wallace. Charles Knight was sixty-two, a maintenance man for the city's subway system, and here he was on a Labor Day Saturday taking a train—a real busman's holiday. The same could be said for Patrick O'Brien, a shipping clerk at the Pennsylvania Railroad for forty years.

Others from Brooklyn included Gordon Sellons, Charles Drew, Robert Lawrence, Raymond Lewis, and Theodore Ogburn. Fourteen-year-old John Furness was on his first big Montauk fishing trip, accompanied by his grandfather, Harold Hertzberg.

There were passengers from Queens, too, who had taken the subway to the Jamaica platform. One was Frank Laurenzana, a watchmaker. Wallace Manko, a mason, was twenty-three and had a wife and baby son at home, but he would dedicate this Saturday to fishing. Edmund White of Corona was looking to use up all his bait on hungry fish.

Queens resident James Hyslop rarely missed a Saturday of fishing. At seventy-five, he was one of the oldest fellows on the train. He sat next to veterans of World War II or even World War I, and did their ears open when he told them of his experiences fighting in the Spanish-American War. What Hyslop looked forward to was telling tales and fishing on a Saturday. He'd been a planner for years at the Brooklyn Navy Yard, then his wife died, and they didn't have children. Saturday was the best day of his week.

Antonio Borruso, an immigrant from Italy, traveled to Montauk almost every weekend. Costas Candalanos was an open-boat veteran too. Brothers Solomon and Victor Finkelberg, both jewelers and on opposite sides of forty, were a bit disappointed; the night before, their brother, Alexander, had decided not to join them. They'd invited their neighbor, Frank Laurenzana, to take his place.

Conversation floated over the train platform in fits and starts.

Several of the waiting passengers had caught an early movie the night before. A couple of films had opened, neither of them destined to be a classic, but they offered marquee stars and passed the time well enough. Ray Milland, Jan Sterling, and Gene Lockhart were featured in *Rhubarb*, about a stray cat who was willed $30 million and a baseball team. Seeing Milland in this fluff, it was hard to believe that he was only six years away from winning the Best Actor Oscar for *The Lost Weekend*.

As the anglers compared notes, it seemed that the Western was the better flick. *Passage West* featured John Payne as the tough-guy leader of a gang of jail busters who tried to escape the law by taking over a wagon train full of religious settlers. The Holy Rollers were getting the worst of it until Dennis O'Keefe came to their rescue. It was not that believable, but it had good scenes, and it was interesting to see Dooley Wilson, the piano player from *Casablanca*, in a Western. *The Frogmen*, with Richard Widmark, had been popular all summer and was still playing.

Conversations stopped as the Fisherman's Special pulled up to the platform, rolling in from a darkened side track, chuffing like a great bull, its clouds of white smoke promising a memorable day to come. But sadly for those waiting—perhaps from considerations of fairness—the Fisherman's Special would not be open to its passengers until the feeder train from Penn Station arrived. This stipulation created more last-minute chaos, but that was the way the Long Island Rail Road did things.

So the train waited, breathing, while its would-be passengers tried to ignore it.

A few in the assembling crowd probably discussed having watched or marched in the big parade a few days earlier in Manhattan. Organized by the Veterans of Foreign Wars, the parade had attracted more than 150,000 onlookers, perhaps due to the expanding conflict in Korea. The marching ranks of uniforms and costumes started at Fifth Avenue and 63rd Street and just kept going and going, beginning at 5:30 in the afternoon and not ending until 9:30, well past dark. The biggest cheers were for former General of the Army

Douglas MacArthur, the official reviewing officer, every time he tipped his cap or lifted his hand in a salute.

Some of the waiting passengers might have discussed with awe the stunning rescue in Wales of two explorers three days earlier. The victims had become trapped in a flooded underground cave, and it took a chain of eighty-five men to reach them and get them out. Very likely, however, no one could pronounce Ogof Ffyddu, where the rescue had taken place.

A few on the platform must have lamented missing out on the pennant race in order to go fishing. With twenty-seven games to play, the Yankees were only a game ahead of the Cleveland Indians and four and a half games in front of the Red Sox. Some must have pondered whether the great Joe DiMaggio would retire after the season; he'd been dropping hints about that. Anglers from Brooklyn, of course, were more worried about the way the New York Giants were gaining on their Dodgers in a race that might come down to the final game.

President Truman was going to be at the Yankees game that day, a special game against the Senators at Griffith Stadium in Washington, D.C. What made it special was that the members of the Giants and Senators teams of 1924 had been invited for an Old-Timers' Day reenactment. Bill Terry, Frankie Frisch, and Bucky Harris would be back in uniform. Johnny Sain, the veteran righty, had just been purchased from the Braves, and it would be good to see him in a Yankees uniform.

But the biggest topic was the weather—as it was wherever fishermen gathered. The metropolitan newspapers the morning before had predicted fair and mild weather for most of Saturday, which was one reason for the big crowd now gathering on the platform. And Saturday's early editions confirmed that forecast. It was going to be a fine day.

All conversation stopped as the rails began a persistent thrum. The Penn Station train rushed into sight, making those on the platform take a step back in surprise and a little awe. Even veteran rail riders had to be impressed by the stallion-like engines that hauled the old steel passenger cars behind them.

When the train rolled to a stop and its doors opened, people spilled out and hurried across the cigarette-strewn concrete platform, juggling fishing rods, tackle boxes, lunch bags, quart bottles of Piels and Ballantine, and whatever else they carried. If the Long Island Rail Road was trying to give all comers an equal chance at their choice of seats, that gesture was diminished significantly by the fact that those who had been occupying the platform for a half hour or more were pressed against the metal exterior of the Fisherman's Special, and the instant the conductors slid the doors open they were the first ones in.

In only three minutes the Fisherman's Special was full and ready to go.

Curiously, with diesel engines just having replaced most of the Long Island Rail Road's coal-burning steam ones, the train still generated a lot of smoke and noise as it pulled away from the Jamaica station. It was like a horse, snorting and kicking, breathing more heavily as it gathered momentum, rushing forward on straight tracks that seemed to converge in the distance ahead, searching for that clear space of fresh air and sunrise where the fish were running.

8

Though the full realization was still a few years away, commercial fishermen and observant recreational anglers were beginning to appreciate that the fishing off Montauk was among the best and most varied—not just in America but in the world. Especially in late summer and early fall, the waters teemed with millions upon millions of fish.

As water temperatures along eastern Canada and New England began to cool in late summer, many species of fish began a journey of a thousand miles or more to winter in the warmer waters off Virginia, the Carolinas, Georgia, and Florida. These included sharks, bluefish, weakfish, tuna, shad, striped bass, and the smaller baitfish they followed, such as swarming schools of herring. If this mass migration took place on land, it would be viewed as one of the most vast and plentiful on the planet. The fish hugged the coast inshore of the northeast-flowing Gulf Stream.

Between Montauk Point and Block Island is a shallow expanse of fast and shifting currents through which the Atlantic Ocean fills and empties Long Island Sound in each twelve-hour tide cycle. These productive waters boiled with life, and Montauk fishermen and their clients could work "The Rip" itself or drift-fish just outside it, east and southeast of the point.

While the big fish took baited hooks, thousands of gulls, terns, and other seabirds swooped overhead and dove for krill and small fish. The cries and twittering of migratory and year-round-resident birds made a wild, diverting chorus. Every so often, clouds of migrating butterflies passed by, and the air came alive with their flickering wings and pinpoint explosions of color.

Although everyone wanted to land a fish, in early September—after an outing off Montauk Point—even returning with an empty bag couldn't spoil a good day.

9

Montauk had been a magnet for opportunists ever since Lion Gardiner first saw it. King James I gave Gardiner the Isle of Wight, between the North and South Forks of Long Island, as a reward for Gardiner's service in the Pequot War of 1637, which put Connecticut under the control of English settlers and virtually extinguished the Pequot tribe. Gardiner moved to what would be known as Gardiners Island with his Dutch wife in 1639, and from there he could see the South Fork stretching out before him from his southwest to his east.

Much of what he saw was uninhabited, but to the south and east were two settlements established by the Montaukett Indians some 4,000 years before. South of Gardiners Island was Napeague, meaning "water land"; east of that, where scrub oak and pine gave way to dune grass, sand, and limitless ocean, was Montauk, meaning "place of observation" or "fortified place." Gardiner and the tribe's sachem, Wyandanch, saw in each other the key to their respective interests— for Gardiner, new territory for his family and other English settlers as well as a good source of prized wampum; for Wyandanch, a means to retain and increase his power.

Gardiner helped found Southampton in 1640 and Maidstone in 1648, the latter on land for which Gardiner's associates paid the Montauketts twenty coats, twenty-four looking glasses (mirrors), twenty-four hoes, twenty-four hatchets, twenty-four knives, and one hundred wampum drills. The Montauk Indians were also promised protection from their enemies and the right to take from any convenient place shells to make wampum. Two years later, Gardiner bought Maidstone, which was renamed East Hampton, from his friends for what would today be $30,000.

What Gardiner then owned was land that extended from the Southampton border to the sandy Napeague Stretch, connecting Montauk to the rest of Long Island. Montauk was not part of the deal, but it offered prime grazing for livestock. Cattle and other livestock would be herded east in spring and fattened up in Montauk until mid-fall. The price paid to the town of East Hampton in the late eighteenth century was $3 per animal for a full summer's pasturage—a nice harvest for the town, considering that there were 7,000 sheep alone munching on Montauk grasslands.

In October, long before there was an "Old West," there would be an Old West–style cattle drive to bring the animals back to East Hampton Village for slaughter or winter shelter. The first cattle ranch in America was established in Montauk in 1658 and and is still in operation, though cattle drives ceased in the 1930s.

In 1686 the Indians, already decimated by European diseases, sold Montauk to English settlers known as "proprietors," who oversaw farming and fishing activities. What land the Montauketts didn't sell they lost to trickery and shady legal maneuvers.

By 1800 the tribe had dwindled below sustainability. Montauk Indians still fished, but rarely for food. Instead they traded almost everything they caught and grew in East Hampton for staples, medicine, clothing, and alcohol. They were trapped in a downward spiral, dependent on the white residents for survival. By 1910 there were so few Montauketts left that, in response to a legal action filed by developers who wanted the last of their land, the New York Appellate Court declared the tribe extinct. The ruling threw Montauk wide open. Farmers anywhere on the South Fork could graze their livestock in the hamlet's hills; developers could build houses for wealthy New Yorkers; and a new generation of fishermen could ply waters once fished by the Montauketts.

Native-born fishermen were joined by migrants from Nova Scotia, among them Gus Pitts's father, who arrived in July 1914 with his wife, two sons, and six daughters. Gus's uncle moved to Montauk from the Connecticut shore three years later, when Gus's cousin Ralph was two years old. Summers were spent lobstering and dragging, and winters long-lining for cod off Culloden Point, at the entrance to Fort Pond Bay. After school Ralph baited hooks for his father's next day's fishing, and during the winter he knitted the entrance funnels for the lobster pots.

Another source of revenue arrived in 1920 with Prohibition, when Montauk became a crucial rumrunner's port serving the New York City market. In an operation orchestrated from the city by Dutch Schultz, Albert Anastasia, and Vincent "Mad Dog" Coll, large boats carrying booze hovered six miles out between Montauk and Amagansett, and fishermen took their boats out at night to load as much as they could carry. Crates of whiskey, gin, rum, and scotch were passed ashore at small, isolated docks, then loaded onto trucks or a train, the crew having been paid off. A fisherman could earn $10 and a case of liquor for a night's work.

Gus Pitts got an early start in the business. When he was only sixteen, his father fell ill and couldn't fish, and Gus smuggled all night and went out fishing every morning. One of his specialties was digging holes in the dunes big enough to hold an entire shipment of illegal booze, discreetly flagged for the bootleggers to find.

As the Roaring Twenties went on, Montauk became a hot spot. The biggest catalyst was Carl Fisher, a man endowed with charm, restless energy, visions, and, for a time, a Midas touch. He founded a company that supplied Detroit with automobile headlights, then built the successful Indianapolis Speedway. Then he built the Lincoln Highway, the first transcontinental highway in the United States, and the Dixieland Highway, which carried people to Florida.

In 1910 Fisher envisioned a huge resort in swampland next to Miami, and he made the vision a reality. His workers cleared and dredged two hundred acres of swamp, then built hotels, shops, and nightclubs. Miami Beach was incorporated in 1915, and by 1925 it was so popular that a conservative estimate of Fisher's wealth was $20 million.

Fisher arrived in Montauk that year with the same vision in mind. This time it would be easier, because the land was already there and didn't have to be carved out of swamp. Fisher's company, the Montauk Beach Development Corporation, set about constructing Montauk Manor, a luxury hotel; Montauk Yacht Club, on Lake Montauk; Montauk Downs Golf Club; and Montauk Playhouse, which housed tennis courts and a boxing ring in addition to a theater. Fisher also built Montauk's first churches, library, school, and railroad station; beach and nightclubs; private homes; and a seven-story office building known as the Tower, which at the time was Suffolk County's tallest building. To connect his yacht club with the ocean, Fisher cut a channel from freshwater Lake Montauk to Block Island Sound.

The new resort was successful. Politicians, noted entertainers, and heirs and heiresses enjoyed the beaches and nightlife. Then came trouble. A hurricane devastated Miami Beach in 1926, and attempts to rebuild used up most of the money that Fisher hadn't committed to the development of Montauk. The Wall Street crash of 1929 followed, and Fisher, heavily in debt, saw his resources and visitors vanish. Several of his Montauk projects remained unfinished, and a few others closed their doors; they would remain empty for decades.

The Star Island Casino continued to operate under a new owner. It shut down, though, after a raid by the anti-alcohol Suffolk County district attorney on Labor Day 1936. One of the customers was New

York mayor Jimmy Walker. Thinking quickly as cops swarmed the place, Walker put a white towel over his arm and walked about like a waiter, eventually slipping out the door. He took off his shoes and walked down the beach to the Montauk Yacht Club. A few days after the raid, the district attorney was fired, but the casino remained closed.

Fisher suffered several other business setbacks during the Depression, and he never recovered. When he died in 1939, he was worth $40,000—a handsome sum for the day, but a long way down from his zenith. When his dream crumbled, Montauk's recreational fishing industry suffered with it. The Depression meant fewer people with money to charter excursions and stay in the hamlet's motels. With the repeal of Prohibition in 1933, even rum-running disappeared. Fishing for a living required working longer hours deeper into the winter for less money.

Then a storm blew in.

On the night of September 20, 1938, a hurricane 611 miles south of Long Island, off Cape Hatteras, North Carolina, was expected to make landfall to the south or turn northeast, out to sea. That was what hurricanes usually did, but this one was different. It hurtled north at 60 miles an hour, packing sustained winds of 121 miles per hour. (Later, the Blue Hill Observatory in Massachusetts would record a gust of 186 miles per hour, the highest ever noted there.) Weather planes in the Atlantic measured the storm's diameter at 500 miles. Though hurricanes weren't named then, this one would become known as the "Long Island Express."

The storm made its first landfall on eastern Long Island at high tide, sending waves of up to fifty feet crashing over the dunes from Westhampton to Montauk. Houses and businesses were destroyed, cars and farm equipment tossed about, livestock drowned, boats flung onto docks and into one another. The wind uprooted trees and stripped the feathers off chickens. Buildings were encased in sand and salt, and blown seawater killed vegetation twenty miles inland.

Fifty-one people died on Long Island, most of them on the East End. (The death toll soared after the storm surged across Long Island

Sound and exploded against the more densely populated southern sections of Connecticut and Rhode Island.) The fishing village at Fort Pond Bay was almost completely destroyed, disrupting what was left of the local industry. To the west, at Shinnecock Hills, the hurricane carved a permanent waterway, now known as the Shinnecock Canal, severing the South Fork from the rest of Long Island. Montauk was devastated.

Thirteen years and a world war later, things were looking up. On fresh-scrubbed late-summer mornings, Montauk seemed to glint at land's end like a shiny penny, its fish-teeming waters reflecting flashes of sunlight as if from silver coins. But in the long winters—when the mansions of the rich were shuttered, and storms twisted the scrub oak and shook the ramshackle fishermen's houses, and the ocean chewed the dunes and the fishing boats were harbor-bound—it was easy to believe that those hard times would come again. So in summer, in Montauk, you made as much money as you could, and called it getting by.

10

The weather that summer of 1951 had been good, attracting crowds from the city, especially on weekends. Yet it had been something of an unlucky summer. In June, the commercial fishing boat *Jack* had sunk east of Plum Island, off the North Fork, and eleven of the fourteen hands on board had drowned. Both the Coast Guard and the Suffolk County District Attorney's office had yet to issue reports explaining what happened. The Sunday before Labor Day weekend, two visitors—Manuel Rosa of Queens, twenty-six, and Joseph Sequeira, only thirteen, of the Bronx—had drowned in Scallop Pond in Southampton. The teenager had been wading casually when he stepped into a fifteen-foot-deep channel and went under. Rosa tried to save him; neither one resurfaced.

Although folks around the Montauk docks acknowledged and lamented these tragedies, life went on through the summer. The weekend of the drownings in Scallop Pond, more than five hundred people showed up for a fund-raising dance for the Montauk Fire Department in the small Fishangri-la recreation hall. On that warm, late-summer evening, most of the captains and their wives (or soon-to-bes) were there. The couples without babysitters brought their children, who sat restlessly at the back tables. Although the fire department was fourteen years old, it still didn't have an ambulance, so every dollar counted at least as much as a dance step.

Life went on for the town's upper crust as well. Local host families threw farewell parties for out-of-town visitors. Miss Annick Szendroi, of Paris, bid adieu to Mr. and Mrs. Arnold Rattray, owners of the *East Hampton Star*. Mr. and Mrs. Richard Petty Sr., of Dayton, Ohio, prepared to motor off after visiting relatives in Amagansett.

Labor Day weekend 1951 would be the most socially active in eastern Long Island since before the war, maybe even before the Depression. Mrs. Frank Dayton and Mrs. George Smith, officers of the board of the East Hampton Library, would be welcoming guests to a party celebrating the library's fifty-fifth anniversary. The third annual Invitational Exhibit by Regional Artists was opening at Guild Hall, across Main Street from the library.

There was special excitement at the Guild Hall's John Drew Theatre, which was offering humorist S. N. Behrman's new play, *The Foreign Language*, starring Edna Best and John Hoyt. Having two prominent actors in town to headline the work of a famous playwright was thrilling enough, but the troupe had been contacted by *Life* magazine for a photo shoot before and after the play. The timing was perfect—Labor Day weekend, opening night of a new play, a theater named for the patriarch of an American theater dynasty (Drew had been the uncle of John, Ethel, and Lionel Barrymore, and much later would be the great-grandfather of actress Drew Barrymore), a glittering Saturday night crowd—and the careers of the two leads could use the boost.

"Life Goes to a Party" was the title of this regular feature of the magazine—photo coverage of a celebrity party. The magazine wanted plenty of "extras," so in addition to the audience, Guild Hall staff and volunteer ushers were invited to pose. One of the volunteers, Kathryn Rauscher, received a call that morning from Inez Whipple, the executive director of Guild Hall, telling her, "You better get yourself really dolled up. *Life* is going to cover you. Cover all you girls." Kathryn called her best friend, Patty Osborne, another usher, and between excited screams they discussed what to wear.

Perhaps the most anticipated festivity that weekend was going to be the annual Labor Day Dance on Saturday at the twenty-two-room Montauk Yacht Club. Preparations had been under way since Friday afternoon, supervised by Roland McCann, the club's manager. The ballroom was lined with colorful banners and flowers, and tables and chairs were moved against the walls to clear a large dancing area. The two bars were fully stocked, buckets on the tables awaited ice and champagne, and the orchestra's stands already held sheet music. By Saturday morning there was little left to do for the gala event. And the forecast, McCann had noted before retiring Friday night, was good.

Not just the hamlet of Montauk but the entire town of East Hampton, including East Hampton Village and—west to east—the hamlets of Wainscott, Springs, and Amagansett, was ready for the holiday weekend and its optimistic forecast. Art exhibits would be opening, with a conservative bias toward nineteenth- and early-twentieth-century paintings and more recent work influenced by the older masters. Hardly anyone in East Hampton knew or cared that their fellow townspeople included Willem de Kooning, Jackson Pollock, and others who were putting abstract expressionism on the American cultural map.

Some people hoped that a clear day would mean a good view of the Stamford Yacht Club's annual Vineyard Race. This year thirty-eight boats—the longest being seventy-two feet—were to race 234 miles around Martha's Vineyard and back to Stamford, and the route would take them through Block Island Sound.

Town businesspeople welcomed the weekend with excitement. The New York metropolitan economy of 1951 offered the prospect of a real estate boom. Deals would be explored over the weekend, and some would be closed. In Sag Harbor one lot would be sold for

$1,000, another for as much as $5,000. In Southampton, a lot on Moses Lane would sell for $4,500. A Montauk Beach Development Corporation lot went for $1,500, and W. O. Boldt sold one of his parcels in East Hampton for $4,000. Longtime residents were astonished at the prices.

Of course, some residents and visitors cared more for the natural world than the world of commerce and society, and clement weather would put the full beauty of the area on display. There was an especially large osprey population in town in 1951, their nests visible atop power and telephone poles. The young had recently fledged, and hardware stores in Montauk and Amagansett were experiencing a run on binoculars.

11

Most of the charter boats were out on the water before seven o'clock Saturday morning. If you couldn't get a charter on the Saturday of Labor Day weekend, you might as well weigh anchor and go back to where you came from.

The charter captains didn't have to wait for a train to show up, just the customers who were going to hand over the money. The customers, of course, whether they were one or two guys or a half-dozen people, wanted the most bang for their bucks, so if captains could leave the dock on Lake Montauk at first light with a full boat, they did. Most charters consisted of six anglers. Customers wanted to divide the fee as many ways as possible, and six was the maximum allowed on boats regulated by the Coast Guard without adherence to much stiffer and more onerous requirements. The captains called these charters "six-packs."

For a few of the captains, there was another incentive for an early start. They might be booked for two half-day charters, and they didn't want to keep their afternoon customers waiting at noon or 1 P.M. And even if they weren't booked, it was still possible that when they brought back the morning party, other potential customers would be waiting.

Carl Darenberg was already out. So was Bob Tuma, though his cousin Frank, on the *Janet*, was still back by the yacht club waiting for his customers to show. There were two or three Pittses steaming northeast toward Block Island—or south of east, deeper into the Atlantic. George Glass, Harry Clemenz, and George McTurk on their boats were about ready to cut their engines and let their customers start fishing.

Lester Behan had a weekday business in College Point, Queens, and on weekends went east to take people out into the Atlantic. He had begun in Montauk as a head-boat captain, steering any boat that was able to push away from the Fishangri-la dock and happy for the work. Many times he and his friend Bill Blindenhofer didn't get to leave Queens until late Friday night or even after midnight on Saturday. Bill drove Les's old Packard, and Les slept as much as he could on the way so he would be fresh to pilot the boat.

But Les had ambition and the smarts to follow it up. By September 1951, he had bought the *Bingo II* and left Fishangri-la behind for the docks in Lake Montauk, doing charters on the weekends. He took out six people at a time who paid good money for a good boat, a good captain with a strong, engaging mate, and the best fishing grounds on the East Coast. On this Saturday, Les and Bill expected an easy trip in easy weather, then a nice payoff and a good dinner and drinks in Montauk that night. They'd sleep aboard the *Bingo II*, then earn another nice payoff on Sunday before heading home.

Both men were starting to think differently about "home." The more time they spent in the waters off Montauk, the less they wanted to leave them and the hamlet's hills and woods. The discussions between them of moving here with their wives and kids had become more frequent and more serious.

Neither man had any inkling that by the end of the day, they would be heroes.

It was a good time to be away from land and on the water, which was turning bluer by the minute. The southwest breeze was clean and salty, and the sun was rising and gathering strength. There wasn't a captain out there at that moment who wished he was doing something else. And there was an added bonus this day for those out early: an eclipse. The sun was partially obscured at 6:21 A.M., and forty minutes later more than half of it was blocked by the moon. The sight resembled a penny on a nickel in the sky.

12

Frank Mundus was typical of the boatmen taking advantage of the rejuvenated Montauk fishing industry and making the port their home. On his *Cricket II*, a powerful boat built in 1946, he had been running charters out of Brielle, New Jersey, but kept hearing tales of the great fishing and great business going on in Montauk (which multigeneration East Hampton Town natives persisted in pronouncing with the accent on the second syllable). Finally, in June 1951, he could no longer resist the siren call and brought his wife, Janet, and their two-year-old daughter, Bobbie, to Montauk.

That was his version, but there was another one. One afternoon, Mundus had returned to Brielle from a charter trip towing a whale he'd caught and killed with his customers. It was early in the year for whales in New Jersey waters, and Frank figured that the whale would interest the folks on land—an amusement for grown-ups, a marine science lesson for kids, and maybe, others suggested, a big billboard promoting the trophies you could chase on a charter with Frank Mundus. He beached the whale and tied up his boat at the dock.

City fathers saw the situation differently. Sure, some of the residents, especially the kids, thought it was exciting to see this big gray whale stretched out on the sand. Teachers even took their classes down to examine it. But town officials saw a big carcass that was going to rot—in a word, a public nuisance. After two days, they ordered Mundus to remove the dead beast.

The young captain was insulted that his gift to the community was being spurned. Still, he complied. After tying a rope to the whale, he dragged it out to sea with the *Cricket II*. The next day, it was back on the beach. Frustrated officials hired an excavation company to bury the carcass on the beach. This appeared to solve the problem.

Then a spring storm hit the New Jersey coast, and when the waves that crashed against the beach retreated, they took sand with them, exposing the rotting corpse.

During the next few days, as the whale began to putrefy under the strengthening May sun, the managers of the fishing docks and Frank's fellow captains grew angry. The stench gave new meaning to "nasty," and the sight of the collapsing carcass was sad as well as disgusting. Parents and teachers kept children away from the beach.

Mundus was told to remove the whale by any means. He couldn't afford to hire a contractor, and he might have gone broke in the time it would take him to chop the thing up and drag the pieces out to sea himself. Instead he took a charter out for three days.

While he was gone, the city fathers hired two companies: one to cut up the reeking carcass, another to haul the liquefying hunks to the local landfill, where they were buried under tons of less nauseating garbage.

When Mundus returned to port, he was presented with both bills and told that if he didn't pay them there would be no berth waiting for him again—in Brielle or anywhere else the beached whale story had been reported. To make matters worse, several of his fellow captains indicated that they would love to have him join the pieces of carcass in the landfill. It was then that Frank remembered hearing about the virtues of Montauk fishing. The next day, he and his wife and daughter left on the *Cricket II* well before dawn.

When Mundus docked at Fort Pond Bay in the first week of July 1951, Fishangri-la was humming. The only drawback was that there was only so much dock space for so many boats. The way to deal with that was to pack passengers like sardines onto the available boats. Especially on in-season holiday weekends, the boats left for sea brimming with fishermen and their gear.

It was a bit of a setback for Frank. In New Jersey, he had been a known charter captain, and the most he took on any one trip was six passengers. In Montauk he was a nobody, a man starting over among strangers, and with an ornery personality to boot. He had no choice but to do open-boat trips out of Fishangri-la. The family slept on the

Cricket II, then Janet and Bobbie wandered the town for the day while Frank was off fishing.

Then Frank found out how good the fishing business was in Montauk that summer. There was good money to be made, and no one did more than wink if you let forty or more passengers on your boat. In a good week you could clear $500 after mate and fuel expenses. And the other head-boat captains weren't bad guys. As Frank Mundus settled in for seven-day weeks of hauling in fish and money, he concluded that this living had to be a lot better than drowning in whale guts in a landfill.

Ornery he might be, but Mundus was also smart, ambitious, and a born promoter. By 1960 he would carve a specialized niche as a hunter of monster sharks. For big-game trophy hunters wanting to match tackle with a brute bigger than themselves, chasing sharks was the best bet, and the whale hunter Mundus was quick to recognize the promotional value there. He refitted the *Cricket II* to handle bigger fish and routinely ferried home sharks weighing more than a ton. His success probably exceeded his own dreams. He became one of Montauk's most in-demand charter captains, and caught the attention of Peter Benchley, whose character Quint in *Jaws* would be based on Mundus. The biggest shark ever caught with a rod and reel would be hauled in by Mundus and Donnie Braddock forty miles off Montauk in 1986, twelve years after *Jaws* was published. It was a great white that was more than sixteen feet long and weighed 3,450 pounds.

But all that was in the future in 1951, when Mundus was one of the newest head-boat captains at Fishangri-la. He was glad to be rid of Brielle and had no doubt that the feeling was mutual. He was a thorn in dockmaster Gene Goble's side now.

13

Charter captains were the higher rung of recreational fishing. A maximum of six passengers meant more room for active fishing than on the unregulated head boats. Charter-boat clientele were typically better-heeled, more serious anglers casting or trolling for surface-feeding game fish such as striped bass and bluefish. Some wanted the big fish—marlin, swordfish, or bluefin tuna. The charter captains made their own deals with the customers, the dockmasters on Montauk Lake, and sometimes with one another. They were independent contractors, their agreements sealed with a handshake. For reasons that included honor among captains, nothing was put in writing.

Not so the open boats. Something of a roguish reputation was attached to these captains, a faint scent of unreliability. Their boats were smaller than fifteen gross tons in order to avoid more than minimal Coast Guard oversight, and they operated under the same regulations that applied to any motorboat regardless of use. They were required to carry a life jacket for each passenger, and that was about it.

Unlike the larger charter boats—and contrary to common sense—open boats could take as many passengers as they pleased, and often did. All their blue-collar clientele demanded was room at the rail to drop a baited hook for bottom feeders—porgies, sea bass, fluke, and the occasional cod.

The head-boat captains weren't rooted in Montauk sand, as were the Pittses and Tumas and other charter skippers who had been born or raised there. The open-boat skippers, even those needing money, could just not show up at all, or they could take the occasional charter and not be there when the train pulled in at Fishangri-la, meaning fewer passengers who went fishing and less money in Fishangri-la's pocket. And these out-of-town guys, essentially itinerants, might be more inclined to hold a little back when turning over the company's portion of fares. It wasn't just the Marx Brothers or the Three Stooges who could play the "one for you, two for me" game when divvying up the take. Open-boat chartering was a freewheeling, survival-of-the-fittest business, and it had a congenial home in Montauk.

Gene Goble, the owner of Fishangri-la, knew all that. He knew he had to guard against getting cheated in order to make some legitimate money. He made the open-boat business possible by supplying the berths, ice, electricity, and advertising to get the people who loved fishing to do it in Montauk, out of Fort Pond Bay. He even provided the all-purpose Eat and Run coffee shop, the Liar's Lair bar, the weather reports, and sometimes just an ear to bark at when the fishing was lousy. He had an investment to protect.

So Goble had contracts. For public consumption, if anyone cared, the contracts didn't exist, but he had them. Even if all the captains could do was put an "X" on the paper, they were obligated to stick to the deal. Howie Carroll, Eddie Carroll, Frank Mundus, Ray Hegner of the *Dixie II*—all of them had signed on the dotted line. In return for everything Goble provided, he received $150 a boat for a dockage fee for the season and 25¢ per passenger—about 6 percent of the captain's take. Goble regarded that as highly reasonable, and he wanted dependable, good-performing captains at his dock. Let the captains grouse behind his back. Business was good. If a captain failed to produce, Goble could choose not to renew his contract the following year.

On a good Saturday, he could easily make upward of $150, even if the captains cheated him a bit, and that was before considering the income from the coffee shop, bar, and concessions. So when the Fisherman's Special showed up and the boats were mobbed, Goble would be the last person to tell a captain not to take on one passenger more.

14

When Gene Goble was called to testify before the Coast Guard board of investigation, he looked uncomfortable in his suit, as if about to burst out of it. He probably had not worn one in years, and he'd put on a few pounds since then. His face, with a prominent double chin, receding hairline, and thin eyebrows set in a permanent expression of disbelief, was surprisingly pale until you realized that even though Goble was in the fishing business, he spent much of his time in his little office at Fishangri-la.

There was, at least, a natty touch to the suit; in his left breast pocket was a white handkerchief, folded so that five sharp points of material protruded. He held a cigarette between the index and middle fingers of his right hand, and he took one last, long drag before stubbing it out in the ashtray at the witness table.

After he was identified for the record as owner of Fishangri-la, Inc., Goble was sworn in by De Carlo. He sat across from the three white-uniformed officers. Olson wanted it noted in the record that Goble had volunteered to be a witness at the court of inquiry and that, in response to the *Pelican* incident, in just three days Goble had developed safety regulations that federal authorities might use to prevent further events such as this.

Goble nodded, listening to the scratching of reporters' pencils on paper. A photographer appeared by his left shoulder and the flashbulb exploded, blinding him for a few seconds.

COURT: Mr. Goble, do you feel so strongly about this issue that you would be willing to testify before a congressional committee to advocate for broader powers by the Coast Guard?

GOBLE: Yes, sir.

COURT: What would be your first recommendations?

GOBLE: First? Limit the number of passengers a vessel can carry. I also think there should be a roster of passengers made up before sailing. Every boat should have a radio, one that works. Centralized weather reports, so we're not getting reports from half a dozen different places. And the Coast Guard has to station a rescue boat out in Montauk. During the summer months, we got two hundred boats out on the water.

COURT: Would such regulations have a financial impact on the boat operators?

GOBLE: Probably, but not much.

COURT: And operations like your Fishangri-la?

GOBLE: Not really.

COURT: But you do have a financial interest in the *Pelican?*

GOBLE: No, I don't.

COURT: [Pause.] It's the court's understanding that Fishangri-la benefited by the number of passengers on the *Pelican* as well as the other open boats.

GOBLE: That's not quite how it works. See, we get twenty-five cents for every passenger on a boat, from the boats being able to dock there. Not that much money. It's a token, not a relationship.

COURT: But it seems that the more passengers a captain allows on board, the more money can be turned over to you.

GOBLE: Sure. But that's the captain's decision. I don't tell him how many people to carry. No one forces Eddie Carroll or anyone else to fill up the boat. I don't control what these guys do. And figure it out, the twenty-five cents that goes to Fishangri-la is nothing compared to what goes in a captain's pocket out of the four dollars and fifty cents, so it's not me they're doing favors for.

COURT: [Pause.] Mr. Goble, do you have insurance on the boats that dock at Fishangri-la?

GOBLE: No, not one.

COURT: Wouldn't that be prudent, in case there were another such disaster like the *Pelican?*

GOBLE: No. Two reasons. One is, like I said, I don't control these guys. Once they leave the dock, they're on their own. Whatever happens, it's on the captain, not me. Why should someone sue me? I didn't do anything wrong.

COURT: And the second reason?

GOBLE: No underwriter in the United States would write such a policy.

COURT: Mr. Goble, do you know if the *Pelican* ever took on more than sixty passengers before?

GOBLE: No. In fact, I don't think Eddie ever took more than fifty.

COURT: How do you know?

GOBLE: From what Eddie Carroll told me, and the ticket stubs turned over to me.

COURT: Each ticket stub represents twenty-five cents to Fishangri-la?

GOBLE: That's right.

COURT: How do you know this is a reliable system?

GOBLE: It's the honor system. We trust each other.

COURT: Mr. Goble, do you allow the selling of beer on the boats?

GOBLE: I don't allow it. It's not up to me.

COURT: Where do the captains get the beer?

GOBLE: We sell them the beer and ice. What they do with it after that and how much they charge is not my business.

COURT: Is this practice legal?

GOBLE: What I do is legal. After that, it's not my business what happens on the water. But once you're more than three miles out, you're in international waters, so the only law is the captain's.

COURT: Mr. Goble, you posted a weather report on the evening of August 31, correct?

GOBLE: Twice, at 5 P.M. and 7 P.M. They were basically the same.

COURT: Where do you get your information for these reports?

GOBLE: The weather bureau, and I have friends who work for airlines.

COURT: On Saturday, September 1, you received a small-craft warning and other information about inclement weather approaching.

GOBLE: Yes, I did. But all the boats were already out. Even if they weren't, the captains made their own decisions. I've flown storm warnings and some of these guys still go out.

COURT: Isn't it your responsibility as the operator of Fishangri-la to provide accurate and timely weather reports?

GOBLE: No, it's not. I do it voluntarily, like I'm here as a witness.

COURT: Once you had the updated weather report, did you try to contact the *Pelican?*

GOBLE: No.

COURT: Any of the boats?

GOBLE: No.

COURT: But they were in the path of a potentially dangerous storm, and didn't know it.

GOBLE: First of all, every time there's a shift of wind, you can't think that means a bad storm or no one would go out on the water. These captains know and have seen a lot more than a piece of paper typed up a hundred miles away. Second, like I said, I don't control these guys. Nothing I said or did would've made a difference.

After a couple of wrap-up questions, the Coast Guard panel was done with Goble. His offering to appear before a congressional committee on behalf of the stronger regulatory authority that everyone knew the Coast Guard wanted had been a good tactic. Maybe it had bought him some goodwill. At the very least, it couldn't have hurt.

15

One of the most popular open boats—perhaps the most popular—was the *Pelican*, and the main reason was Captain Eddie Carroll. Folks thought he was lucky, though Eddie scoffed at that. He preferred to say "experienced."

True, Eddie sure was experienced on the water. Just turned thirty-four on the previous Tuesday, he had begun his marine apprenticeship racing sailboats as a boy on Staten Island, a full twenty-four years before, and later had worked as a professional yacht skipper. By 1940 he had served as a merchant seaman on voyages to the Far East and Mediterranean for the American Export Line, to the Caribbean for the United Fruit Line, and to South America for the Grace Line. At twenty-three, Eddie had raced a fifty-five-foot schooner from Staten Island to Puerto Rico with two other men.

Then the United States entered World War II. Eddie saw it coming, so four months before Pearl Harbor he enlisted in the navy.

He moved up fast in the noncommissioned ranks, and in 1942 was put in charge of a fleet of small naval craft ranging from fifty-foot motor sailers to eighty-five-foot crash and torpedo-type boats. After that, he was aboard LSTs (Landing Ship Tank) in several assaults, including Okinawa. Soon after the war ended, around his twenty-eighth birthday, Eddie was honorably discharged as a chief boatswain's mate.

He loved the water and wasn't about to leave it, so he found work as captain of a sixty-five-foot yacht, but it bored him to see the same people and sail the same routes every day. In 1947 he spent time in Montauk as a relief captain on board the open boat *Bell Boy II*. He loved the boat, but there weren't enough jobs to make a living, so he took a freelance job delivering boats from New England to Florida. He got to know the Atlantic seaboard well.

Eddie was back in Montauk in 1949 as captain of the *Jigger II*, an open boat sailing out of Fishangri-la. That was a good year, good enough that in 1950 Eddie bought the *Bell Boy II* and renamed it the *Pelican*. The summer of 1950 was even better, because by then Eddie's brother Howie had settled in Montauk for the good fishing. Already married to Rita, and with a son, Howie had been in the Coast Guard during the war. Eddie had told him about his captain experiences in '47, and the following year Howie had come out for the summer to be the relief skipper on the *Bell Boy II*, a job that Eddie had held the previous year. Howie kept the family house on Staten Island, but Rita and the kids—Jean had joined Howard Jr., by then—lived for the summer in a bungalow near Fort Pond Bay.

Howie made good money in 1948, and he was back in '49. By 1950, Howie was fully sold on Montauk. That year, he replaced his brother on the *Jigger II*, and Howie, Rita, and the kids—Susan had joined Jean and Howard Jr.—bought a house. (When Eddie applied for a federal boat operator's license that May, he listed his address as "Railroad Pier, Montauk," which meant he slept on his boat.) Right before the summer of '51 got under way, Howie had enough money to buy the *Jigger II*.

For Eddie, the 1951 season was full of customers and fish, and something else. Closing in on thirty-four, Eddie was ready to get married, and he'd found the right woman, a Swedish woman named Inger Perrson who waitressed at the Open Kitchen, within walking distance of Fishangri-la. Inger was staying for the summer with the Pilbros, who owned the restaurant.

According to one contemporary write-up, "Capt. Carroll, since sailing from the Fishangri-la Dock, has been a perfect gentleman at all times and is not a drinking man. His conduct in carrying out his business and the maintenance of his boat has been of the very best. Because of his pleasant manner, he has countless friends and customers who enjoy fishing aboard his boat."

Eddie was a handsome guy. That didn't mean anything to Montauk's fishermen, but open boats in 1951 welcomed children and women willing to go after good-size fish or at least have fun in the chase. Kids thought Captain Eddie looked like a dashing pirate for the way he could wiggle his brown eyebrows, change his voice, and handle his boat. Adults, especially women, noticed the rakish tilt of his cap, the sun-tanned light brown of his face and arms, the wide and slightly gnarly spread of his fingers, and the jut of his beaked nose that almost obscured a full, wide-toothed grin that said "welcome" and "this will be the best trip on the ocean you've ever had."

The *Pelican* had been built in 1940 in Brooklyn as a recreational fishing boat. The boat was fitted with two six-cylinder Chrysler Crown gasoline engines rated at one hundred horsepower each. She had a lapstraked wood hull and a thirty-inch-high metal railing running around the entire boat. In front of her spacious aft deck was a narrow deckhouse, and forward and below that was a cabin under the raised foredeck. The interior of the cabin was a bit dark, because the only way in and out was from the deckhouse, and there were only six small portholes to allow light in. From the flying-bridge helm station atop the deckhouse, engine controls ran through tubes to the main steering station in the deckhouse below. This gave Eddie full control of the boat from the flying bridge, with its unobstructed view of the boat and the sea, leaving passengers free to crowd the wide side decks and foredeck as well as the big aft deck.

The *Pelican* fit into a good fishing-boat slot at Fishangri-la. At forty-two and a half feet long, she was one of the bigger boats—and thus, thought many anglers, one of the safer ones—and could easily accommodate more passengers than the thirty originally recommended by her manufacturer. Yet she remained just below the fifteen-gross-ton mark that would have required an annual inspection under the U.S. Marine Safety Statutes.

The only important regulation she was subject to was the Coast

Guard rule that there be as many life vests as passengers on board. Eddie Carroll had eighty-two vests stashed away in two lockers on deck abaft the deckhouse. As long as she kept out of trouble, the *Pelican* could pretty much do as she pleased, and Captain Carroll never had any trouble.

Certainly the engines were in tip-top condition. Eddie had just laid out a whopping $3,000 for a complete overhaul of the two engines—the equivalent of $12,000 to $13,000 fifty years later. The engines were running smoothly and were clean enough to fry an egg on, and then eat it.

Yes, the *Pelican* was the boat to be on.

16

If there had been a prize for the most hours logged on the water for weekend fishing, it might have gone to two good friends, Harold Pinckney and Grover Menton. They were only a year apart in age— Harold, at forty-seven, was a year younger—and both had longtime jobs. Grover was a taxi driver, Harold a bank custodian. They lived near each other—Harold in Hempstead, Long Island, and Grover in Garden City. Both were married and had sons named George (Grover also had a daughter, Gladys); both loved to fish, and both were African American, which put them in a decided minority among Long Island's weekend anglers.

There was a big difference between them, though: Harold had not gone fishing out of Montauk before. Over the years he'd been content to fish in the Nassau County bays and from a small boat just off the south shore of Long Island. Every once in a while, Grover had gone out to Montauk and fished from open boats in the Atlantic; finally Harold was curious enough to try it. So Friday night, when Grover had suggested spending the next day fishing out of Montauk, Harold was all for it.

They drove east early Saturday morning. The trip by car took longer than the train—on the Long Island highways of 1951, nothing went as fast as the Fisherman's Special—but neither man wanted to backtrack to Jamaica and leave a car there. Grover drove because he knew the way. They had coffee, egg sandwiches, the radio, and discussions of their prospects for the day to pass the time.

Martin Berger, twenty, drove out from Brooklyn with his brother Lawrence, three years younger (and already a student at City College); his friend Seymour Gabbin, also twenty; and three girls from the neighborhood. One was Lawrence's girlfriend, Cynthia Zurendorf, sixteen. The other two were nineteen: Renee Sherr, who was with Martin, and Seymour's girlfriend, Cynthia Chamades. Martin was looking forward to the outing. He had just returned home from a hitch in the navy, and it would be like old times to go fishing with his brother. Martin had never fished out of Montauk before, but he and Lawrence had logged a lot of time on Sheepshead Bay. According to Lawrence, Montauk was the place to be.

The three girls were mostly along for the ride: sunshine, fresh air, maybe catch a fish by accident—that would make it a good day. There was no way that Cynthia Zurendorf could *not* go. As soon as her boyfriend suggested the outing, she had said yes. Then her father said no. He argued that it was dangerous for a nonswimmer to be on a boat in the deep waters off Montauk Point. Cynthia, with help from her mother, had worn him down. She didn't want to miss an adventure like this.

17

The Fisherman's Special rocked and rattled loudly on the tracks as it neared fifty miles per hour, the highest speed of the entire trip east. Here, nearing Riverhead, there was nothing but open track bordered by the thousands of thin, shiny green spikes of the pine barrens.

Craning to look ahead out of windows crusted with dirt, passengers could see that the eastern sky was clear, the sun was floating perceptibly higher like a yellow fishing bob casually rising toward the surface, and the moon was disappearing. Each time the train mounted an incline, it appeared to be heading directly into the sun.

When the train crested a rise and went downhill, the sun's ascent in the clear blue sky was suddenly accelerated.

Here and there in the crowded cars of the Special, windows were yanked down. The air that rushed in felt cold and damp at first, but that was okay after almost two hours of strong coffee, stale cigarette smoke, and tightly packed human bodies. Muttered curses and pounding fists identified the inoperable train windows; they had probably stopped working around the time of the Berlin Airlift or V-J Day. The train's engine was the only thing new.

The Special usually had enough seats to go around, but not on the Saturday morning of Labor Day weekend. Still, it was rare that someone stood the whole way, because many of the passengers knew one another and there was a lot of sharing of seats, particularly when those who had been asleep woke up and wanted to stretch by walking up and down the car's narrow aisle.

It was more important to find a seat on the trip back; otherwise, you could fall asleep standing up and keel over. During the return trip, people who had been on the go (and possibly drinking) for fifteen hours would need some shut-eye. One of the cars on the train back to the city was a sort of icehouse. Upon returning to Fishangri-la, fishermen labeled the fish or bags of fish they had caught and tossed them into that car's ice bunkers, to be retrieved when the train arrived in Jamaica.

Helen Friedel especially appreciated the cool, fresh air. Only on trips like this to the Montauk docks did she spend so much time in such close quarters with men. Her husband, Jack—unlike most of the other fishermen, who wanted a womanless weekend, even if it was a holiday one—liked her to be with him. For much of the ride Helen breathed through her mouth to keep the odors at bay and kept envisioning being on a boat on the open sea. She hoped once again that she and Jack would get aboard the *Pelican* along with her brother-in-law and nephew.

Three friends who had traveled out together woke up and double-checked their gear. Antonio De Jesus was from the Bronx, and the other two fellows, Constantin Acevedo and Manuel Ramirez, were from Manhattan. They were following their usual routine: meet up on the Fisherman's Special, grab some sleep on the ride out, get on the *Pelican*, and catch bags full of fish.

Portable radios were tuning in more static than music this far from New York City (it would be twelve years before WLNG in Sag Harbor broadcast to all of eastern Long Island), so some frustrated listeners switched off their radios. Veteran riders of the Fisherman's Special, however, tuned in Connecticut stations.

Most of the popular tunes getting airtime were about love, including the year's biggest, "Too Young," by Nat King Cole. It was hard to find a station that wasn't playing something by the hot new singer Tony Bennett—his "Because of You" and "Cold, Cold Heart" were huge hits. "Come On-a My House" by Rosemary Clooney, "Be My Love" by opera singer Mario Lanza, and "Tennessee Waltz" by cute Patti Page were big, too, and Les Paul and Mary Ford had made the big time with "How High the Moon."

But the music wasn't as important as the weather reports. The ones from Connecticut were predicting a fine day, but those reports weren't very reliable; most were for the entire state, with an occasional nod to New London or Mystic on the coast, and their relevance to the waters off Montauk was limited. Still, good news about the weather was encouraging, no matter what. Who wanted bad news early on an eighteen-hour day that could cost more than fifteen bucks with beer and sandwiches factored in?

As more passengers woke up, conversations began or were resumed. Of the nearly four hundred people on the Fisherman's Special, more than three hundred were men, and probably half of those over twenty-five had been in the army, navy, or marines in World War II. (To say nothing of Antonio Borruso, who had served in the Italian navy in World War I.) Stories and jokes about basic training, favorite and hated officers, first sights of Europe or the Pacific, and tales of combat floated through the cars. A few veterans discussed going back into the service now that the conflict in Korea seemed as though it wouldn't be over soon.

Early-edition newspapers provided other topics. The new movie

David and Bathsheba reportedly included some steamy scenes between Gregory Peck and Susan Hayward, and the same was said of *A Place in the Sun*, with Elizabeth Taylor and Montgomery Clift. Book readers could discuss the bestsellers *The Caine Mutiny* and *Kon-Tiki*, or the latest Mickey Spillane novel.

Sports was a popular topic, especially boxing and baseball. Joe Louis had come out of retirement within the past two weeks to win a decision over Jimmy Bivins in a Baltimore ten-rounder, and Kid Gavilan had taken a split decision over Billy Graham to keep the welterweight title (a few of the passengers had probably seen that one at Madison Square Garden the previous Wednesday night). Joey Maxim had kept the light-heavy crown by beating Bob Murphy. The Yanks had finally brought this kid Mickey Mantle back up from the Kansas City farm; good young buck, but he couldn't even shine Joe D's shoes and had better not think so. And what about that clown Bill Veeck, hiring a midget, Eddie Gaedel, to pinch-hit for Veeck's St. Louis Browns? The guy had no respect for the game.

Some of the passengers had been following events down in Argentina, where Juan and Eva Perón had just been nominated for president and vice president. Imagine that, a husband and wife running a country together, and Evita so much younger. Forget the country—how was the marriage going to work out?

When the train reached the crisscross-beamed metal bridge over the Shinnecock Canal, veteran passengers knew they were on the home stretch. The canal was only about eighty yards wide at this point, less than a football field. If the Army Corps of Engineers didn't dredge it every two or three years, it began to close up, sometimes literally trapping boats on their way in or out. Those unfamiliar with the hurricane of '38 no doubt questioned the wisdom of digging a canal that had to be continually re-dug.

By 7:30, as the Fisherman's Special steamed through eastern Southampton Town, the sun was climbing above the windows, and there would be no more hills before the Napeague Stretch to bring the sun back into view. The wind through the open windows was beginning to lose its early-morning chill, and the air felt drier even though the train was closer to the ocean than it had been at anytime during the journey. The blue of the sky was deepening, especially far from the sun, reminding a few former marines of mornings on Pacific islands.

The train itself seemed to hum with anticipation. It was going to be a beautiful day for fishing.

18

Not everyone heading east to fish that Saturday was aiming for Montauk. Charters and a few open boats out of Shinnecock and Canoe Place in Hampton Bays offered good fishing too. Docked boats, bait and tackle shops, and fuel stations lined the canal. Stopping at Shinnecock took a good half hour off the journey from the city, especially for anglers traveling by car. When the locks were open and the tide was ebbing, finding good fishing grounds in the Atlantic was a breeze.

Shinnecock got its share, all right, but Montauk had a mystique. It was "The End," as many of its own residents called it, the last stop for civilization—if the waterfront life of Montauk could be called civilized—before 3,000 miles of ocean. Montauk was the place to go, and that was why almost as many anglers were driving there that morning as were riding the train.

Albert Snyder, a thirty-year-old fur manufacturer from New Hyde Park, was one of them. Though his drive was close to a hundred miles, he met few other cars on the roads at 5 A.M., and he had plenty of coffee. He stopped in Huntington, on Long Island's north shore, to pick up two friends, Max Stein and Ben Tasman.

It was a shorter drive for William Hoak, who had to travel only from Babylon. There were good fishing spots off this south shore village, but they weren't Montauk.

Angelo Testa, forty-eight, wasn't all that keen to be driving east from his home in Patchogue, more than an hour west of Montauk. A masseur at the Manhattan Club, he'd been commuting all week. But he was taking his son, twenty-three-year-old Angelo Jr., open-boat fishing for the first time since the younger man's discharge from the army a couple of years before. Angelo Sr. didn't see his son often enough now that the boy was working at Republic Airport in Farmingdale, and maybe they'd have luck with the fish. Angelo Sr. had persuaded his friend and neighbor Nicholas Trotta to come along too.

Forty-eight-year-old John Griffin and his wife, Josie, had driven out to Montauk on Friday from Brooklyn and slept overnight in their car. John wanted to be early to Fishangri-la to be sure of getting on the *Pelican*, and this time his wife had agreed to travel with him. John had gone open-boat fishing many times, and the *Pelican* was his favorite boat. Being a bricklayer in summer in Brooklyn was not the easiest job, so for this holiday weekend he and Josie were going to live it up as much as their limited means allowed.

But Josie almost spoiled it when they woke up well before dawn on Saturday. Actually, she woke up first and shook John awake. "Don't go," she whispered urgently.

"What?" John mumbled, thinking he was dreaming.

"Don't go," Josie repeated. "Don't go out on the *Pelican* today."

"You crazy? That's why we drove out here. I can't wait to get out on that boat."

"I had a dream," his wife said. "I dreamed the boat turned over in a big storm. Everyone drowned."

"Oh, come on," John said with a groan. "There isn't any big storm. Look out the window. The sky's clear as can be."

"I know what I dreamed."

"And boats just don't flip over. Plus that Captain Carroll, he knows how to handle a boat."

"I'm not going."

"Josie . . ."

"I know what I dreamed."

John sighed. He felt like scoffing some more, but that wouldn't work; it would just get her back up even further. He urged her to go back to sleep, thinking she'd feel better with another hour of shut-eye. She said all right. But as John stared out the window, waiting for the first sign of the sunrise, he could tell that his wife was awake too.

19

The head-boat captains finished breakfast before 7:30 and could have left the coffee shop to make sure the mates had their boats ready, but the fresh pot of coffee would serve at least another twenty minutes of chatter. Frank Mundus would have preferred silence, but he was sitting at the counter with the Carroll brothers, and Eddie couldn't stop talking about Inger, the girl he was going to marry in two weeks.

"That's right, fellas, no more roaming for me, except on a boat," Eddie said for at least the fifth time.

"She's a fine girl, that's true," Howie repeated to his younger brother and anyone else within earshot.

"Jesus," Mundus said, groaning.

Mundus was seven years younger than Eddie, but with a wife and daughter already, he couldn't share Eddie's optimism. For one thing, he'd had too much to drink the night before over at Salivar's on Lake Montauk. The bar at Salivar's stayed open until 4 A.M., and when it closed you could simply step—or stagger—across the front entryway to Salivar's coffee shop for breakfast.

If the cook didn't show up on time, the bartender went around the back and entered the kitchen, changed from a blue apron to a white one, then made coffee and fired up the grill. Meanwhile the drunks and drifters migrated to the coffee shop, where they would take up the same relative positions they'd had at the bar since midnight or before.

After a couple of hours of coffee and cigarettes—and breakfast, if they could afford it or keep it down—they would stagger out one by one, to be replaced by charter captains. The waitresses kept an eye on the ones leaving, making sure they pushed open the front exit door instead of the rear one. Every few months, an errant customer had to be fished out of Lake Montauk.

"Shit, Eddie, you're not bringing that on the boat with you," growled Mundus, motioning with his coffee cup at the wedding ring once more being held aloft.

"Hell, yeah, Frank," said Eddie Carroll. "It's not leaving my sight until I put it on Inger's hand at the wedding."

Eddie stubbed out his cigarette and got off his stool at the same time Mundus did. Howie got up too. The three captains paid at the cash register by the front door and left together, squinting in the sudden strong sunlight.

On the way to their boats, they encountered Gene Goble emerging from the Fishangri-la office to meet the Fisherman's Special. He'd say he wanted to ensure passenger safety and satisfaction, but the captains knew that Goble would be counting the passengers; his share of ticket receipts had better reflect that, or the captains would hear about it.

Like the charter captains a couple of hours earlier, the Carrolls and Mundus looked at the weather report that Goble had tacked on the Fishangri-la bulletin board the night before and drew the same conclusion. If a blow out of the southwest got too frisky, they could always duck north of Montauk Point to dodge it. And a shift to the northwest at the end of the day would find the fleet back at the dock. It was a good forecast, but with caveats—enough to make a captain wonder whether he'd have a sick or unhappy passenger or two by day's end, but not enough to cause any real concern.

"Well, it's flat calm now," said Mundus. "You could roll a marble to England."

Eddie walked past the ranks of head boats, docked with their transoms to the pier. They looked eager to get going, though the real reason for docking them that way had more to do with ease of passenger boarding and efficient use of dock space. When Eddie took up his station next to the *Pelican*'s transom, he gave the boat a searching look. She'd seen a lot of fishing action over the summer but was still in solid condition. He'd put most of last year's profits into a few upgrades—the new wood paneling in the cabin impressed customers—and he'd do more this winter, though it was time, too, to think about saving for a house for Inger and the kids they were going to have.

People smiled and waved to Eddie from the *Pelican*. There were two dozen passengers, maybe more, aboard already. He acknowledged them by tipping his cap. Many of these folks were his hard-core regulars who weren't going to take a chance on missing out on his boat. They were among those who had driven out, arriving as early as two hours ago. A few may even have arrived the night before. It made Eddie feel good that, as usual, he probably had more people waiting on board than the other boats. He could even shove off now if he wanted to. But that wouldn't be smart money-wise. Anyway, there were more hard-core regulars on the Fisherman's Special whom he couldn't disappoint.

Eddie turned and tucked his hands into his back pockets. The top button of his shirt was open. His boots felt firmly planted on the wooden dock. One hand rose up in a characteristic gesture to check that his captain's cap was fixed on his head the way he liked it, back off his forehead and tilted toward the left—the way Bogie had worn his in *To Have and Have Not*. Eddie was no movie star, but on some Saturdays—and he was certain that this would be one of them—he felt a little bit like one when the folks off the Fisherman's Special came running up, eager to be on the *Pelican*.

He glanced around the dock, hearing Bobby Scanlon busy behind him with final preparations. Eddie caught his brother's eye as he stood behind the *Jigger II*, and they nodded to each other. Frank Mundus squatted before the stern of his boat, yawning between drags on his cigarette. The other captains stood or squatted, smoked or yawned, took off their caps and scratched their heads. One or two whistled quietly.

All of them heard the sound at the same time—the far-reaching tenor horn of the Fisherman's Special. It was off the Napeague Stretch now, steaming through that last bit of brush and pine, then it would turn north to the docks. No matter how many charters these captains had logged, there was always something special about hearing that horn on a summer Saturday morning.

20

Northeast storms off the Atlantic are uncommon over Montauk in early September. The nor'easters that can descend on the coast without warning in autumn and winter—when the polar front moves south over North America and low-pressure cells track up the eastern seaboard—are rare in summer. The approach of a warm front might bring wind and rain from the east, and a cold front might be preceded by strong southwesterlies and accompanied by a stiff blow from the west or northwest, but southerly sea breezes dominate the summer days in Block Island Sound. Of greater concern in 1951 was another hurricane like the Long Island Express of 1938, but the summer of 1951 had been free of storms like that.

Ordinary summer storms were little more than an inconvenience for tourists and shopkeepers in 1951, and were welcomed by Long Island farmers for the moisture they dropped on parched corn, potatoes, tomatoes, and other crops. Such a storm announced its approach with high, filmy clouds, a backing wind, and a slowly falling barometer, to say nothing of the weather reports filling the airwaves from across New York State and southern New England as the warm front traveled east.

On the morning of September 1, 1951, in Montauk, the wind was gentle from the southwest. The typical late-summer day it promised couldn't come at a better time. The sea off Montauk would be filled with sailboats, charter boats, open boats from Fishangri-la, and commercial fishing boats hauling in striped bass and cod.

There were no predictive weather computer models in 1951. A forecasting experiment at Princeton University involving mathematics and radar, which had been developed during World War II, had successfully predicted the 1950 Thanksgiving Day nor'easter that roared in from the Atlantic. This led to the U.S. Weather Bureau, navy, and air force combining to form the Joint Numerical Weather Prediction Unit, but that wouldn't be operational until 1954 or considered reliable until 1958. The first U.S. weather satellite wouldn't be sent into orbit until April 1960. In 1951 it was not yet possible to detect weather patterns and storms from above.

Residents in major metropolitan areas had begun to receive weather reports on a daily basis via two means other than radio—TV news and newspaper graphics—in the late 1940s. Initially, newspapers were more useful because they were far more available. By 1950, the Associated Press was able to offer its newspaper subscribers a detailed weather map that purportedly could predict the weather an entire twelve hours in advance. Newspapers in the New York metropolitan area on Friday, August 31, predicted fair and mild weather for most of Saturday. When the first edition of Saturday's papers carried the same forecast, there was no reason to suspect that the weather would be any different.

Within the limitations of weather forecasting in 1951, the notice posted by Goble on the bulletin board outside the dockmaster's office on the evening of August 31 was, by comparison, authoritative. But it was also wrong. The cold front predicted to arrive in the later afternoon was attached to a strong low that, the previous afternoon, had swept across eastern Wisconsin, pelting the Great Lakes with rain and line squalls. Moving across Lake Ontario that night, the low caused "unprecedented wave heights and considerable shore damage," according to one report. But then the depression weakened, and by Saturday morning it was stalling over Pennsylvania. That in itself might have left the day's weather over Montauk even more benign than predicted, but as the Fisherman's Special sped eastward on Long Island, something of far greater consequence was transpiring four or five miles above the train, undetected by surface observations. An upper-atmosphere trough of cold air with its axis running northeast to southwest—a deep southward kink in the polar jet stream—was approaching Long Island Sound from the west. As the late-summer sun warmed the surface air beneath this subzero air aloft, a dangerous instability would result. If a tipping point were reached, cold, dense air would descend rapidly and violently to displace the lighter air beneath it, and that warm, moist surface air, shouldered suddenly aloft, would build towering cumulonimbus clouds and unleash squalls and thunderstorms on the waters beneath. Meteorologists of a later generation would call this chain of cause and effect a "meso-scale convective event," but mariners have always known it as a sudden storm.

The Montauk captains knew none of that early Saturday morning. They relied for their weather reports first on what was posted at Fishangri-la, then on what they told one another based on past patterns, observations of the sky and water, and pessimistic or wishful thinking. The Coast Guard, the U.S. Weather Bureau, the New York marine operator, and radio stations—these were considered secondary sources.

And by Saturday morning, with Goble's forecast from the previous evening still on the bulletin board, none of the captains was reporting anything more alarming. If that was the worst-case scenario, it wasn't bad.

21

Pelican survivors at the investigation came to dread each announcement by Admiral Olson that the court of inquiry would be taking a short recess. It was during the recesses that widows, siblings, sons, and daughters of victims pushed photographs at them.

And with the photographs came questions, pleas for scraps of recollection, no detail too small: Do you remember him? Were you standing near my husband? What did he say? My brother, did you see him die? Did he try to save others?

The survivors knew that anything comforting they supplied would be welcome, and they were sympathetic. What they dreaded most was meeting loved ones of the missing, because these were people who hadn't yet given in completely to grief or resignation. They still had a tiny, windblown flicker of hope in their eyes and voices that, miraculously, a missing *Pelican* passenger would suddenly arrive home, having been plucked from a yielding sea by a dragger that was only now, days later, inbound with full holds.

With each recess the loved ones grew more pushy, more desperate, thrusting their clutched photographs ever more insistently forward—photos sometimes posed with the very people now pleading for information.

The survivors hurried from the room at the barest hint of a recess, and if they couldn't escape, they made up details. Oh yes, they would say, the man in that photo died a hero—I saw it myself. What they didn't tell was the truth—that it had been every man for himself out there when it happened, that it was confused and chaotic, that people died alone, or that, because of panic, they—the survivors— couldn't remember a thing.

22

Those charter and open-boat captains not plagued by repairs and AWOL mates shared a calm confidence about Saturday's prospects. The younger men wished they had twenty hours of daylight to work with. There would be time enough to rest in the off-season, when the season's profits would pay for rent, food, and clothes for the kids. Older captains looked forward to the season's end, having wearied of the almost nonstop trips since the beginning of May. What was a so-called holiday weekend when it just meant more work than usual? Those with good, dependable mates gave silent thanks.

One such mate, Lenny Riley, was only nineteen but had spent most of his life on the water, having been raised in New Bedford, Massachusetts. He didn't care to fish on one of the big draggers, though, so he'd spent the summer in Montauk as mate on the *Marie II*. There had been little downtime.

It had been an especially good week, and in fact his best summer ever, but Jim Miller was glad that Labor Day weekend had finally arrived. He was dog tired. Jim was only sixteen and a mate on the *Kingfisher*, berthed opposite the *Pelican*—their sterns facing each other across the intervening wooden dock—and next to the *Cricket II*. Jim had been worked to the bone that summer. He had come out from Merrick, up-island, almost a hundred miles west, to find a job as a mate with the Montauk fleet. Taken on by Captain Bill Reichert, he slept aboard the *Kingfisher*. He had been a mate before, on a charter boat out of Freeport, but the experience in Montauk was more exhilarating, albeit exhausting. Jim hoped for a quiet end to the season. He had to get back to school in Merrick, and he didn't want to start the year by falling asleep at his desk.

Bob Conklin was also thinking about going back to school next week. Not high school, though, because he was only thirteen. Bob was too young for most boats, but his captain was his father, owner of the *Arab*, and Bob knew boats up and down, back and forth. During World War II, his father had been in the Coast Guard, patrolling the waters off Montauk and breaking ice in New York Harbor. The talk in the family had always centered around boats and fishing.

Jimmy Hewitt was even younger, only eleven—too young to be a mate, but the Duryeas, who supplied the ice and packed up the fish in crates, paid him a few bucks to wash off their dock on Lake Montauk and alert them if anything needed repairing. Jimmy liked the work, and he didn't mind getting up before dawn. The best part was watching the charter boats leave from the town dock and the dock outside Gosman's Restaurant. One by one they backed away from the dock and turned toward the channel out of Lake Montauk, full of promise. Jimmy couldn't wait to start working on one of those boats.

The older mates turned their transistor radios up loud as they went about their last-minute tasks before the Fisherman's Special arrived. Soon they would be doing their best to supervise an orderly boarding process, but they knew from past experience how difficult it would be for teenage mates to oppose the stampede of arriving anglers. Since their radios were turned up loud, it was fortunate that they were all listening to the same station, one from Rhode Island that came in clearest.

At any given moment on the docks, they could hear from a half-dozen speakers Frankie Laine belting out "Jezebel," Perry Como crooning "If," Dinah Shore warbling "Sweet Violets," and the Weavers giving shape to heartbreak with "On Top of Old Smoky." Even if a song was played that they didn't like—they thought "The Thing" by

Phil Harris was pretty dopey, though the movie was scary—it brought back hazy, beer-soaked memories of the night before, dancing with current and potential girlfriends in front of the jukebox at the bar downtown.

23

Harold Bishop and his wife Jeanne had risen with the sun. They had the routine down pat: Get dressed in the *Betty Anne*'s snug cabin, pack lunches and drinks, and step out on deck with a mug of coffee in hand—all in less than a half hour.

The *Betty Anne* was a good, solid boat and reasonably roomy at forty-two feet long and more than eleven feet wide. With its flat skiff bottom, it drew only two and a half feet of water. Originally called *Gadfly*, the boat had been designed and built in 1926–27 in Freeport, Long Island, by Fred Scopinich, whose sons later became highly respected sailboat designers and builders. Some of the boats constructed at the Freeport Point Boat Yard in the '20s were strictly for recreation, but the *Gadfly* was not one of those. She was a rumrunner.

Built for renowned gangster Dutch Schultz, the boat had two 500-gallon and two 250-gallon tanks encased in bulletproof metal. In its early years the *Gadfly* carried up to eight hundred cases of scotch, packed in sawdust in wooden boxes, from "mother ships" out in the Atlantic to small, dark harbors on the Long Island coast, where they would be unloaded for trucking to New York speakeasies.

At the time, heavy water-cooled Sterling engines powered the Coast Guard boats, and the *Gadfly*, with its two Packard Liberty 500-horsepower air-cooled engines, could outrun them in all but the roughest seas. The few times the Coast Guard got too close, the boat's crew dumped the booze overboard in an anchored fishing net and marked the spot. Even if caught and boarded, the boat was clean.

When Prohibition ended in 1933, Dutch retired the *Gadfly* to a more peaceful and legal life (though a tad immoral) as a pleasure boat. But the pleasure ran out for Dutch in an October 1935 hail of lead, and the *Gadfly* was purchased at auction by a Freeport real estate broker. Every year he hired a captain and cruised the Intracoastal Waterway to Florida with his mistress. Though he renamed the boat after his wife, Betty Anne, he did not allow her on it.

After the broker died, the Bishops purchased the *Betty Anne* and moved it to Asharoken, on the north shore of Long Island. In summer, they would often drive the boat east late on a Friday afternoon and occupy one of the few Fishangri-la berths not reserved for open boats.

On this Saturday morning when they emerged on deck, Harold and Jeanne—he was thirty-five, she nine years younger—were pleasantly surprised to find their three guests, the Smiths (Jeanne's parents) and Jim Bolton (the teenage son of a family friend), already standing on the Union News Dock waiting for them. Though clearly sleepy, their guests would soon be bright eyed on the blue water.

It was hard for Harold Bishop, a member of the naval reserve, to remember a time when he had not been on the water. He backed the *Betty Anne* out of her berth, and they were on their way by 7:30, heading out toward the Atlantic in a gentle southwest wind.

24

Aboard the Fisherman's Special, police captain John Carlson knew what to expect after the train blasted past the wooden and well-weathered Amagansett station. This was also true of at least thirty other people he could see in his car this morning.

But there were a lot of first-timers today—men, women, and kids who were giving Fishangri-la a try. These folks didn't know what they were in for on a morning like this, at a little before eight o'clock. When the moment came, Carlson and other Fisherman's Special veterans could hear them gasp, even the men who had served overseas.

The train crested a forested hill and burst free of surrounding trees to be bathed in bright sunlight again. On both sides of the Napeague Stretch was glistening blue water. The Atlantic Ocean expanded to the distant southern horizon; Napeague Bay drew the eye north to Gardiners Island in the distance, and beyond it the white coast of the North Fork terminating in Orient Point and Plum Island. The glistening blue surroundings were breathtaking. It was as though everyone on the Special had suddenly entered a new and shining world far, far from home.

There was no sitting still after this. Radios were shut off, cigarettes stubbed out, newspapers and 50¢ paperbacks with lurid covers tucked away. The few who still slept were roused and informed of what they had just missed. Fishangri-la was only minutes away. Already the train was starting to slow, and for the last time it entered woods of pine and scrub oak.

Had it been a weekday passenger train, upon emerging from the woods the engineer would have aimed for "downtown" Montauk—the business district south of Fort Pond—and its train depot. The small station building, resembling one of the waterfront white bungalows that dotted the Napeague Stretch, appeared even smaller and more obscure thanks to the dozen side tracks and rail spurs on its south side. Because it was the end of the line—or, to Montaukers, the beginning—the Long Island Rail Road used the station as a storage area for out-of-service trains in addition to the necessary turn-arounds of engines and passenger cars.

Downtown Montauk featured a few shops, a movie theater, White's Drugstore in the middle of the Circle, an IGA grocery store, a large village green, and an Esso station. Visitors could stay at the Memory Motel or The Tavern. Except for the great sweep of the Atlantic spread before it, this could have been Main Street in any small hamlet or village of the Northeast that hadn't changed much since the Depression.

But the Fisherman's Special didn't stop there. It turned northeast before the village and headed for Fort Pond Bay as eager passengers stretched and reached for overhead bags and tackle boxes. John Stein had slept much of the trip and Rudy for some of it; the nervous Kolesar had nodded off briefly a few times. The older man knew it wasn't too late to back out, but he got up and began to gather his gear like everyone else.

Slowing considerably, the Special eased onto the tracks of the siding that the navy had built during the last war. Fishangri-la was straight ahead. Dozens of passengers were out of the train before it stopped—an instant after it began to chug slowly along the asphalt platform. The more alert ones had positioned themselves by the doors and could skip down the stairs and onto the platform. Others, foolhardy as much as anxious, and small or thin enough, squeezed out of windows and plunged to the asphalt, trying to stay on their feet and hold onto their rods and tackle. A few were rewarded with a twisted ankle, bruised shins and knees, even a scraped forehead.

Once the train came to a complete stop and everyone could get off, the rush across the docks resembled Ernest Hemingway's description of the running of the bulls in Pamplona. (His next book, in 1952, would portray the struggles of an aging fisherman.) Although people were running toward something—not away—the mix of excitement and anxiety on their faces was similar.

What they ran toward was the Fishangri-la dock entrance, chained to hold back the human tide. The anglers who had arrived by car viewed the oncoming horde with alarm. It was as if the Long Island Rail Road and Fishangri-la *wanted* pandemonium and took some perverse pleasure from it.

The waiting anglers included Albert Snyder, the New York furrier, and his friends Max Stein and Ben Tasman. Angelo Testa, the Manhattan Club masseur, was waiting with his son, Angelo Jr., and his friend Nicholas Trotta. And John Griffin was there, too, still trying to shake off the lingering discomfort of his wife's bad dream. The surging crowd did nothing to reassure him.

According to the Coast Guard report on the events of this day, early-arriving anglers had been allowed to board their chosen boats, and two dozen or more were already on board the *Pelican*. But at least one of the early arrivers, Paul Pasqualini, would remember it differently. "What they would do," he said years later, "was to have a chain across the dock so that everybody could have an equal opportunity to get on board the boat they wanted. When the train came in, the chain came down." Perhaps the chain was put in place only a few minutes before the train's arrival.

As usual, Pasqualini was determined to get on the *Pelican*. He'd been on it many times. He had a good feeling about the boat—inspired by the number of fish he'd taken home to the Bronx—and he liked Eddie Carroll. In his view, the chain was unfair to anglers who arrived before the train. Paul and his father-in-law had left home at three o'clock, and they had earned the privilege of being first on the boat. But every week it was the same story.

"At last, at last!" Pasqualini almost sang out as the chain was yanked loose and those first in line could beat the train passengers to their favorite boats. Shouting "Follow me!" to his father-in-law, Paul surged forward—and tripped over the chain.

Down he went, face first, landing on the dock with a loud thud. His tackle box crashed onto the hard wood, too, and sprang open, spewing its contents. Moments later, his father-in-law fell on top of him. As Paul and his father-in-law tried to stand, the wave of train passengers washed over them.

25

The rush of people wasn't good news for the concession stands that lined the old Union News Dock. Arriving anglers had to funnel between the stands that sold beer and other beverages, sandwiches, shirts and hats, souvenirs, and fishing tackle. But no one could risk not getting on a boat, especially a favorite boat, by stopping at a stall, even for cigarettes. The sellers weren't that concerned, though. They'd get plenty of business when the boats got back, and from those anglers left behind.

As the captains watched the wave of fishermen and the few women and kids rush toward them, some recalled what had happened one Saturday morning the previous year: An angler, running with the rest, suddenly fell and lay writhing and gasping on the dock like a big marlin. He'd had a heart attack. No one noticed until just about all the folks had found boats; then a few people spotted his contortions. He was dead well before they got him to Southampton Hospital.

Now it was business first for Eddie and Howie Carroll, Frank Mundus, and the dozen or so other captains. Each man, standing on the dock behind his boat's transom, put his hand out to slow the wave of people and motioned them to form a line behind the chain that had been placed across the stern entrance to his boat. The anglers reluctantly settled down, grumbling and shifting restlessly, eyeing resentfully those already on board. A few men, obnoxious by nature or perhaps already drunk, had to be physically restrained by the captains and their mates.

The price of $4.50 a head included tax, bait, and ice for the all-day trip, with kids under twelve free. Beer, on the "wet boats" (captain's choice), was extra. The afternoon before, each captain had filled a battered metal bait box with dollar bills and quarters. But to be on the safe side, they called out, "Exact change appreciated, folks!"

The longest line extended from the *Pelican*'s stern down the dock. Eddie's regulars—a sizable lot—wanted to be back on board. Then there were the ones who had fished on other boats, and a few first-timers. All of them had heard about the *Pelican*'s luck and the entertaining yarns of its captain, so they too wanted their little portion of deck space. And besides, the crowd of anglers already on board told the new arrivals all they needed to know.

Once on the *Pelican*, and after he'd caught his breath, Rudolph Stein looked up and down the boat. The oval railing was lined with anglers; there were no gaps. He turned to his younger brother. "There are too many people on this boat. It's very crowded."

"What are you worried about?" John replied.

"Fishing. That's what I'm here for. How are we going to find room at the railing?"

John grinned. "Rudy, I've been on this boat many times before. By the time we're ready to drop our lines in, there will be plenty of room."

"What, you going to throw people overboard on the way out?"

"Won't have to." John paused to scan the passengers' faces. "There's always new people and people who haven't been out for a while. They'll get seasick and hide in the cabin. Trust me."

"Trust you? You're not the one running the boat."

"Rudy, I've gone fishing with Eddie Carroll plenty of times. We can trust him."

John and Rudy glanced at John's father-in-law, who shrugged. "We're here, and the other boats are full too. Let's go fish," Kolesar said, though he looked pale and nervous.

John Furness found a spot at the railing only because his grandfather created one for him by elbowing other passengers away. Now John clung to the railing, fearing that if he got squeezed out he'd never get back there again.

The Testas and Trotta had lined up for the *Jigger II*, but when they were almost to the stern entrance they heard the anglers ahead of them protesting. "I'm sorry, fellas, I'm full to the brim," Howie Carroll said as he stretched his chain across the opening. "Go see my brother on the *Pelican*."

Trotta and the two Angelos didn't hesitate. They turned and ran to the *Pelican*, which was still taking on passengers. "Boy, that was lucky," Angelo Jr. said.

After ten minutes it was obvious that every boat would be full, and in another ten minutes the captains could see that a few boats might be too full. There were no legal passenger limits. The Coast Guard could and did regulate boats of more than fifteen gross tons, imposing stiffer licensing requirements on boats and captains and limiting the charter fishing passengers to six or fewer. But some of the head boats were built or rebuilt under fifteen tons precisely to avoid such requirements. A head-boat captain imposed his own limits.

Although the *Pelican* carried eighty-two life jackets, her Brooklyn builder had specified a thirty-passenger limit, because more than that would begin to affect the boat's stability. But the *Pelican* was one of the sturdiest boats in the open-boat fleet, and they'd all taken many more than thirty passengers at one time or another.

As the minutes went by and the *Pelican* filled up, Eddie Carroll kept thinking about calling a halt. But always at the head of the line, or two or three back, was a repeat customer saying with his eyes or his voice, "C'mon Eddie, you've got room for me, don't you?" Those personal connections that Eddie had with his customers made it hard to disappoint them at a time like this. And there at the head of the dock was Goble, surveying the scene with a fish hawk's eye. With boat payments and a pending marriage and every intention of being back at Fishangri-la next year, Eddie didn't want to get on Goble's blacklist. And this was the last big weekend of the season. After this would come the short glide into autumn and the long winter, and Eddie could use a big payday after buying that wedding ring.

Eddie looked at the *Pelican*, crowded with humanity. Had he really let so many on? It didn't seem possible. It occurred to him that some might have stepped across from the *Dixie II* or the *Frances Anne*, which were docked on either side of him. That happened sometimes to a popular boat like the *Pelican*. He didn't think Bobby Scanlon would have the fortitude to prevent it. Were there more in the cabin? Eddie couldn't be sure. He looked out at Fort Pond Bay, still flat as a millpond. He looked up at the cloudless sky. He looked at the anxious milling crowd on the dock—so many still without berths—and he decided to take just a couple more.

At that point Frank Mundus shouted his name. Frank had moved his boat away from the dock so no more passengers could get on, and *Cricket II* was idling just ahead of the *Pelican*, blocking her in her slip. Frank had kiddingly predicted this at breakfast, saying that he'd let Eddie out only if Eddie gave him a dollar for every one of his passengers. Eddie looked over at his brother. Howie believed that Frank was serious, because even after just three months in Montauk, Frank had acquired a hard-nosed reputation.

Maybe he really was serious, Eddie thought. But he smiled anyway and called, "When I'm ready, I'm heading out—next to or through the *Cricket!*" Frank laughed, a rare occasion; he liked it when someone found a different way to tell him to go to hell.

"Eddie, no kidding, I think you've got too many today," Mundus called, the laugh over. He compared the *Pelican*'s waterline to those of the nearest boats. Eddie's boat was the lowest in the water.

"How many *you* got?" Carroll asked, smirking.

"I stopped at forty-one," Mundus replied. Unlike Eddie, Frank cared little for personal connections, and he had no trouble saying no. He would have taken fewer still except that the forecast was fairly good and he too needed the money. He tried another tack. "Don't listen to these bastards here. They just want the money. They don't care about us captains, you know that."

Carroll seemed to think it over, his eyes roaming over the shoulder-to-shoulder passengers packed onto the *Pelican*. He called over to his brother, "Howie, how many you got?"

"Fifty-three," Howie called back.

Well, his brother had set a limit, even though the *Jigger II* could carry more. "Bobby, how many on the *Pelican?*"

"I counted fifty-four," Eddie's mate replied.

That number seemed low to Eddie as he once again surveyed the deck below. But it was time to go. Boat engines thundered, and Goble and others yelled from the almost-emptied docks.

"Going to be a great day, Frank!" Eddie shouted.

"Like hell it is," Mundus shouted back, but he let himself smile a little bit. It *was* a beautiful morning, and he had a full boat. Too full, probably, but at least he wasn't pushed deep in the water like the *Pelican*. Well, he'd tried; now it was Eddie's problem.

Time to stop the fooling. Mundus backed his boat away, which opened up a lane for the *Pelican*. "You follow me, Eddie, and I'll take care of you!" Mundus shouted.

"I can take care of myself, you son of a bitch!" Eddie Carroll shouted back, laughing. Then he turned away to cast off.

There were still about eighty unhappy people on the dock, shifting from foot to foot and hoping for one more spot on a boat. Most wore baseball caps, jeans, boots or sneakers, and sweatshirts or button-down shirts with a white T-shirt visible at the neck. As Mundus motored away, he heard Eddie yelling, "No more! No more!"

Dark Noon

'Aye,' said the Captain, reverentially; 'it's a almighty element.
There's wonders in the deep, my pretty. Think on it when the
winds is roaring and the waves is rowling. Think on it when
the stormy nights is so pitch dark,' said the Captain, solemnly
holding up his hook, 'as you can't see your hand afore you,
excepting when the vivid lightning reveals the same; and when
you drive, drive, drive through the storm and dark, as if you
was a driving, head on, to the world without end . . .'

Dombey and Son,
CHARLES DICKENS

A man can be destroyed but not defeated.

The Old Man and the Sea,
ERNEST HEMINGWAY

26

Among the people Eddie had left on the dock were Paul Pasqualini and his father-in-law. By the time they'd collected their tackle and themselves and run down the dock, the *Pelican* was pulling out. Paul couldn't believe his rotten luck. There was one boat that hadn't left yet, the *Rex*. "Room for two more?" Paul yelled. The captain just stared from the bridge as the two men stepped aboard. Paul was already thinking that this Saturday was a day of wasted gas and time.

Eddie had mixed feelings about running an open boat instead of doing charters. One downside was getting a late start—it was 8:32 when he throttled away from the Fishangri-la dock—which meant not taking advantage of the good fishing to be had in the first hours of daylight. And in open-boat fishing you could make money only by volume, carrying a lot more people who paid a lot less money than charters did.

A charter, Eddie thought, like what Bob and Frank Tuma did most of the time, was only a handful of people, usually more serious and knowledgeable about fishing, who hired the boat for the day or half day. Things just seemed more relaxed. If you got going at 6 A.M., you could do one twelve-hour or two six-hour trips. If the fishing was good you would get a little bonus, and you could share in the proceeds from the sale of a big tuna. With the open-boat trips, you could do just one a day, and, whether the fishing was good or bad, back at the dock everyone raced off to catch the train back west and the only tips you were likely to get were the odds and ends of tackle that people forgot. All things considered, a captain stood to make more money from charters than from open boats.

But open boats had their advantages. No uncertainty, for example: especially on the weekends, you knew that a passel of people was coming to Montauk to fish, no worries about a canceled charter. It was guaranteed income.

But Eddie was rethinking open boats because of the way Fishangri-la was shoving passengers onto the decks until they were practically falling off the other side. He looked down at the deck again, seeing how the men, women, and a few teenagers were elbow to elbow at the railing around the entire boat. Rods, fishing lines, even hats and handkerchiefs were repeatedly getting tangled, and this was before they got where they were going and started fishing.

Eddie wondered whether he was going to have a few fights on his hands. He'd never carried this many people before. Thank goodness the weather was holding. As he surveyed those below him—some of them already flushed from sun or booze—he was grateful for the many familiar faces, experienced anglers with level heads to help keep tempers from boiling over.

But there was nothing like good fishing to keep the folks happy. Maybe today they'd be pulling up enough sea bass and porgies to keep everyone occupied.

The open boats fell into formation, a single line chugging toward the wide mouth of Fort Pond Bay. The *Pelican* was about in the middle. From the dock, Bill Morris of *Outdoor Life* magazine snapped a photo that showed the *Pelican* loaded with more passengers than the two nearest boats, Eddie Carroll up on the flying bridge, his light-colored clothes gleaming in the sun, his hat at the preferred angle, chatting over his shoulder with a man in a plaid shirt and dark pants.

A few of the passengers waved back at Fishangi-la, but most were busy with their tackle and jockeying for a bit more space at the rail. The water in the bay was calm.

27

Some 18,000 to 20,000 feet above Fishangri-la, the axis of the upper-atmosphere trough was passing eastward, piling cold polar air overhead. Already the rising sun was warming the surface air, promising a hot late-summer day. With each passing minute, the cold, dense air pressing down on the warm surface air beneath it was becoming more and more unstable, like pressure building behind a dam.

This upper-atmosphere instability would fail to show on the 1:30 P.M. surface weather map that the *New York Times* would publish retrospectively in its Sunday edition—too late to make a difference. What that map would show, however, was a large area of high pressure northeast of Lake Superior. Packed between the high and the trough, a band of tightly spaced isobars—signifying strong winds—would be depicted running east to west over Block Island Sound. In most places the storm would dump up to two inches of rain and move on, erased from weather maps and from memory with equal speed. But not in Montauk.

28

As the open boats entered Block Island Sound, they turned east at Culloden Point and started to spread out, heading for their chosen spots for the day. The southwest wind gave the *Pelican* an easy, gentle push. Eddie felt it on his neck as he steered up on the bridge.

He had already decided on his destination: the Frisbie Bank. Four miles southwest of the Montauk Lighthouse, it was about a mile off the beach. The total run out there would be eleven miles or so, and the *Pelican* would make good time on the calm water. Eddie's passengers could experience the sensation of the open ocean, with a limitless horizon to seaward, but if the southwest breeze should start to build, as predicted for later in the day, he'd have a short downhill run back to Montauk Point and a sheltered passage from there back to the barn. And he knew from experience that they'd find good fishing and less competition on Frisbie.

Eddie gestured for Bobby to collect fares from the people who had forced themselves on the *Pelican* at the last minute. There were always a few. Eddie believed that all his passengers would get their money's worth today.

After the turn east, the *Pelican* cruised between the sun-spangled waters of Block Island Sound on the port side and a shoreline of rocky beaches and sandy bluffs to starboard. Fishers Island, ten miles to port, was visible on the horizon. The island constitutes the northeast boundary of The Race, the tide-choked passage through which Long Island Sound empties into Block Island Sound on each ebb, then fills again with the flood. Just beyond Fishers was the Connecticut shore.

A little more than a mile past Culloden Point, the *Pelican* passed the mouth of the channel from Lake Montauk. Another mile and a half took it past Gin Beach to Shagwong Point. Taking the shortest route, Eddie Carroll cut inside the Shagwong Rock can buoy, marking an eight-foot depth a little less than a half mile off the point. By this time the outgoing fleet of open boats more closely resembled Brownian molecular motion than an orderly procession, as captains veered off for favorite fishing spots. The *Cricket II*, however, was still chugging along near the *Pelican* on a similar course. In another two miles, the *Pelican* rounded can buoy number 3 off False Point, so named because of all the mariners who, over the years, had mistaken the outcropping for Montauk Point.

Eddie negotiated the flood tide in The Rip with ease, leaving Block Island Sound and entering the Atlantic Ocean. Frank Mundus on the *Cricket II* had engine trouble near can buoy number 3 and stopped to take care of it. His customers wet their lines and immediately started catching fish, so Mundus stayed in the area even after fixing his engine.

On the *Pelican*'s starboard side now was the Montauk Light, the fourth-oldest active lighthouse in the United States. President George Washington and Congress had agreed in the early 1790s that a lighthouse should be built on Montauk Point as an aid to shipping, and Congress authorized construction at a cost of $22,300. Operational in late 1796, the octagonal sandstone structure, standing eighty feet tall on an eighty-eight-foot bluff, was first lit by whale oil lamps. By 1951 the Montauk Light was electric, visible from nineteen miles at sea in clear weather. Because of the incessant pounding of the waves eroding the cliff, every year the lighthouse came a foot or so closer to tumbling into the water.

The tide at Montauk Point was high, but the flood current through The Race into Long Island Sound would continue another hour or more. The ebb tide around the point would then reach its maximum at about 12:30, continuing at two knots or more for two hours after that. By four o'clock or so, when the *Pelican* figured to be inbound around the point, the last of the ebb would be hardly noticeable.

While piloting his boat from the flying bridge, Eddie chatted with passengers, putting a new shine on old stories about fishing, foreign lands, and the war, and making idle predictions about the day's potential for porgies and sea bass. He kept one eye on those lining the rail below who were already drinking. If there was trouble later, he wanted to know who to confront first.

A few captains didn't allow booze on their boats. Ironically, a couple of the old-timers who felt that way had smuggled case upon case of hard stuff onto Long Island in those same boats during Prohibition. The Pittses alone had run enough hooch to give all of Manhattan a hangover.

But most of the open-boat and charter captains didn't mind if their passengers drank, and it was good for business. On the charters, captains usually supplied beer along with bait and ice as part of the day or half-day fee. Beer was for sale on the open boats, but in truth that generated only a little extra cash, because many anglers brought their own cans of Schlitz, Rheingold, Piels, and Ballantine, and flasks full of who knew what.

Some anglers were there for the adventure, but others regarded drinking as the sauce of fishing out of Montauk—like cream cheese on a bagel or corned beef with cabbage. So Eddie kept his eyes peeled, because too much of anything could make a mess, and he knew that Bobby didn't have the experience to settle any unpleasantness himself.

Leaving the point behind just before 9:30 A.M., Eddie steered the boat southwest, following Montauk's seaward shore. He liked the Frisbie Bank—the local name for what was really just a seaward bulge of the ten-fathom-deep contour off "downtown" Montauk. Eddie always found plenty of fish and plenty of elbow room out there. His destination today was the near end. He could be there by around ten o'clock, and it was a good choice for the expected weather.

To Eddie and to most of his passengers, this was turning into a typical late-summer trip. Those looking ahead or off to the sides watched the boat's expanding wake and the sparkle of blue water as far as they could see, as though jewels had been cast from a giant net. But a few passengers looking back from the stern saw clouds approaching from the northeast, large white ones and smaller gray ones. Gazing at them for a few minutes, a couple of passengers discerned that the gray ones were moving faster and starting to outnumber the white ones. After fifteen minutes, most of the sky just above the northeast horizon was dotted by moving gray clouds. It was an unwelcome intrusion on an otherwise glorious day.

A few other passengers were uneasy for a different reason—the way the *Pelican* was riding. Those who had been on the boat before would later report that it was riding low, a sensation that became more obvious once they rounded Montauk Point and met the gentle North Atlantic ground swell. They didn't like having their feet so close to foaming seawater, and the boat felt strangely sluggish and listless.

These passengers looked at the crowd on board and put two and two together. The *Pelican* was overloaded, the sheer weight of fifty-five to sixty or more people pushing the boat a few inches deeper than normal into the water. That made them uneasy, even though Captain Eddie up there on the bridge, with his tilted cap and grin, in the middle of another story, looked as though he didn't have a care in the world.

Eddie didn't know that there were sixty-four people, including himself, on board the *Pelican*, although he thought Scanlon's earlier estimate of fifty-four was low. He knew that he could have been deceived by a common trick: some anglers, worried that a boat might be considered overloaded, would immediately head for the cabin and hide there until the boat was on the ocean. They knew that if they were put off before leaving the dock, it would be too late to find a spot on another boat. On board the *Pelican*, there was nothing Eddie could do about those who had hidden.

The *Pelican* should have arrived in the familiar waters of the Frisbie Bank an hour after rounding Culloden Point at 8:45, but the boat still had a mile or so to go at 9:45. The tide had been flooding around Montauk Point, but the breeze was light and the engines sounded fine. No one knew the *Pelican* better than Eddie, and he knew that the boat was sluggish due to overloading. He resolved to pull Gene Goble aside when he got back to Fishangri-la and talk to him about ceasing the practice of driving people down the dock toward the open boats like cattle through a chute.

The seabirds as well as his experience told Eddie when they arrived at Frisbie Bank. As he glanced at the *Pelican*'s surroundings to judge where to stop—a little more than a mile off the beach in the Ditch Plain section of Montauk, with the Coast Guard station there clearly visible—he saw the clouds astern. The horizon was thick with them now, gray outnumbering white. They could mean something, or nothing. It was a blow from the southwest that the weather report had cautioned him to watch for, and for the moment the slight southwest breeze felt good, as did the waves that lolled genially against the *Pelican*.

The way Bobby was looking at him, Eddie knew exactly what his mate was thinking: are we there yet, boss? The farther the boat got from the dock, the more nervous Bobby grew. Put him behind the counter or in the kitchen of the greasiest Montauk eatery, and he was fine for as long as you needed him. But as mate on an open boat on summer weekends, he counted the minutes until it was time to turn back. Eddie loved the trip out, the expectation of it, the sun easing up in the sky like a yellow balloon. For Bobby—well, being mate meant some extra money and a chance to impress the young girls, especially the ones out from New York City for the summer.

Eddie reached in his pocket and twirled—but didn't take out—Inger's wedding ring. Two more weeks. She was beautiful to look at and beautiful in spirit, and he was ready for the minister.

When Eddie made a motion that told Bobby he was about to stop, the relief on Bobby's face was obvious. Eddie told himself that he had to seriously consider hiring a more experienced, seaworthy mate. On the other hand, the way business was now, Bobby could have his pick of other open boats.

The season was almost over. They might as well just ride it out together.

29

At the board of inquiry hearing, Albert Snyder, the thirty-year-old furrier from New Hyde Park, was sworn in. He sat across from the three officers, who asked a few warm-up questions. One was about his military service. Snyder pointed out that he had served in the navy and was familiar with boats.

SNYDER: The fishing was good. Took a little while, but then we were pulling in bass and some porgies.

COURT: So staying out at the Frisbie Bank was okay with you?

SNYDER: Well, no, actually.

COURT: Please explain, Mr. Snyder.

SNYDER: There were just too many people on the boat.

COURT: Did you do a count?

SNYDER: No, that wasn't my job. It was the captain's, or the mate's. I didn't need an exact number to see how we were all squeezed together, even with people puking in the cabin or off the stern. I figured if something happened, we were sunk.

COURT: What did you think might happen?

SNYDER: Well, look what did happen.

COURT: Mr. Snyder, did you talk to Captain Carroll about your concerns?

SNYDER: No. Once we got going, we just wanted to fish.

30

Bobby Scanlon didn't have to tell the anglers twice that it was okay to put their lines in the water. As soon as Captain Eddie cut the engines just before ten o'clock and allowed the boat to drift in the gentle ground swell, the fishermen began to jostle for position.

To the surprise of most, including Rudy Stein, every eager angler found a spot at the rail. His brother had been right, which was annoying because it was a trend that went back to when they were kids. This time Rudy was glad, though. A few of the passengers were queasy and thought that squatting in the wheelhouse or cabin might help. They were wrong, of course. Sure, you could avoid watching the water rise up and down along with your guts, but the small cabin, in particular, was hot, stuffy, and closed. Fresh air was better medicine. So was fishing, now that they could get to it.

A good half-dozen passengers were too boozed up to bait a hook, let alone stand fast at the rail and fish without tangling a neighbor's line. Instead they sat on Coke crates and coolers, or sprawled against the cabin sides, perhaps still greedily sucking on a flask or a beer can, which reflected the sun's light like a mirror.

The air had warmed as the sun inched higher, the southwest breeze still little more than a riffle. Most of the passengers wore baseball or fishing caps, but few wore sunglasses. They had to squint against the brilliant sparkle of blue water.

The younger Angelo Testa kept glancing at his father, and was relieved to see Angelo Sr. enjoying himself. The older man and his neighbor, Nick Trotta, had been annoyed by the crowd, but now that their lines were wet, they looked happy.

Angelo Jr. remembered that this was what it used to be like when they fished regularly. It would be fun to see his mother's face when they got home with a tub of fish packed in ice. He was glad he had decided to come along.

Cynthia Zurendorf didn't know much about fishing, but she baited her hook with her boyfriend's help. When Lawrence Berger said to drop the hook, she did, watching it sink out of sight. She was afraid she might actually catch a fish, but at the same time she hoped she would. It would be fun to show her catch to her father.

She and Lawrence, his brother Martin, and Martin's girlfriend, Renee Sherr, had found spots at the rail, and so did Seymour Gabbin and his girlfriend, Cynthia Chamades, but Cynthia Zurendorf was a little uncomfortable. Everybody was still shoulder to shoulder. She wasn't used to being so close to so many strangers, unless you counted being at the movies. Somehow this was different, out on the ocean on a bright, hot day, with most of the people around her men and many of them a lot older than she.

"How many people do you think are on this boat?" she asked.

Lawrence shrugged, as did Martin. "A lot," the other Cynthia said, and laughed. Then an older man standing next to them whom she didn't know said, "I heard there are fifty-four passengers. That *is* a lot."

Cynthia glanced around. A quick count showed twenty-four people fishing on her side of the boat and three drunken men sitting. She saw some people in the cabin. The captain was up top, and that cute mate was standing on the ladder going up to the bridge. So that was at least thirty people. That would mean only twenty-four on the other side, though she didn't know why one side would be less popular than the other. Maybe it had something to do with the breeze or the current. Still, the boat was crowded, for sure.

She stared down into the water, willing a fish to bite her hook. Then she could go home and say—without crossing her fingers— that this was one of the best times she'd ever had.

31

About the time the *Pelican* arrived at Frisbie Bank, Gene Goble answered the phone in his small office at Fishangri-la and heard the voice of his Pan Am contact at Idlewild Airport, then in its third year of operation and still twelve years away from being renamed the John F. Kennedy International Airport. "A new forecast is being distributed here," the voice said.

"Good or bad?"

"Not so good. Couple of our pilots coming in from the northeast saw a nasty little storm."

"Heading?"

"You might have to batten down the hatches there, Gene. But it's early yet."

"All right, thanks for the update."

He replaced the receiver and thought for a minute. He hadn't expected more details. After all, the pilots didn't work for the weather bureau. All he ever asked for, and what he usually got, from the guy at Pan Am was the signal of a major change, and if there was a storm, what direction it was heading.

He made a quick call to the Coast Guard, which had no updated forecast to share. Again, not surprising. When weather brewed at sea, the flyboys going back and forth across the North Atlantic were likely to see it first. Maybe this thing would blow itself out, or just brush the fishing fleet off Cape Cod.

Goble got up and walked outside. The dock was quiet. With the exception of one boat undergoing repairs—bad luck for a captain on Labor Day weekend—all the open boats were out, and all should be drifting by now, lines streaming into the swells.

He thought about radioing at least a couple of the captains and telling them what he'd just learned; they could pass it around among themselves. Then he dismissed that thought. A captain wouldn't abandon good fishing and anger paying customers because a storm might head his way. If something serious started to show, the boats could hightail it back pretty quickly. Until then, Goble's intervention wouldn't matter much.

He nodded hello to a couple of dock rats who were picking up gum wrappers and cigarette butts to earn loose change, and decided to go get a cup of coffee.

32

Even when he had no strong reason to do so, Frank Tuma Jr. always kept his eyes and ears open for news about the weather. So Saturday morning, while waiting for a late charter party to arrive at the *Janet*'s berth at the town dock next to the Montauk Yacht Club, Tuma listened to the radio and to the idle chatter on the dock.

He rated it a fine morning. What could be better than a Saturday like this on Labor Day weekend? The charter had been booked a good month before; charter captains charged extra for the holiday weekend, and it was hard on the wallet when bad weather caused customers to cancel. Frank expected no trouble getting the full price today.

But not long after ten o'clock, he heard something—not from the radio but from one of the dock rats doing odd jobs for cash. Frank heard his name called and yelled down, "What is it?"

"You still going out, Cap'n Tuma?"

He knew the man—a veteran of around thirty, his clothes looking as though he'd spent half the war on a deserted island in the Pacific. "Yes. My people are late. Probably stayed out last night. Why?"

"New weather report came in. It's not friendly."

The man said the report was predicting a wind shift into the northeast, with a chance of a storm. His source was a dishwasher at the Montauk Yacht Club who had overheard Roland McCann, the manager, telling one of the chefs about it. The club was trolling for weather reports, hoping for time to prepare should bad weather threaten to interfere with the big holiday party that evening.

Tuma thanked him and flicked him a dime. Then he saw a half-dozen people approaching with rods, tackle boxes, and two coolers.

He was glad to have the information, but it wouldn't change anything. No captain would make a living if he stayed tied up every time there was talk of rotten weather. Besides, who knew where the club had gotten this report or how reliable it was? On the other hand, Tuma could now see a few clouds to the northeast, over Block Island Sound. Maybe he should get on the radio and give his cousin Bob, on *Dawn*, a heads-up.

But then it was time to greet his customers and collect the fare. Anyway, Bob could see more than Frank could from his fishing spot near Block Island. Bob would just laugh at the notion that he needed to be told there might be a squall coming through.

33

At ten o'clock Eddie Carroll was allowing the *Pelican* to drift east. He liked being out there without engine noise or exhaust, but, more important, his passengers' lines hung straight while the *Pelican* drifted at the same speed as the water beneath it. That meant fewer tangled lines and the chance to drift baited hooks alluringly just off the bottom.

There was no room at the rail to cast a line. From the bridge, Eddie watched his passengers drop their lines in the water, let them drift for a few minutes, reel in, stare at the untouched bait as if at a stubborn child, then drop the line in the water again. After a few minutes without bites, even the anglers who weren't seasick or busy untangling their lines from their neighbors' looked unhappy.

Well, it was just rotten luck, and you had to work through it. Eddie had chosen the Frisbie Bank in part because it had been a good spot all season. His passengers almost always went home happy. On Labor Day weekend, he especially wanted satisfied customers. That would ensure good word-of-mouth advertising to carry the *Pelican* into the next year. Frisbie was letting them all down so far, but they'd been there only a few minutes. You had to be patient.

At about 10:15, John Griffin reeled in and stood his rod up. "Hey, Captain," he called up to Eddie. "Maybe we can try another place."

"Hell, John, we just got here."

"They ain't biting."

"The fish haven't been properly introduced yet," Eddie said. "They've got to warm up to you. You should've brought flowers, some chocolates."

Several passengers laughed. Many knew that moving the boat might be the wrong thing to do. They hadn't been at Frisbie Bank long, and things could change in a minute. The *Pelican* could move to another spot five miles away that wouldn't work either, and along the way no fishing would get done.

But Eddie had another consideration in mind: the clouds on the horizon to the northeast had been building, and now the wind was starting to shift. This was not a good time to take the *Pelican* farther west.

Griffin called out, "Okay. I'm going to tell the fish you said to bite."

"It's worked before," Eddie replied, nodding.

Only another minute passed when an angler shouted as he reeled in. A good-size sea bass danced at the end of his line. Only a few seconds later, another bass rose flipping from the sparkling water. Soon, porgies and bass were arriving each minute, to be thrust into net bags by excited anglers.

Eddie winked at Bobby. Everything would be fine.

34

The captains off Block Island, ten to thirteen miles east-northeast of the *Pelican*, were growing increasingly uneasy. The wind was backing from southwest into the northeast and stiffening, and they too had observed the increasing number and size of the clouds to the northeast. They chatted a bit about it on the radio among themselves and with a few captains drifting elsewhere—Ray Hegner on the *Sea Rover*, to George Moore on the *Anona*, to Lester Behan on *Bingo II*, to Frank Mundus on the *Cricket II* still over by False Point, to George Glass and Wally Drobecker on their boats, to Howie Carroll on *Jigger II*. The consensus was to keep a weather eye on it.

If Hegner had been feeling less apprehensive, he would have patted himself on the back. He'd had an uneasy feeling about today. He'd been unsettled enough by the forecast tacked on the Fishangri-la bulletin board, and perhaps by some mariner's intuition, to limit himself to thirty-one passengers instead of the expected forty or more. George Moore had done the same, but neither could have said exactly why. Hegner glanced at his mate, Ray Jr., all of seventeen, and nodded. Things would be okay.

They waved to a couple of draggers heading back to Montauk, but thought little of it. The draggers might simply be heading in with full holds after a two- or three-day trip.

Shortly after 10 A.M. the radios crackled, then a clear message came in from the captain of a trawler east of Block Island. He was passing along the small-craft warning he had received from the Coast Guard in Boston—a warning that the Long Island–area Coast Guard had not yet broadcast. As a postscript, he reported that more and darker clouds were approaching his location from the northeast, and the waves were beginning to build.

At 10:20, Chief Boatswain's Mate Purnell Curles, the Coast Guard officer in charge of the Ditch Plain Coast Guard Station in Montauk, picked up the telephone. The Shinnecock Coast Guard Station relayed a message from the Coast Guard Operation Center in Manhattan, which had gotten it from the weather bureau office in New York, which had received it from Washington. Curles copied down:

> Priority X 011340 Zebra. From CGD 3 to Group Command Moriches, List 4 through 6. Small craft warnings indicated 5 A.M. today south of Block Island to Delaware Breakwater. Wind shifting to fresh to occasionally strong northeasterly around Long Island this morning and southward to Delaware Breakwater during afternoon. Cloudy with thunder squalls. Poor visibility with fog.

A small-craft advisory meant winds of up to thirty-three knots, and embedded thunder squalls could magnify that intensity locally. And here, for the first time, was a prediction of squalls from the northeast. But Curles had no formal procedure for sending this message to the Montauk fishing fleet; in any case, it was far too late. A warning referenced to 5 A.M. was just reaching Montauk almost five and a half hours later, a woeful performance that the Coast Guard would, in the future, take steps to correct.

By 10:20 A.M. on September 1, the fleet was out. Whatever was going to happen would happen.

35

Bob Tuma had taken the *Dawn* out early, at sunrise. Like Drobecker, Darenberg, Glass, and a few others, Bob had boarded a charter at Lake Montauk that morning. It was a half-day charter, which meant an early start in the hope of getting hired by someone else for the afternoon.

Not being able to leave until the Fisherman's Special came in was one reason why Bob didn't go for being an open-boat captain. He liked that early start, even before 6 A.M. in June and July. That, and not having to deal with the craziness when the train got in.

Most people in Montauk and most of their regular customers thought that Bob and Frank Tuma Jr. were brothers. They might as well have been. They had grown up together in Montauk, each the son of a fishing captain, gone to grade school together in Montauk and then to high school in East Hampton. (Frank was quick to point out that he was four years younger.) As teenagers, each had been a mate on his father's boat. After serving in the navy in World War II, both had returned to Montauk, become captain of their own boats, married, and started families.

In fact, they were cousins. Bob was the son of Charlie Tuma, Frank the son of Frank Sr., brothers who had come to Montauk during the Carl Fisher boom years in the Roaring Twenties and had helped establish a recreational fishing fleet when Fisher went bust.

A little after 10 A.M., Bob had spoken to George Glass on the radio, both commenting on the wind's swing to the northeast and how brisk it was becoming. The boats closest to Block Island were feeling it first, so it was up to them to spread the word. Now Bob could see that the weather was changing rapidly.

"Jeez, we better start going home," Bob told his charter customers after another few minutes.

The wind was blowing a steady twenty miles per hour by then. No sooner were the words out of Bob's mouth than a stronger, chilling gust buffeted them.

Over the radio he heard George Glass say, "It's really picking up here. We better move on toward home."

Others on Bob's boat heard that too. They nodded and started reeling in their lines. They were losing very little fishing time from their half-day charter anyway. Bob turned the boat southwest, aiming for False Point. The *Dawn* would be all right, running with the wind, but he knew that some captains, including Les Behan on the *Bingo II*, had headed south of east that morning, out to sea in pursuit of tuna or swordfish. Things might get rough for them coming in.

36

By 10:20, the sudden wind shift into the northeast and what Howie Carroll was hearing from other captains had him thoroughly skittish about the weather. Yet he decided to hold off on contacting his brother. For one thing, it was possible that Eddie had been monitoring the captains' weather chatter and already had all the information that Howie did, though this was far from certain. VHF radiotelephones were available in 1951 but not yet in common use, and the Montauk captains still relied on portable amplitude-modulated (AM) radiotelephones operating in the marine bands around two megahertz. These low-power, twelve-volt, vacuum-tube radios had limited range even in the best of times. Prone to atmospheric static from local or even distant storms, and vulnerable to salt and moisture, they were most unreliable just when most likely to be needed. Howie couldn't know whether or not Eddie, on the Frisbie Bank, had heard what captains twelve or more miles away were saying.

But other considerations contributed to Howie's hesitation. Eddie was an easygoing guy, but he could get prickly when Howie pulled any older brother stuff, which was how Eddie would interpret Howie's warning. On the other hand, hailing Eddie on the radio would be passing along the weather report to another captain—one of his open-boat brothers, so to speak—and that was not just accepted but expected practice.

Still Howie hesitated. In the Montauk fleet pecking order, he was on the B-list. So were Eddie, Frank Mundus, and the other open-boat captains. All were considered newcomers. Somehow, broadcasting weather warnings to the fleet felt pretentious.

The distance from Fishangri-la and the docks between Gosman's and Duryea's on Lake Montauk was a lot wider than the two miles shown on the map. The Tumas, the Pittses, and other charter captains had literally built Montauk. They were good people, and Howie and Eddie got along fine with them, but it was like the difference between grade school and high school. You didn't tell the older kids about storms; they told you.

Howie listened to the chatter of his passengers. Most were aware that some kind of weather was closing in, and he saw a few anxious expressions. About a dozen terns and small gulls had gathered above the boat, attracted by the scent of bait and fish and the food that passengers were pulling out of brown paper bags. And every time a tern tittered or a gull squawked, anyone who looked up saw the gray-white sky in transformation. But mostly Howie's passengers were talking about the fishing and still looked pretty relaxed.

Howie's mind drifted back to a few nights before, when Eddie had come over for a small party to celebrate his birthday. Rita had cooked a nice meal, and they'd had a few beers and swapped stories about growing up on Staten Island, loving boats and the water.

Starting when he was four, Eddie used to tag along when Howie went down to the Richmond Yacht Club. There the boatowners gave the kids quarters for sweeping out the boats and polishing brass. The boys liked the money, of course, but for Eddie the incentive was more to hitch rides on the boats, even if the owners would just coast out of the harbor and back. Howie laughed when he told his brother, "You're only thirty-four years old, but you've already got thirty years on the water."

They had talked well into the night, never running out of childhood memories to share. Finally, Eddie got up to leave. He said to

Howie, "After all we've been through, we're on top at last and it was worth every minute of the effort to get here." He showed Howie the wedding ring, then left.

"Goddammit," Howie muttered as he reached for the black radio mike. He was going to call his brother. Now he chided himself for hesitating. If Eddie got irritated—well, the Carroll boys had been through worse disagreements, and none had ever lasted.

37

It was noisy on the *Pelican* even with the engines off. Two passengers had brought portable radios and both were blaring music, one on the starboard side and one to port. At least they were tuned to the same station, so whenever "Aba Daba Honeymoon" by Debbie Reynolds or "Undecided" by the Ames Brothers played, the voices and music rose up from each side and blended at Eddie's helm station on the bridge.

But it would have been noisy even without the radios. Now that the fish were biting, there had to be at least a dozen different conversations going on.

Many were about fishing, of course—the merits of different fish on the hook and the dinner plate, varieties of tackle, open boats versus charter boats, favorite spots to fish, the fish that had gotten away, and the ones that hadn't. A few talked about families, jobs, and neighborhoods; others talked about national and world events. Eddie liked to think that he never had to read the paper or turn on a radio to keep up with the news; he could just listen to what his customers were saying.

The war in Korea was a popular topic. A few World War II veterans sounded as though they wanted to be back in uniform and give the Commies a good licking. The heaviest fighting on the ground now was in the Yanggu sector, and a guy from the Bronx reported that his wife's nephew had been wounded there and evacuated to Japan.

Eddie gleaned other news: The FBI had rounded up seven Reds in Hawaii, including Jack Hall, the labor big shot whose union must surely be a Communist front. The navy had just sent up an experimental superjet from a base in the Mojave Desert and broken the altitude record of 13.7 miles (maybe more impressive, that record had been set in 1935 by two guys in a hot-air balloon). Everyone agreed that the higher federal taxes on cigarettes, liquor, gasoline, cars, and some household appliances were bad news.

The women and kids on board, and a couple of the men, were talking about movies, but Eddie rarely got to the movies, especially this time of year. He was too busy to make the early show, and getting up at 4:30 every morning made it easy to sleep through the late shows. Inger liked the pictures, though; they helped her to speak English better, and she was wild about a few of the big movie stars.

By 10:30 or so, a few of the more experienced fishermen were noticing what Eddie had—that the breeze was strengthening and backing into the east. Also, there were more clouds on the horizon.

At that point Eddie heard an incoming call and picked up the mike on the flying bridge. (The radio itself was in the wheelhouse.) His brother was on the other end. "Eddie, I'm going in," Howie said.

"You okay?"

"Yeah, I'm fine. It's you I'm worried about."

"Why, other than being an older brother?"

Howie didn't laugh. "You should head in too."

"We're getting a few fish. It's pretty good down here."

"Not so good Block Island way, Eddie, and I'm not talking about the fishing."

"Yeah, I've seen a few clouds. Felt the wind picking up a bit."

"Worse up by me, and it's heading your way."

"My guys are still pulling them in," Eddie insisted to his brother. "I think I'll stay here awhile."

"All right. I'll call again right after I get back in."

"Just don't make it collect," Eddie said.

He heard Howie laugh this time before he cut off the call. Still, it bothered Eddie that his brother had contacted him, not because Howie was playing the big brother but because he was skittish enough about this weather to want to head in early. Howie was a good seaman and had a seaman's intuition.

Eddie saw that the railing around the *Pelican* wasn't as crowded as it had been a few minutes before. The stiffening breeze was whipping up a chop, which had sent a few more anglers into the wheelhouse and cabin to squat with their heads between their knees. Eddie couldn't see them from the flying bridge, but he could see three or four queasy-looking passengers doing the same thing on deck.

He'd wait a little longer, then call Howie and maybe one other skipper to see what they were encountering. Maybe it was a reluctance to disappoint his passengers or to have to deal with demands for refunds; maybe it was just stubborn pride. At any rate, Eddie would hate to have the *Pelican* be one of the first boats back at the dock if this blow turned out to be nothing worse than a passing shower.

38

Janet Mundus and her two-year-old daughter were spending that day, as they spent most every day, at Eat and Run, the Fishangri-la coffee shop. Everyone knew the situation—her husband new to Montauk, the young family too broke to rent a house or even an apartment above one of the shops in Montauk village, sleeping on the *Cricket II*, then getting through the day until Frank got back in.

So no one badgered her to order food as she sat with Bobbie at a small wooden table. She drank coffee, and they ate toast with jelly for breakfast. It was always busy when Janet and Bobbie arrived in the morning, because fishermen would hurry in before the boats left to buy the box lunches that the coffee shop had been preparing since 5 A.M.

For lunch, Janet and her daughter would share something simple and inexpensive, like a grilled cheese sandwich and a glass of milk. Janet felt bad about always leaving a small tip, especially because she was practically living in the place, so a couple of times a day when the waitress took a break to smoke a cigarette and put her feet up, Janet collected plates and glasses and ashtrays from the tables and carried them out back. Little Bobbie was fascinated by the kitchen area and sometimes stayed there for a while with the cook, allowing Janet time to look at a magazine.

On nice days they could walk as far as Bobbie's legs would carry her, which usually meant just up the road to the Open Kitchen. It wasn't a big place, but it was more than a coffee shop. If it wasn't busy there, they would visit with Inger, the pretty Swedish girl who was about to marry Eddie Carroll. She always brought out something for Bobbie, a cookie or a small scoop of ice cream.

But by 10:45 today, it looked as though a walk was out of the question. Through the Fishangri-la coffee shop window, Janet saw angry, dark clouds approaching quickly, then sweeping overhead. The breeze turned into a gusting wind, making the shop's front door rattle. She wasn't worried about Frank—not yet anyway. Folks in New Jersey used to say that he was meaner than any storm. He liked to hear that.

The door opened with a rush, and Gene Goble entered and slammed it closed. He went right to the front counter for a container of coffee, his second of the past half hour. He usually acknowledged Janet and sometimes stopped by the table to chat and do coin tricks for Bobbie. Once on the boat when Janet said that Goble's hands had a way with money, Frank had cackled and said, "You got that goddamn right. It's all that experience reaching into other people's pockets."

This morning Goble appeared distracted. He poured milk in his coffee, palmed the lid on, and headed for the door. Then he paused and looked over, gave a quick smile, and touched the brim of his cap. Bobbie hadn't even noticed him, but Janet smiled back. When Goble turned the handle, the door almost flew into his face.

39

Harold Bishop, on the *Betty Anne*, didn't like what he saw, and he didn't like what he felt either. The others, so far, hadn't noticed.

He knew that the *Betty Anne* was a strong, stable boat that had handled its share of weather. Most likely it could take whatever was coming at it. But Harold also knew that the boat wasn't as important as the people on it, and he had four people to look after.

It was around 10:30 when the clouds moved swiftly in from the northeast, threatening to cover the whole sky. The *Betty Anne* was lurching and rolling increasingly as the waves got steeper. The freshening wind was damp and cutting, a far cry from the gentle sea breeze of a half hour before, and the boat was southeast of Block Island and twenty miles from Fort Pond Bay.

Harold glanced at Jeanne. His wife was a good sailor but lacked his experience on the water. She was a small, slim woman, and Harold didn't like the image of her on a boat in bad weather. Jeanne's parents and his friend Jim still appeared more interested in getting bass to bite than in what was happening around them. Well, time to let the real world intrude.

"Everybody, I think we should go back in," he said.

There were groans of "Oh, so soon?" and "Why, what's the matter?" But it was as if he had snapped them out of a trance. Harold saw his wife, her parents, and Jim look up at the changed sky, then recognize the direction and urgency of the wind.

"Something coming this way, looks like," John Smith said.

"Yes."

Jim asked, "Anything on the radio?"

"Not that I heard." Harold gave Jeanne a quick smile. "But I have to admit, for a long while things were so good I wasn't keeping my ear to it."

"What about now?" his wife asked.

Harold went to the radio and turned the knob. It picked up some chatter, some static, and an annoying electronic whine. Then they thought they heard a voice from a boat near Block Island report, "It's getting nasty here," but that was all, and they couldn't be positive.

"Your call, Captain," Jeanne said, and the others saluted and grinned with her.

"Yep, I hate to cut off the festivities, but I got a bad feeling, and every time I look up it gets worse."

Harold started the engines and aimed the *Betty Anne* for the point.

40

Had satellite images existed in 1951, they would have showed—at 10:30 A.M.—a thin band of clouds running southwest from the waters seaward of Cape Cod into Block Island Sound. The building clouds, squeezed between the upper-air trough to the east and the big cloud-less area of high pressure north of the Great Lakes, would have looked dense but narrow, like a snake gobbling up Block Island and Montauk and reaching into Long Island Sound beyond.

The upper-air dam had burst, and cold air was falling to earth, forcing warm air aloft to be rapidly chilled. That was the source of the building wind and the clouds. The squall lines and thunderstorms would follow.

As rogue storms go, this one was no monster, no "storm of the century." It would leave scarcely a ripple in the weather annals. Had it occurred in November, it might have gone unnoticed. But it appeared fast and struck fast on a day with hundreds of boats on the water. The cold, stinging northeast blast it threw from offshore came without much warning, and came first at Montauk and Block Island.

All wise mariners fear storms at sea. Sailors through the ages have cursed storms, assigned them supernatural characteristics, and suspected them of malevolent intent. But a storm at sea—like a volcano, an earthquake, or a tornado—has no intent. It is simply a natural event. What it has are consequences. And what it shows to mariners are the consequences of their own decisions—decisions they may not even have realized they were making.

41

Frank Mundus sensed something odd at around 10:50 A.M., seconds before he felt what it was—the cussed wind had clocked around the lighthouse. The *Cricket II*, her engine back in action, was east-southeast of the point by this time. Suddenly the wind was blowing from the northeast and getting stiffer by the minute.

What Mundus had heard on the radio from the captains near Block Island hadn't really registered with him; he believed only what he could see and feel himself. "What the hell is this?" he muttered.

None of his passengers looked up. By this point in the trip, little more than two hours after leaving Fishangri-la, they were already used to his muttering—which was just as well, because much of the time he was muttering about them.

Goble's weather report hadn't mentioned this development. Southwest wind, my ass, Mundus thought. Well, you got what you paid for.

First engine trouble, and now a penny-ante storm in the middle of what had started out to be a classic Labor Day Saturday. It was bad luck, and bad luck was just one item on the long list of things that made Mundus mad. His list also included elected officials; officials appointed by elected officials; Gene Goble and any other crook who overcharged him for bait, gas, and ice; 99 percent of his passengers; 50 percent of the other captains; just about every mate he'd ever had; hangovers; bad fishing; and sometimes his wife and kid.

But this sudden intrusion of a raggedy-ass squall was particularly galling because it was so unfair. It defied explanation, and, in Mundus's experience, events without obvious explanations were usually perpetrated by someone or something determined to do him harm. This was supposed to have been a great day for fishing, and now this. He saw and felt the waves picking up, and the wind was strong enough already to stand them up like small white-capped walls.

Mundus would later say that if he had been a dog, his ears would have pricked up and his nose would have started sniffing like mad. "This ain't any goddamn good," he heard his instincts telling him.

"Folks," he called out, "I'm not liking this stiffening wind and its direction, plus these waves here. We might have to think about cutting this trip short." It wasn't yet eleven o'clock.

His pronouncement did not go over well. The way everybody started yelling, Mundus would recall, you'd have thought the *Cricket*

II was on a waterfall rushing down the mouth of hell. "Idiots," he muttered to himself and to anyone else nearby who cared to listen. "You'd tell the captain to get lost for the sake of four and a half bucks."

He called out again, "All right, all right. Let's see how it goes. Keep your hooks in. Go on fishing."

42

Only two Montauk captains showed up at Lafayette Street to testify: Raymond Hegner of the *Sea Rover* and George Moore of the *Anona*. Others had been invited to appear, but it meant losing at least a day of income, with each day in September becoming more precious. And some of them just didn't want to appear before a court of inquiry. What good would it do now?

Hegner and Moore seemed uncomfortable answering questions from the court of inquiry. They too could have avoided the hearing, but they felt compelled to put in a good word for Eddie.

Hegner was called first, and answered the necessary preliminary questions about his fishing background.

COURT: Mr. Hegner, where was your boat berthed the morning of September 1?

HEGNER: I was in the Montauk Harbor that morning, operating out of Gosman's. [Pause.] That's on Lake Montauk.

COURT: What were the weather conditions that morning?

HEGNER: I was going through the channel as the sun was rising, and everything was fine to me.

COURT: The weather report posted Friday evening at Fishangri-la described a possible change in conditions on Saturday. Were you aware of the chance of foul weather?

HEGNER: I don't know what the open-boat captains knew or were being told about the weather. Around the harbor where I was, some skippers were talking about stormy weather moving in.

COURT: Do you know the source of this information?

HEGNER: The usual ones.

COURT: Which are?

HEGNER: [Shrugs.] We hear things, we see things, we talk to each other. The captains, I mean.

COURT: That's what you go by?

HEGNER: It's pretty reliable. We're the ones out on the water, not the guys wearing ties in New York.

COURT: Given what you consider a "pretty reliable" chance of stormy weather, did you or any of the captains consider not going out that morning?

HEGNER: I wasn't *not* going to go out. It was Saturday of Labor Day weekend; the weather was fine. No Montauk captain's going to stay tied to the dock. What I did was, I took on thirty-one people. I usually take forty-one. The lighter load means I can get back in faster if a storm shows up.

COURT: Did you do anything differently that morning because of the possibility of a storm?

HEGNER: I headed east, just a few miles, far enough to fish. I didn't want to have far to go against a storm on the way back. But Eddie, if he just had only that Friday report, just like the other captains out of Fishangri-la, then he had no advance warning.

COURT: When the storm approached, what did you do?

HEGNER: Headed back to Montauk.

COURT: Was your boat caught in the storm before you reached Montauk Harbor?

HEGNER: Yes.

COURT: Did you tell your passengers to put on life preservers?

HEGNER: No.

COURT: Wouldn't that be a sensible precaution?

HEGNER: The weather was rough, but it would have to get a lot worse before I'd tell people to do that.

COURT: Why?

HEGNER: Because if nothing happened, then they'd laugh at you.

COURT: Is this the feeling of the Montauk captains, including Edward Carroll?

HEGNER: [Shrugs.] I'm not speaking for anybody but myself.

COURT: Mr. Hegner, we are in the unfortunate but necessary position of determining if Captain Edward Carroll made a fatal error or errors while out with the *Pelican* and its passengers last Saturday, or even that he erred by taking his passengers out at all, and the consequences of that.

HEGNER: Let me tell you something. Eddie Carroll's as good a man and as good a captain as you'll find out here. I mean Montauk. No one gave a damn about the people on his boat more than Eddie.

COURT: Then why didn't he bring the *Pelican* in earlier?

HEGNER: I can't answer that, because every captain is different and has to make his own decision. He would not deliberately put his passengers in danger. What happened was Eddie Carroll and the *Pelican* were in the wrong place at the wrong time, and things happened.

43

At first the *Pelican* had drifted gently east, but by 10:30 the building wind had started pushing the boat southwest. More to the point, the *Pelican* was hanging side-to the four-foot seas that were now curling around Montauk Point, and starting to roll heavily. Not much longer now, and those not already sick would be bowing over the rails.

Eddie eyed the sky to the northeast, as he had been doing with increasing frequency for the past fifty minutes. Like a movie speeded up to show the passage of time, dark gray and black clouds were hurrying the *Pelican*'s way, gobbling up the remnants of clear sky. The wind had risen to twenty knots or so, and every sudden, sharply higher gust was a slap in the face. The wind was damp and chilling, too, though it didn't feel as though the air temperature had dropped much.

At 10:50 A.M., Eddie leaned over the bridge and caught Bobby's attention down on the deck. He made twisting gestures with his hands: turn off the radios. In the abrupt silence that followed, Eddie cupped his hands to his mouth.

"Folks, in my opinion it's time to head back in," he called down.

A few anglers looked relieved, and Eddie figured he could count the proxy votes of the sick passengers in the cabin. Not that this was a democracy. Eddie Carroll could decide to go in or stay out with complete authority. The wind dropped momentarily, allowing some unhappy mutterings to waft upward. He noticed several fishermen glancing at watches or at the contents of their fish bags. They had counted on more time and more fish.

"Hey, Captain, you going to let a few clouds bother you?" one man shouted.

"This is a storm out of the northeast, ladies and gentlemen," Eddie replied. "Those clouds will be followed by their big brothers."

"Let's see how bad it gets first," another passenger suggested.

Eddie hesitated. The suggestion was a stupid one, but he understood that more than a few people on the *Pelican* felt that way. These people had paid $4.50 each—more like $15 if you counted train fare and incidentals—for a full day out on the Atlantic catching big, tasty fish for Sunday dinner or, for the Catholics, next Friday's meal if kept iced. And it was Labor Day weekend, the last trip of the year for many of these folks. This was more than just a job for Eddie. He liked his passengers—most of them, anyway—and he didn't like disappointing them.

He compromised. "I don't like the way things are looking, folks," he called down. "But fish for another fifteen minutes. Catch what you can. Then we'll make a run for it."

He added, "Whoever's not satisfied with what you caught today— or didn't catch—I'll refund half your fare."

That announcement was greeted with smiles and nodding heads from most of those on deck. Eddie saw lips move, but this time he couldn't hear any voices. The strongest gust yet shrieked around his ears and blew all other sounds away.

44

Les Behan was stronger than he looked, thanks to his years in the marines and his hard work on the water, but he was not a big man. Now, at eleven o'clock, he had to face down a half-dozen passengers who wouldn't like what he was about to say.

At least he had Bill Blindenhofer, his mate, to back him up. Bill looked like a big, strong guy, and he was. He was smart too. In the 1930s Bill had graduated from the Massachusetts Institute of Technology, then had gone to work helping design bridges for Consolidated Edison in New York City. He loved boats and could take one apart and put it back together again, so when the Depression bit harder and wouldn't let go, he found he could make better money on the water. He and Les had been working together since the war.

It was for the passengers' own good that the *Bingo II* try to beat this storm back to Lake Montauk, but the passengers wouldn't understand that until later. They wanted to keep fishing no matter what and get their day charter's worth. But Les thought he knew when the weather gods were taking control, and this felt like one of those times.

Plus, Les was tired. Between open-boat work, the occasional charter, and his up-island business, he'd worked just about every day this summer. Enduring the seemingly endless weeks in winter when all you did was wait for the ice to melt didn't make you any less exhausted on September 1.

Les turned on the engines to get the passengers' attention. He liked to tell other captains that if you say you're going somewhere with the engines still off, your passengers will think they can talk you out of it.

Les pictured passing Shagwong Point and soon after arriving at Gosman's dock in Lake Montauk. He would get his passengers off safely no matter how surly a few might be, then double his dock lines and lash things down on the boat. Then the squall could hit Montauk like a truck for all he cared. He and Bill would drive over to Fishangri-la to meet up with the head-boat captains and mates whom they were friendly with for a couple of drinks. He couldn't think of a better way to get warm after a chilly northeast squall.

Les knew he wouldn't be alone. Mundus would be there, and one or both of the Carroll brothers. Maybe all the open-boat skippers would be there. Might as well have a few pops to soften the blow of a Labor Day Saturday's business blown kaput. The storm was winning today's round, but maybe tomorrow would be better, after a good night's sleep.

Les felt his eyes closing. Jeez, he *was* tired. His six passengers were looking up at him on the bridge. As predicted, the engines had caught their attention.

He signaled to Bill, then started down to the deck. Time to deliver the unwelcome news. This squall smelled bad to him, and nothing was going to stop him from reaching the safety of his berth.

45

In the Light House Photo Shop in Montauk, Betty Edwardes enjoyed listening to the radio on Saturday afternoons. Even this far east of the city, she could receive three or four of the New York stations with surprising clarity. The station she preferred offered a steady diet of music from the best Broadway musicals. Right now, she was listening to *South Pacific*.

She could give the show almost her full attention, because there were few customers. The morning had started out busy, but as it grew cloudy and the wind picked up, most of the holiday visitors seemed to find shelter or maybe get an early start up-island. Then the rain started, and she was by herself for long stretches of time.

Her husband, David, had stopped in a couple of times and would probably be back for good in a little while. He was a photographer, and on a holiday weekend like this he would normally be busy shooting pictures of tourists, boats, craft fairs, concerts on the village green, and other holiday sights. But as the storm got worse, there would be less to photograph.

Betty Edwardes felt the building shudder as a gust of wind

slammed against it. It was eleven o'clock. She wondered whether all the boats had come back in yet. She was pretty confident that the open and charter boats would be okay; those captains knew storms and how to get home through them. But some of the out-of-town people with boats might be foolish enough to try to ride it out, or they might not even understand the growing danger until too late.

Another wind gust spattered raindrops on the front window. She went to the big Zenith multiband radio in her back office and switched over to the marine AM band, on which she might overhear the chatter of the Montauk fishing fleet. If anything was happening out there, it could be more dramatic than any Broadway show.

46

When Bill Reichert aboard the *Kingfisher* declared, "We're going in," his sixteen-year-old mate, Jim Miller, didn't have to hear it twice. Miller had been on boats out of Freeport when storms came running, but he'd never been far offshore. Freeport fronted the sheltered waters of Hempstead Bay, and even outside the bay you were never far from the nearest inlet if things got rough. Out in the ocean near Block Island was a different story, and Jim didn't care for it.

Up on the flying bridge, Reichert headed the *Kingfisher* west at a few minutes past eleven. Steep, short seas slapped the starboard side of the thirty-eight-foot boat, but at least the *Kingfisher* was heading in. The weather promised to get worse before it got better. The sky grew darker by the minute, the wind increasing, the rain lashing. Jim would have gladly admitted that he was scared by the squall's escalating intensity, but no one bothered to ask him.

Things did indeed get worse, and faster than he could have anticipated. He heard a high-pitched sound that he realized was the bilge alarm, and a few seconds later the similar-sounding engine alarm went off, piercing the noise of the wind. When Jim looked up at the bridge to make sure the captain had heard the alarms too, the bridge was empty.

Captain Reichert must have gone over the side! Now it was up to a sixteen year old to pilot the passengers to safety.

Jim pushed into the wheelhouse. If the wind was strong enough to blow the captain off the flying bridge, it made no sense for him to try to get up there. The *Kingfisher* was already turning southwest, steered by the overbearing wind. Fishermen were sliding all over the deck, and a few began to shout that the boat was out of control. For the moment, they were right.

Jim had a big decision to make: should he turn the boat around to try to find the captain? He was out there with no life jacket on. He might even be unconscious if he hit his head on the way overboard. Unless another boat came along on the exact same track, he would die in the water if his own boat abandoned him. That settled it for Jim. He was not going to leave a man in the water, and certainly not his skipper. Anyway, if he did find Reichert, the *Kingfisher* stood a better chance of returning safely to Montauk.

Jim steeled himself to tell the fishermen that the captain had gone overboard, and that he would need their help to get Reichert back.

Meanwhile, heart pounding, palms sweating, Jim told himself to start a circling pattern. Grabbing the helm in the wheelhouse, he tried to turn the boat to starboard, but it wouldn't budge. The northeast wind and waves fought him. Hoping to work with rather than against the elements, he tried swinging to port, but the storm fought that turn too. It was as if another hand was on the wheel, opposing his every move.

It turned out that there was. Reichert's head suddenly popped into the wheelhouse. "Hey, let go of the wheel!" he shouted.

A wave hit the *Kingfisher* at that moment, and when the boat heaved, Jim's head banged against one wall of the wheelhouse. He was grateful for that, because now he could believe he wasn't dreaming. "Thought you were overboard," he gasped.

"You crazy?" As Reichert withdrew, he added, "Go see after the passengers."

Jim learned later that when the alarms sounded, the captain had ducked under the console to check the wiring and was out of sight from below. In a few days, with time to think about it, the young mate would feel pretty foolish. But right now he was heading west in a very rough sea, and his long day had hardly begun.

47

It was eleven o'clock, and in just ten minutes the waves had gone from four to six feet. Eddie Carroll had promised his passengers another fifteen minutes of angling, and they'd had only ten. But it was time to take the *Pelican* in.

Eddie knew that the *Pelican* wouldn't make good time heading into the wind and waves, especially given the weight on board. From the Frisbie Bank he would have had a downhill run to Montauk Point if the wind had increased from the southwest as expected, but now he faced an uphill climb into the teeth of a rising squall. The tide would be ebbing in The Rip, too, and that would make things interesting.

Eddie signaled Bobby to get the lines reeled in; more than half were in already. Then he pressed the starter button for the starboard engine. Unexpectedly, it coughed and hesitated before rumbling to life. When he pressed the button for the port engine, nothing happened. Eddie tried again. Nothing. He gestured for Bobby to climb up to the bridge.

Softly enough that no one else could hear, Eddie told him, "The port engine won't start. Take a look down below."

Bobby was immediately nervous. "What am I looking for?"

"Maybe we took on water and don't know about it. Or we got a busted hose. Or maybe there's a problem in the starter circuit up here. Try the starter in the wheelhouse."

Bobby nodded and climbed down. Eddie didn't have much confidence in the outcome, but it was worth a shot. For his passengers' peace of mind as well as his own, Eddie was reluctant to abandon the bridge himself. Several passengers, having heard one engine start but not the other, had watched the exchange between captain and mate with intense interest. Unable to hear what was said, they nevertheless inferred what was going on.

After trying the wheelhouse starter circuit without success, Bobby walked back to the main deck. He picked up the lift ring in the hatch over the port engine, and people made room for him to swing the hatch open. Staring into the dim light of the bilge was to Bobby like trying to decipher hieroglyphics in a cave; he didn't know what to look for. The engine looked clean, with no fluids leaking out and no wires or hoses hanging askew. Bobby thought a minute. There were fifty-something people on the *Pelican*, all ages and jobs and smarts. Navy guys, maybe, or some kind of mechanic—cars, trucks, whatever. Engines are engines. Bobby would find a mechanic among the passengers, the guy would poke his head down the opening here, spot something wrong right away, fix it, and Bobby would thank him and climb up to the bridge, problem solved.

As Bobby turned, he got a faceful of salty, cold spray from a breaking wave. A few people were still struggling to fish and had their backs to him, but others were just holding onto the railing, and they stared at him.

Bobby called out, "Anybody here know anything about engines?"

The good news was that Bobby was smart enough to recognize immediately that he'd made a mistake. The bad news, of course, was that now everyone within earshot was staring at him, including a woman and a couple of teenagers. Clearly, they were all thinking the same thing: We're all up the creek.

A voice said, "Sure, kid, I can fix it."

"I ain't said they're broke," Bobby sputtered as though he'd taken another wave in the face. "It's just . . ."

"Yeah, okay, lemme see."

A middle-aged man with a crew cut—Bobby didn't recognize him—rose from his crouched position against one side of the cabin and staggered toward him. Bobby figured that another wave had struck the boat, but then the man fell forward. Bobby had to catch him.

"My name's Swede," he said between belches.

With a red face and foul breath, the guy was obviously soused. "That's all right, buddy," Bobby yelled into his ear. Then, almost pleading, "I'm sure there's someone else who . . ."

"Yeah, they're all lining up. Get out of the way."

Bobby let him go, and the man straightened up. He gazed down at the silent port engine, then slowly and deliberately kneeled down, then stretched out with his head below the deck, out of sight. Bobby smiled at the passengers. No one smiled back. Two people were shaking their heads.

Bobby was just turning toward toward the bridge when Eddie dropped down in front of him. "What's going on with the engines, Bobby?"

"Looking good, Captain Eddie. One of the guys volunteered to . . ."

"Okay, Bobby, I'll give it a shot. Stay up at the wheel. When the engines get going, turn us east right away. Then I'll be back."

"Yes, Captain."

Eddie turned away, not wanting to say any more. He should have gone himself, right away. He'd lost valuable time.

Eddie crossed over to where the man was lying on the deck. What he wanted to hear was the engine turning over, but what he heard instead was the man's snores. Eddie rolled him aside and took his own look at the engines. Nothing appeared to be wrong. This was so damn aggravating—he'd had the engines overhauled to the tune of $3,000, in large part to avoid a predicament like this: engines not working, a rookie mate, and a boat full of people who had to be getting sicker and more concerned by the minute.

All right, Eddie concluded, sighing. One engine's enough. We're not that far out.

48

Gene Goble liked to meet the boats returning to Fishangri-la on Saturday so he could collect his portion of the fares from the captains and mates. He wasn't used to seeing them inbound around Culloden Point as early as 11:30 in the morning, though.

If the weather was bad enough in the morning, the captains wouldn't go out at all, telling the customers to try again later, or tomorrow, or next week. But if they did go out and the weather turned, they'd usually just ride it out. Most of the passengers would push for that, wanting their money's worth.

Today was different, though. Something had spooked the captains, something beyond the darkening sky and the lashing wind and the rain that was now spattering Goble's head and shoulders. Because he hadn't passed along the weather warning he'd received from his Pan Am contact more than an hour before, he wondered what they'd heard or sensed. A few could get reports over the radio, but they often ignored these in favor of seeing for themselves.

But there they were, rounding the point and steaming into the bay. Goble watched three open boats make the turn and chug toward the dock.

In less than a half hour, they were tied up at Fishangri-la, sterns to the dock. If this wasn't such an unusual event, Goble would have been amused at the differing expressions on the faces of passengers as they got off the boats and trudged up the dock. Some looked angry, some merely annoyed or mildly frustrated, some relieved. A few others, obviously drunk, didn't seem to realize where they were or why.

The captains and mates would be the last off—and not for a while yet, the way they were tying things down. All the boats were empty of passengers now. It would be a good six hours before the Fisherman's Special made the return trip west. With that kind of wait on their hands, many of the passengers who were sober would be drunk by then, and those who were drunk now would be passed out or nursing hangovers. One way or another, it would be miserable on the railroad station platform.

Goble walked over to one of the boats and called to the mate, "Getting bad out there, is it?"

"Yep." The man didn't look up. He was coiling thick manila rope. He wore a Red Sox cap, a black T-shirt, and jeans. Two toes on each foot protruded from his worn black shoes.

"What's the wind?"

"Getting stronger."

"Tell the boss to stop by the office when you're done."

"Yep."

Goble didn't like being treated like a dock rat. Half of these open-boat mates would be nothing but dock rats themselves if not for captains who were desperate during the high season. Goble wandered three berths down to the next boat, whose captain was securing a green canvas tarp over the bridge. "Looks like you think we're getting something."

"I know we are." The captain paused to stick a Camel in his mouth and light it, even in the stiffening breeze. As soon as the smoke left his nostrils, it dissipated. "It was getting bad fast out there."

"So you're okay with coming in this early?"

"Hell, no. I had a dozen people wanting half their fares back."

"Then why . . ."

" 'Cause everyone else couldn't wait to get out of there. And me and my mate are going to spend the rest of the day on this fucking boat mopping up puke." He talked without taking the cigarette out of his mouth.

"Want me to send down a couple of rats?"

"Would be appreciated. I'll come by with your take."

"No rush. Mind your boat."

Goble headed back to his office. A gust of wind pushed him from behind, as though announcing more to come. Noticing motion out of the corner of his eye, he looked toward the bay and saw two more boats on their way in, passengers lining the decks. He knew the boats. Goble ticked off in his head the open boats still out on the ocean and in Block Island Sound.

He paused when he thought of the *Pelican*. The boat had certainly been full when it left that morning. He liked Eddie Carroll, a good man. Goble considered him one of the more cautious captains in the fleet, so he was surprised that the *Pelican* wasn't back already.

49

With the wind increasing and the sea surging against his boat, Frank Mundus knew for certain that the day was shot. But he smiled his typically sardonic smile, not because he was happy—far from it—but because twenty minutes after he'd first announced that they should head back in, at least half of his passengers had, to put it politely, lost the stomach to oppose him.

He would have been happy to tell his passengers that he was more worried about tidiness than he was about them, and he might even have meant it. Some of them would soon be vomiting all over the *Cricket II*, oblivious to the fact that the boat was home to Frank and his wife and kid. To a born pessimist like Mundus, this fouling of his home was inevitable. And just as certainly, when the real weather began, they'd blame him for not getting them back to the dock sooner.

But he was also smiling because he was about to employ a favorite trick to convince the last holdouts that it was time to head in. Mundus switched on the engines and gave them just enough throttle to point the bow into the wind and waves and keep it there.

Within a few minutes the passengers began to complain, especially the ones closest to the bow who were getting showered with spray. Even the ones not getting wet looked increasingly unhappy with this bucking bronco.

Mundus cupped his hand around his mouth. "Sorry, folks!" he mouthed as the *Cricket II* lifted, dropped, shuddered, and lifted again. His facial gestures implied that he was yelling as loud as he could, but he actually let his voice fade. "Whatever's coming this way is coming hard." For all he knew, he might not be exaggerating. "If we don't head in now, we might be too late!"

Even then there was some hesitation. Mundus carefully gave the engines a bit of juice every time a wave approached the bow, and the impacts gave the *Cricket II* fits. A guy on the starboard side leaned over and offered up his breakfast for public examination; shortly after that, a guy on the port side did the same. Having seen this particular routine many times before, Mundus knew how quickly it would spread. Suggestion was a powerful thing.

A wave washed over the bow, drenching more anglers, who watched as their gear sloshed around the deck. "Let's go in, Captain!" someone shouted. A chorus supported that.

"Okay, folks, get your lines in and let's head back to the barn," Mundus said. He gave them a minute, then turned up the throttles and changed direction, heading home to Montauk. He looked down at his forty-one passengers, then smiled and tipped his cap. They waved back and offered grateful grins. "Idiots," Mundus muttered.

Ten minutes later he looked again. Most people were hunkered down on deck, huddled into their sweatshirts and jackets. A few hardier souls were standing and talking. One guy in particular caught Mundus's eye, a guy after his own heart. The elderly man squatted by the stern and was eating what Mundus would later recall as an entire roast chicken stuffed between two pieces of white bread.

50

As soon as Frank Tuma's *Janet* had cleared the channel out of Lake Montauk—sometime between 10:45 and 11 A.M.—and turned east, Tuma and his late-arriving charter party felt the increasing wind and wave action. The weather was coming from the northeast, confirming the forecast that had been buzzing around the Lake Montauk docks for the past half hour. Confirmation of a bad forecast was the last thing Tuma wanted.

Conditions worsened when they rounded False Point. The tide was just starting to ebb, so the water in The Rip was running right into the teeth of that northeast blow, although it wasn't yet flowing fast. When a current opposes the wind, the result is short, steep, vicious seas, and today would be no exception—Tuma was sure of that. By the time the *Janet* made it past the lighthouse, Frank had decided he wasn't going far. He went a couple of miles toward Block Island and called that good.

His charterers caught a few fish, mostly bass, but they looked unhappy with the weather. With yellow and dark green slickers and baseball and fishing caps pulled down low, they might not be getting wet yet, but they were chilled and looked a little fearful. It was beginning to rain—stinging, cold, wind-driven drops. Summer seemed to have given way to autumn in the space of a half hour. Frank was relieved to see their obvious discomfort. It would make his decision easier to sell.

But then he decided he wouldn't even bother trying to sell it. He might have to refund some of the charter, because they'd had only a half hour of fishing, but he was prepared for that. Yes, they looked unhappy enough.

"Hey, folks!" Frank shouted down through cupped hands. "We're getting the hell out of here!"

They looked up, rain bouncing off their faces, eyes squinting in the wind. "What's that?" one called.

"This storm!" Frank replied, gesturing toward the northeast. "I'm making a charge for the beach!"

With fortunate timing, two other boats appeared nearby, both heading back to Montauk. Frank pointed to them, then started the engines. No one said anything, and when he glanced down, they looked a tad less unhappy. It was not yet noon.

51

Rear Admiral Olson, Captain Roundtree, and Captain Shackelford—the board of investigation members—were unhappy, and so was Commander Joseph De Carlo, the lead investigator. The reporters attending the hearing every day were confused by testimony that conflicted with what had been given earlier in the inquiry, and a couple were smelling a rat. Worse, the Coast Guard officers could see that the victims' family members who had been there day after day were getting upset by the inconsistencies.

The panel sent for Bobby Scanlon again. A few days previously, the *New York Daily News* had referred to him as "an inarticulate young man," but the real problem was that what he had previously testified to had been contradicted by one witness after another. The chronology that Scanlon had given was wrong: he had testified that both engines were working until the *Pelican* arrived at The Rip, and he claimed to have helped rescue people in the water when other witnesses recalled him doing nothing more than clinging to the hull.

So, on the morning of September 14, more than a week after his first testimony, the first mate of the *Pelican* was back. The room on Lafayette Street was again full. Scanlon seemed not to have changed his clothes since his previous testimony. More likely, it was the only decent shirt and pair of pants he owned. His light brown hair was more askew this time, though, as if he hadn't had time to comb it. For someone who had spent at least weekends on the water, the taut skin of his face was surprisingly pale.

COURT: Mr. Scanlon, is there anything about your previous testimony that you would like to retract, or in any way change?
SCANLON: No, sir.
COURT: Is there anything you would like to add to your previous testimony?
SCANLON: No, sir. I answered every question.
COURT: Yes, you did, Mr. Scanlon. Our problem today is that much of what you've testified to has not been matched by the testimony of others who were aboard the *Pelican* on Saturday, September 1.

Bobby may have told himself not to shrug, but he shrugged anyway.

COURT: Mr. Scanlon, it is quite obvious that you hesitate exceedingly.

Bobby wasn't sure what that meant. Then Joseph Meehan, the attorney representing the Carroll family, stood up. "Admiral," he said, "I don't understand why this is continuing. Mr. Scanlon has given his testimony and just said that he has no desire to change it." Bobby looked gratefully toward the lawyer.

Olson, visibly irritated, told Meehan that it was the panel's decision to call Scanlon, or whomever else they wanted, as many times as they felt necessary. Then he told Meehan to sit down.

COURT: Mr. Scanlon, for the record, would you describe again the trip out by the *Pelican* and what happened?
SCANLON: Sure.

He was silent for a few seconds.

COURT: Mr. Scanlon?
SCANLON: Sorry, sir.

De Carlo, who was leading the questioning, was becoming more and more frustrated. The *Daily News* had been right. Why Captain Carroll had chosen this kid as a mate, he couldn't understand

COURT: Please proceed.
SCANLON: Sure. We went about eleven miles from the dock to the fishing grounds in the Atlantic Ocean and started fishing. It took us about one hour and twenty minutes running time to reach the fish grounds after we left the dock. At the time the wind was light, southwest, and the sea smooth. At about 10 A.M., we had a violent northeast squall.
COURT: This was at 10 A.M., you say?
SCANLON: Yes.
COURT: [Pause.] Continue, please. Mr. Scanlon?
SCANLON: Right. We were also having trouble with the port motor. We canceled out fishing and started back for the dock. When we reached the lighthouse and were near Jones bar [just inside Montauk Point], about six miles from the fishing dock, having passed most of the Montauk Light rip, the port motor stopped entirely.
COURT: [Pause.] And then?
SCANLON: The starboard motor was working when a big sea hit

the boat broadside, rolled the *Pelican* at about a sixty-degree angle, and caused the passengers to fall to one side.

He stopped talking, staring ahead, his features working. He might have been watching the events of that day on a movie screen in his mind.

Meehan rose once more. Addressing Olson, he said, "It seems to me that this court of inquiry is trying to impeach the witness."

Olson responded, "Mr. Scanlon has nothing to fear from this investigation as long as he has told the truth." Then he added, "But he seems reluctant to tell the truth."

Meehan responded, and while he and Olson argued, Bobby said nothing. None of this was his fault, he seemed to be thinking, and he wasn't going to stumble into being a scapegoat.

52

Eddie glanced down at his passengers. It was close to noon, and if this was as bad as it was going to get, the *Pelican* would make out fine. Eddie kept looking from the sea to the sky and back, feeling the wind, tasting the salt on his lips, his eyes stinging and tearing, trying to weigh the growing seas against the dwindling distance to Montauk Point. They were making progress against the Montauk shoreline, but it was painfully slow.

The sky was covered with a mattress of darkening, swift-moving clouds, and the horizon to the northeast had vanished behind a curtain of onrushing rain. The wind had to be a good twenty-five knots now, with regular stronger gusts that whipped the water into breaking seas that topped six feet.

Eddie could see familiar faces on deck: John Griffin, Tony Borruso, the cops John Carlson and Stanley McKeegan, Jim Hyslop, and John Stein. They had been out fishing off Montauk plenty of times, and they knew boats and storms and this boat's captain. They wouldn't scare easily.

It was the other people he was worried about—the first-timers, the women, that group of kids. If things got bad enough, someone might panic, and the panic might spread like wildfire. He couldn't handle that while steering the boat too.

Eddie thought of the good time that he and Howie had shared the other night celebrating his birthday, then took a deep breath. It occurred to him that the way the mist—flecked with salt spray—filled his lungs must be almost like drowning. The wave of rain rolled closer. After a strong gust of wind, Eddie pulled down his cap and tightened his grip on the wheel of the *Pelican*.

53

Every time Roland McCann looked out any of the windows at the Montauk Yacht Club, what he saw depressed him. The sky was fully gray now, awnings were flapping wildly in the wind, and he'd told the staff to bring in all the table umbrellas and bar setups. He had to accept that no part of the holiday party this evening would take place outside.

But how bad would it get? Would it be an inconvenience or a total washout? McCann could make sure that guests were dry, comfortable, well fed, and well oiled once they arrived, but he had no control over how many would decide not to venture out at all if the weather got nasty enough.

He paused at noon to gaze down at Lake Montauk. The docks were filling up fast. That was a bad sign too. The charter captains were a tough bunch, and if they were returning to the docks—perhaps refunding some of what they had pocketed that morning—it could only mean that they were genuinely worried about what was on the way.

McCann stepped away from the window and glanced around the ballroom area. All the tables were covered with white cloths and plates, gleaming silverware, sparkling wine and water glasses, and vases of colorful flowers. His staff had done a fine job. McCann wondered whether only he and they would end up taking notice of that.

Up on the bridge, Eddie was above most of the cold spray from wave after wave of gray-green water. On the other hand, he was fully exposed to the wind and rain, obliged to thrust his face directly into the weather coming in over the bow. And the boat's motion was decidedly exaggerated on the flying bridge. As the *Pelican* pitched and rolled, Eddie's perch described crazy arcs ahead, back, and from side to side. To keep himself rooted, he had to grip the wet, slick wheel ever more tightly, bracing himself first with his right arm and then his left. His neck and shoulder muscles were cramped and aching.

Then the *Pelican* bucked into a rearing seven-foot wave, and the water running down Eddie's face was instantly salty rather than fresh. He was soaked through by now, and so was everyone else.

He wished he could push the boat faster. Judging by its progress, the *Pelican* was making no better than two or three knots. He and the passengers were looking at a good two and a half hours to get back in.

Down on the main deck, many of the passengers clung miserably to the railing. The lucky or smart ones stayed where they could see the waves coming and thus had a couple of seconds to brace themselves before each impact. Others, perhaps too wet and cold or too frightened to care, took little note of those foaming gray walls of water suddenly emerging from a curtain of rain and mist.

The wheelhouse—ten feet long by seven feet wide—offered standing-room-only shelter for ten to fifteen people. Eddie was willing to bet that a few were packed into the enclosed forward cabin—which could seat eight or nine people tops—not realizing or caring that the motion in the bow was worse than amidships.

Noon, a dark one, came and went, and at 12:30 the *Pelican* was still struggling toward Montauk Point. The sky blackened further, and the wind showed no sign of letting up; it was still a good twenty-five knots with higher gusts, and the seas were still building.

The rain was more annoying than painful. It was like being struck by a whip that had thousands of tiny ends to it; it didn't hurt, but it couldn't be ignored. Eddie wondered vaguely whether this might not be the worst of it, but that question was answered just moments later when clouds of white mist rolled out of the storm ahead as if drawing water up from the crests of the waves. The thin, undulating spouts disappeared into the advancing clouds above.

"Hang on!" Eddie shouted down at the passengers. "Hold onto anything you—"

The mist parted to reveal the largest wave yet. Eddie hunched over the wheel as the wave thundered down and exploded over the bow, stopping the boat cold. Then the bow rose, shedding green water, and slowly, haltingly, the *Pelican* resumed its forward progress.

55

Cynthia Dunwell arrived early for her 2:30 to 11 P.M. shift at Southampton Hospital that Saturday afternoon. She always tried to arrive early; she was a student nurse, and earliness could count in her favor during evaluations. It would, as usual, be a long day.

The three-story brick building on Meeting House Lane in Southampton Village was quiet in the early afternoon. True, a holiday weekend could be expected to bring the usual wave of injuries and illnesses, but that mostly affected the emergency room. The days before a holiday weekend were the least likely time for surgeries, so there were few people in the wards for post-op recovery. The traffic in Obstetrics continued unabated, of course, but otherwise only a third of the beds were occupied by people who had been unlucky enough in the previous day or two to come down with pneumonia, suffer an attack of appendicitis, or relapse into a chronic illness.

Cynthia hoped it would stay that way. Not only was there a skeleton staff at the hospital on a holiday Saturday, with few exceptions the staff consisted of student nurses such as herself who had no choice but to accept a shift unwanted by the experienced nurses.

Long before the advent of the modern Coast Guard, from the 1700s on, the town of East Hampton had puts its faith in "lifesaving stations" spread out from Wainscott, the westernmost hamlet, to Montauk. These stations were manned by volunteer lookouts who patrolled the beaches watching and listening for foundering boats, debris, distress calls, or anything else that told of a vessel in trouble.

By 1873 there were four lifesaving stations within a reasonable distance of the Montauk Lighthouse. One was established on the Napeague Stretch in 1856. Next east was the Hither Plain station, established in 1873, then the Ditch Plain station (1856), and finally Montauk Point (1836).

Given their primitive communications and equipment, the stations and the crews who manned them were remarkably effective at finding and saving foundering ships, their cargoes, and those aboard. In one example, the schooner *Elsie Fay*, with a cargo of coconuts and logwood, lost its way in a heavy snowstorm and foundered on the rocks west of Montauk Point on February 17, 1893. The keeper at the time, William B. Miller, swung into action with his team. Despite the wind, snow, and low temperature, they managed to rig a breeches buoy—a lifebuoy to which were attached canvas breeches for a victim's legs—between the lifesaving boat and the *Elsie Fay*, and carried all seven crewmen safely to shore. They retrieved some of the cargo as well, though much was lost and some found its way into locally baked coconut cakes and other treats.

In 1878 the country's network of locally supported lifesaving stations became the U.S. Life-Saving Service—its motto was "You have to go out, but you don't have to come back"—and Congress appropriated $200,000 to build another 189 stations. The Revenue Cutter Service was formally established in the 1890s, and the two services were merged to create the modern Coast Guard in 1915.

By 1951 all the eastern Long Island lifesaving stations were closed, replaced by a lesser number of Coast Guard stations and boats. Some of the old stations had been derelict for so long that they had disappeared into the shifting sands of the south shore. A few others were destroyed during the hurricane of '38. (The town's Dory Rescue Squad, a reduced consolidation of the lifesaving station crews, endured until 2005, when it disbanded.) Though the Coast Guard had bigger boats and better equipment, the Montauk fleet was vulnerable when any boat was in trouble because the Coast Guard itself was in trouble.

At its peak in the mid-1940s, the Coast Guard had had over 30,000 officers and enlisted men. By the end of 1949, Coast Guard personnel numbered just over 5,000 nationwide, and its boats were being decommissioned and sold to private interests.

Coast Guard officials argued that it was becoming impossible to provide basic services along three coasts, let alone quick action to save lives with fewer stations and ships. The service requested $4 million from Congress to recruit and train new members, but in July 1950 Congress approved just one-quarter of the amount sought. The outbreak of the Korean War that year brought no additional funding because, unlike World War II, there was little threat to home waters.

What was available to the east end of Long Island from the Coast Guard in 1951 were three vessels at the Ditch Plain station. One was a thirty-six-foot diesel-powered lifeboat, built in the 1920s, that had three crew and could carry up to twenty-seven survivors. It was the best bet in heavy-weather search-and-rescue operations.

The other two boats—neither one designed for storm conditions—were a twenty-six-foot motorboat, which was kept in a boathouse on the ocean side to be launched into moderate surf for quick, close-range rescues, and a thirty-eight-foot patrol or picketboat, which, like the lifeboat, was moored in Lake Montauk. Because there was no anchorage on the Atlantic side, a distress call from a boat south or east of Montauk Point required deployment through the Lake Montauk channel to Block Island Sound, then around the lighthouse to the ocean, a time-consuming trip. Like the lifeboat, the picketboat had been built in the '20s, its original purpose being to chase down rumrunners, usually without success.

In a storm too strong even for the lifeboat, a call would go out to the Coast Guard station across Long Island Sound in New London, Connecticut, where two cutters, an eighty-three-footer and a seventy-five-footer, were stationed. Depending on weather conditions, however, it might take up to an hour for either boat to reach the point. Montauk would not get its own cutter, the eighty-two-foot *Point Wells*, until 1962.

Even as personnel and equipment were becoming more scarce, the number of rescues was increasing. In all of 1950, the Ditch Plain station had responded to thirty-nine distress calls. In July and August 1951 alone, there had been twenty-four distress calls, among which were the usual assortment of wild-goose chases. Some boat operators were quick to contact the Coast Guard, then fail to call off the rescue if they resolved the problem themselves. It was not unusual for a rescue ship to conduct a fruitless search, only to learn later that it had been unnecessary.

The line of defense against tragedy in Montauk waters was stretched dangerously thin.

It became thinner early in the afternoon of September 1, with the waters off the east end of Long Island already teeming with Labor Day weekend nautical traffic. The Ditch Plain station received a distress call from three people in a boat in Napeague Bay. Boatswain's Mate Purnell Curles took the lifeboat and set off in search of the boat in jeopardy, turning left out of Lake Montauk, then heading west, urged on by the increasing wind.

That left a twenty-year-old radioman, Boatswain's Mate Third Class Kenneth Whiting, at the Ditch Plain station, and the picketboat on Lake Montauk. Whiting was alone, with Curles twelve miles to the west and the storm's intensity mounting.

57

For years, Coast Guard station personnel and officials in Washington had been warning about overcrowding on recreational fishing boats, but Congress had taken no action. Regardless of how much it might have wanted to, the Coast Guard had no legal authority in 1951 to restrict the number of passengers on boats of under fifteen gross tons.

The *Pelican*'s eighty-two life jackets were stacked in two lockers on the main deck aft of the pilothouse. Only passengers who had been on the boat before knew this, and it didn't occur to Bobby Scanlon, as first mate, to offer life preservers to passengers. If it did occur to Captain Eddie, he was too busy on the flying bridge to do anything about it.

There were a few life preservers in the cabin, which the seasick passengers were using as pillows. Other people sat on deck with arms entwined; still others found ways to fasten themselves, standing, to the railing. Harold Hertzberg had taken this a step further, lashing his grandson, John Furness, to the railing on the port side of the bow with a wire fishing leader. He thought that the fourteen year old would have more protection there, especially when the *Pelican* turned west after the lighthouse, and he wanted to prevent the wind and waves from sweeping the youngster into the sea.

But only one passenger, John Griffin, donned a life jacket. When he appeared on deck from the pilothouse around 1 P.M. wearing a white life preserver, he found at least a dozen passengers staring at him.

"Hey, fella, going for a swim?" one man asked.

"Hell, *he's* got a lot of confidence in the captain," said another.

"Captain Eddie's a fine captain," Griffin responded, "but why not be careful? There's more of these in the lockers."

The passengers near John were silent. The roar of the wind and crash of the waves sounded louder than ever, seeming to surge every ten seconds. Griffin could see from their faces that some of the anglers were tempted to go after life preservers for themselves.

But others, even a couple of guys he'd fished with before, were just revving up. Griffin knew what they were thinking, because he'd thought that way himself when he was out on rough seas: you're showing fear when you put on a life preserver. You could be jinxing the journey back. Put on a life preserver and you're almost guaranteeing that the boat won't make it.

But given how the boat was pitching and the waves were growing, with water and sky whipped to a commingled froth, a life jacket made sense to Griffin. He hadn't been out in weather like this before; it was mean stuff. And there was his wife's dream to think about. Of course, he'd rather drown than tell anyone on the *Pelican* about that. So he'd keep the preserver on and his mouth shut.

"John, maybe you want to hand us your personal effects, so we can give them to your next of kin."

"I'll hold your fishing rod for you, 'cause it takes two hands to pray."

"Do me a favor, Kilroy. When you're the only one fished out of the drink, tell my wife I got three porgies and two bass."

"You must be chicken."

"I'm not afraid, just careful," Griffin responded, then shut his mouth again.

"You *are* chicken," John Stein scoffed.

Griffin took the taunting, thinking maybe he deserved it. He *was* afraid, and he wasn't going to let stupid pride get in the way of good sense.

So he grinned back, nodded his head, even turning a couple of times to show off the preserver as if it was a new shirt. Suddenly an especially big wave hit the *Pelican*, sending it reeling, and everyone grasped for something solid to hold. When the boat righted and the water receded, people shook their heads like dogs and glanced down at their feet, as though to check that they were still on the boat.

A few looked at Griffin as if reconsidering their ridicule of life preservers. No one moved, but after that they let him alone.

58

Antonio Borruso's brown suit hung on him. Either he'd lost weight in the past week or he preferred suits a couple of sizes too big. His mostly silver hair was combed straight back. The knot of his white and red tie was neat, but the last yank had twisted it toward his right shoulder. He told the court that he had served nine years in the Italian navy before World War II. Then he added, with an odd expression of pride, that he was the oldest survivor of the *Pelican.*

COURT: Mr. Borruso, were there life preservers on board the *Pelican?*
BORRUSO: Yes.
COURT: How many?
BORRUSO: I don't have a number. More than the passengers, 'cause that's the law.
COURT: Captain Carroll followed the law, you're saying?
BORRUSO: Yes. He was a good captain. A good man.
COURT: How many times were you a passenger on board Captain Carroll's boat?
BORRUSO: The last time was . . . maybe fifteenth time.
COURT: When did Captain Carroll tell the passengers about the life preservers and where they could be found?
BORRUSO: He didn't.
COURT: Did Mr. Scanlon tell the passengers?
BORRUSO: No. See, we know they're on board. We need them, we'll get them. But nobody thinks we need them. We're just going out to Frisbie Bank, not off Nova Scotia.
COURT: At any point, as the storm intensified, did Captain Carroll or Mr. Scanlon tell passengers to put on the life preservers?
BORRUSO: No. One guy put one on, though. They laughed at him.
COURT: Mr. Borruso, having been on the *Pelican* many times, have you ever seen it as crowded as on September 1?
BORRUSO: No. That was the most.
COURT: Did you say anything to Captain Carroll?
BORRUSO: Yes. I say, "Why are you taking so many people?" He say, "Next week you will see everything all right. For now, you take the place of the next person who gets seasick."
COURT: Is that what you did?
BORRUSO: Sure. But I tell the captain, "I don't catch any fish, I want my money back."
COURT: What was Captain Carroll's response?

BORRUSO: He smiled. He liked to smile. Then he says, "I'm good-natured. I can't refuse anybody."

59

Eddie stared into the swirling gray curtain of mist and rain, steering half by compass and half by intermittent glimpses of the Montauk shoreline until his eyeballs felt as though they would burst out of their sockets like cannonballs. Any hope he might have entertained that the storm would exhaust itself quickly seemed misguided by 1:15. He was soaked, and his face felt pricked and sore from the spray that the wind was hurling like tiny javelins. Why his hat was still on his head he couldn't explain.

His passengers were wet, sick, and scared, and Eddie felt awful about what they were going through. He heard Helen Friedel screaming, "When will we get back?" Even if he could have taken the time to answer, he wouldn't have known what to say.

When they *did* get back to Montauk, he'd treat them all to a drink, and they'd laugh about a close call. It would be a good story to tell their grandchildren.

As recently as fifteen minutes before, some of the passengers had been joking about the storm and the impact it was having on the *Pelican*. "Oh, we're going to go over!" one had said loudly in mock fright. "Well, not this time," another lamented. "Maybe next time." Every time a fresh wave approached, a few of the fishermen laughed.

To Seymour Gabbin, it wasn't funny anymore. Looking at the faces around him, it was clear that no one else thought so either.

Gabbin hadn't been on the *Pelican* before, and he was sure he'd never been in a storm like this out in the Atlantic, so it wasn't a game to him. His girlfriend, Cynthia, had sought shelter in the wheelhouse. He would have joined her, except there didn't seem to be room for another person. Now when a wave approached, several people shouted out warnings.

Helen Friedel screamed again, her voice piercing the wind, "When will we get back?"

John Vallone heard the scream, too, and wondered the same thing. This trip was getting old fast. He decided that putting on a life preserver was not a bad idea, but he had to find one first. This was his third time fishing on the *Pelican*, but he had yet to see any life preservers, and this was no time to go wandering around the boat looking for anything. Every time the boat lurched, he feared he'd lose his lunch and go slipping and sliding across the deck and under the railing. What a switch, he thought; the fish would catch him.

Andrew Kolesar had gotten separated from his son-in-law John and John's brother Rudy. As the weather worsened, Kolesar felt the fear rising in him—the fear of being trapped in his worst nightmare. But this was no nightmare. He was out on the water—exactly where he *didn't* want to be—and on a boat being tossed around like a toy in his grandson's bathwater.

Kolesar couldn't stay outside. Everything was reeling, he was getting soaked, and he was afraid of being tossed overboard by a sudden lurch. He wrenched open the door from the side deck into the wheelhouse. Several people were already squeezed into the small space, but he pushed himself in and vowed to stay in the wheelhouse until the boat was out of trouble.

Max Stein moved around the boat, heading for the port side, making sure before each step that he had something solid to hold onto. As each wave hit, the *Pelican* nosed up and over the breaking crest, shuddered, then fell into the valley between waves, shipping green water over the bow. Then the bow would begin to rise again to meet the next onrushing sea. To Stein it felt like being stuck in an out-of-control elevator that was filling with water.

When the next wave hit, a locker flew open and life preservers spewed out. Some fell on deck and were dragged overboard as the water receded. Others were cast by the wind toward the gray-black sky like so many torn-off roof shingles. Then the locker door slammed shut and stayed closed.

Turning to the side, Stein saw a wave rising like a frothing wall. He grabbed something—later he wouldn't be able to remember what—and held tight as the hissing, cold water covered him. As bad as things were, Stein intended to make it back to Montauk. He couldn't wait to tell the authorities about conditions aboard the *Pelican*. There would be hell to pay.

60

By 1:30, most of the stragglers had made the turn into Fort Pond Bay, and only two berths at the Fishangri-la dock remained empty. One was the *Betty Anne*'s; the other was the slip that the *Pelican* had left five hours before. That empty space between the *Dixie II* and the *Frances Anne* appeared much larger than it had at eight o'clock that morning. Usually, all the open boats came in about the same time, and if two or three were late, the other captains had at least seen them on the way in or been in touch by radio.

But no one had seen the *Pelican* on the way in, and Eddie Carroll could not be raised by radio. Perhaps the *Pelican*'s radio had gotten wet, or Eddie had lost the use of his microphone on the flying bridge and couldn't get down to the wheelhouse, or his transmissions were lost in storm static. Still, his radio silence made several of the skippers uneasy.

By this time a few Montaukers were calling the storm a nor'easter, but most of the captains and mates referred to it as a "son of a bitch nasty bastard squall that came out of nowhere." Whatever it was, it had passengers running for cover as soon as they got off the boats. For some crew members and Gene Goble, peering out of his office window, the sight was both amusing and remarkable.

The amusing part was watching things in reverse. That morning, many of these same people had hurled themselves out of the Fisherman's Special and rushed down the dock like stampeding cattle. Now it was the opposite, with passengers jumping off boats and combining to form a horde of wet, shivering, disappointed people seeking shelter. Too bad the Fisherman's Special was hibernating on a side track, its crew sleeping or at one of the Montauk bars within walking distance.

What was remarkable was that it seemed like two different days. The morning had been bathed in sun, warmth, and expectation. Now the day was already done. The storm had changed everything. The next hours would be long and wet, full of plaintive irritation.

The wind and rain weren't as intense onshore, but people there weren't as accustomed to such weather as those who spent most of their time on the water. The people of Montauk—perched on the exposed tip of a 110-mile-long island—had seen nasty storms before. You couldn't swing a dead cat on the village green without hitting a man or woman who had somehow survived the '38 hurricane. But this holiday weekend, year-round residents represented less than half the people in town.

The rain stung. It was cold and sharp, and it found your face and neck, your arms, even your ankles. It was like being attacked by a swarm of bees. The wind was chill, and gusted just when you raised your head to glance at the malevolent sky. Most weekend visitors couldn't wait to head home.

Frank Mundus was ready to get out of the weather himself. He'd had the *Cricket II* secured at the Fishangri-la dock by 12:30 or so, then helped his passengers step off. He wanted no trouble with someone being tossed in the water by the wind or slippery footing.

It wasn't going to be that easy. "We want our money back!" one old guy shouted. "That wasn't even half a trip," complained another guy.

"Hey, folks, I can't control the weather," Frank said, forcing a friendly grin.

"Neither can we. We paid for a full trip."

Frank sighed. He'd been in this position before in New Jersey, though this was the first time in Montauk. It just confirmed his belief that there were idiots everywhere.

With more effort, Frank forced another grin. He said he understood what they were saying—the trip had been a stinker for all of them. But they had caught some fish. He reminded them how he had agreed to stay out longer, against his better judgment with the storm coming, and how they'd never find a nicer captain and one more concerned about his passengers than Frank Mundus. The storm had screwed him too, he said. He had used up the same amount of fuel as if the day had been beautiful, and sold less beer on board. He still had to pay his mate, insurance, and other expenses.

A few of his customers didn't buy it, which made Frank mad, because this time he really was telling the truth. But they just shook their heads and appeared anxious to get off the boat. Others bought it and were also anxious to get off. Frank made sure each one got ashore safely.

Howie Carroll had docked the *Jigger II* not long after Frank got back. Right away, passengers started clamoring for their money back. Howie figured that it wasn't because they needed the $4.50 as much as they just wanted to pocket the cash and get off the boat. No doubt most of them would spend the $4.50 at whatever bar they fancied. When the boat emptied, Howie still had money in his hand. Some of the wetter, more impatient, and thirstier anglers had simply made a quick getaway.

After securing and cleaning his boat, Howie took another look around. Boats lined the Fishangri-la dock, some with people still staggering off them. A few captains and mates were lashing things down. But by this point, with the storm caterwauling above their heads and the sky still descending, most of the boats were empty.

Then Howie's eyes went to the berth he usually checked first when he got back. It was empty. The *Pelican* still hadn't come in.

Howie walked over to where his brother's boat should be, as though a closer view would change reality. The gasoline-smelling brown water slapped against the dock pilings and bounced off the boats on either side. Howie glanced around. Of the few people left on the dock and on boats, no one appeared concerned.

"Hey, Frank!" he called to Mundus, who was finishing up on his boat. Howie shouted again, louder, though the *Cricket II* was right there. The wind was alternately shrieking and moaning.

Finally, Mundus looked up from what he was doing. "Have you seen the *Pelican*?" asked Howie.

Mundus shook his head. "He was only going to Frisbie, so he'll be here any minute."

"Everybody but him is back," Howie said, cupping his mouth with his hands.

"He stayed out longer than the rest of us." Mundus shrugged, then looked up at Howie. "You know Eddie, he's careful enough."

Finished, Mundus jumped off the *Cricket II*. He told Howie, "I'm going up to get some soup and a shot. Come on along."

"Thanks. I'll wait just a little longer."

"Suit yourself. Goddamn miserable out here. So much for the goddamn holiday weekend."

"See you in a bit, Frank."

Howie watched the other captain, hat pulled down low on his head, as he walked away. A couple of other skippers and a group of mates—those old enough to drink—fell into step behind him.

With the exception of Howie and his brother, the captains had gone home or would be leaning over the bar next to Mundus. Howie should be heading home to Rita. She had to be worried. Well, word about the fleet traveled fast, and she probably knew already that he was back. Just the way people at Fishangri-la were finding out that every boat except the *Pelican* was back.

Jesus, Howie thought, I'm his brother, not his mother. Eddie can take care of himself and his passengers. This is no hurricane, after all, it's just a nasty squall.

And that's what worried him. Eddie had been through nasty squalls before in at least three oceans. So why wasn't he back?

Howie knew he should be on his way home to his wife and kids, but his feet wouldn't move. He pulled his hat lower on his head, turned up his jacket collar, stuck his hands in his pockets, and walked up the dock to the slight shelter of the Fishangri-la roof overhang. He saw a light on in Gene Goble's office, but he preferred to stay outside. Howie wondered, though, if Goble too was going to stay until the last boat was in.

Howie couldn't see the entrance to Fort Pond Bay. Swirling mist and rain covered the northern half of the bay. But he would be the first to see the emerging *Pelican*. He shivered, wet and getting cold, and told himself that he would see the boat in less than five minutes. He started to count.

61

Back in Brooklyn, Irene Stein wasn't listening to the radio. She'd been busy all morning, getting the kids ready for the day and shopping for dinner—not Saturday night's dinner, because the men would be back from Montauk too late for that, but Sunday's. Some of the markets on and near Kingsland Avenue were closed on Sundays, so if you wanted certain things and a choice of prices, you did your shopping on Saturday—and early, too, to get a good selection.

She and the children had lunch, then Irene got them to lie down for a nap. She waited fifteen minutes, thumbing through an issue of *Reader's Digest*. When she was certain that John Jr. and Judy were in dreamland, she started her big project for the day: rearranging the living room furniture. It would have been easier with her husband's help, but she had a clear idea of what she wanted, and John's suggestions, well-meaning as they were, would have been only a distraction. He probably wouldn't notice the change tonight, but he'd be pleased tomorrow morning.

Irene was busy with this task until two o'clock. It was tiring, and even though she would get less done once the children woke up, she needed a break. She filled a glass with water from the tap and stood by the kitchen window. She had waved good-bye from here to John and her father all those hours ago, when it was still dark. The breeze felt good, cooling.

Then it occurred to her that there hadn't been a breeze all day on Kingsland Avenue, but now there was a strong one. Leaves fluttered and branches swayed all along the block. She couldn't tell from what direction it was blowing; it seemed to be swirling. Was the wind this strong, or worse, off Montauk?

John Jr., aware of his father's absence, thought of raspberry candy. Often when his father came home from a trip, he gave the kids little raspberry candies in red and orange wrappers. John Jr. hoped his father got home soon so they could play with the little lead World War II soldiers on his bed. He loved doing that with his dad.

But his father had been gone an awfully long time. Maybe his mother knew when he would be home.

Irene heard John Jr. calling for her, and she turned away from the window.

62

"I'd give this boat and everything on it to be back on dry land," Harold Bishop said to his wife. Jeanne simply nodded. He wondered if she was too scared to speak.

It was just before 1:30, and the *Betty Anne* had been struggling northwest for the better part of three hours. They'd been a long way out when the squall hit—too far, Harold realized now. The waves had to be topping off at twelve feet now, and if anything the wind was getting stronger. Harold had to fight the boat constantly to stay on course. Even with some protection from the flying bridge enclosure, he was soaked and cold. His wife wasn't any better off. At least he could brace himself against the wheel—he and the boat were steadying each other. Jeanne, smaller and with nothing stable to hold on to, was getting bounced around and nearly knocked off her feet by each new and powerful wave.

"So, what's new?" Harold asked, trying a smile. "Let's keep talking, it helps me concentrate."

They talked about movies they wanted to see once they got back home, laughing at each other's predictable choices. Jeanne voted for *On Moonlight Bay* with Gordon MacRae and Doris Day. Harold wanted to see *The People Against O'Hara* with Spencer Tracy. Jeanne countered with Humphrey Bogart and Katharine Hepburn in *The African Queen*, and mentioned wistfully that if their kids were younger they could drive up to White Plains tomorrow where Bozo the Clown was making a personal appearance. Harold said the trip today was more than enough for him, and he was kind of interested in *Bullfighter and the Lady* with Robert Stack and Joy Page.

Harold looked back at Jim and Jeanne's parents. They were huddled together, clutching part of a tarpaulin over them. He called to Jeanne, who was on her way back to rejoin them, "Do they have life preservers on?"

"I don't think so!" she shouted back.

"I think it's time," he said, just as a blast of wind carried his words away.

63

Eddie had heard some of the other captains around Fishangri-la criticize the *Pelican* for being nose-heavy, which was supposed to make her less stable than other boats in rough weather. But Eddie had made it through a lot of weather on the *Pelican*, and he wasn't giving up on her now.

Almost as if that vow turned the trick, at 1:30 Eddie's tired eyes saw what he'd been waiting to see for some time. Through the obscuring, aggravating mist he caught another glimpse of the lighthouse, and now it was bearing just a little north of west, well back on the *Pelican*'s port side. That meant the *Pelican* could begin to turn north and chug past the point, taking them that much closer to home.

Eddie could feel the boat struggling with just one engine, like a man trying to walk with one leg. He knew as he initiated the turn that he'd have to be careful. The seas in The Rip would be piling up against the ebb tide, making them higher, steeper, and more unstable, and the farther to port Eddie turned, the more he would expose the *Pelican*'s starboard side to those breaking seas, which up to now had been coming from directly ahead. Ironically, leaving the open ocean for the more sheltered waters of Block Island Sound would place the *Pelican* in greater danger.

The captains of the Montauk fishing fleet had plenty of experience negotiating The Rip, because they had to do so on an almost daily basis from May into October. Eddie Carroll, like most of them, rarely had trouble there because he respected the area, as an experienced swimmer respects an undertow. He was cautious and attentive.

But this day was different. The Rip was roiling, driven by the northeast gale whipping into a two-knot contrary current, just one more piece of bad luck at this critical spot in a strong ebb with one engine. Eddie and Bobby, who had reappeared from below, looked ahead. There was no choice, no detour except back out to sea.

Eddie pulled Bobby next to him. "I don't know how well she's going to move in The Rip," Eddie told the mate. "There might be a few minutes when we're going to be stuck."

"What do you mean 'stuck'?"

"When I'm trying to turn her west. Our starboard's going to be one big target for the waves. The bigger ones have to be ten feet, maybe more now, and The Rip is making them steep."

Bobby swallowed. His face was pinched and pale. "How big are we?"

"Big enough. But we got some problems." Eddie motioned for the mate not to interrupt. "I'll take care of the problems, but I can't take care of the passengers too."

"Okay, Captain Eddie, what do you need?"

Eddie squeezed his shoulder. "That's what I wanted to hear. Keep them calm, like we do this every day of the week, twice on Saturdays. Make sure they're holding on tight, because the waves are going to slap us around some. And get life jackets out for anyone who wants one."

"Won't that scare them?"

"Some. But others will feel safer. And if something happens, they'll be better off."

Bobby swallowed again. "You think something's gonna happen?"

"Yeah. We're going to get through The Rip and all be laughing about this at the Open Kitchen while Inger serves us beers." He gave Bobby's shoulder another squeeze. "Go on, kid."

The mate was halfway down the ladder when Eddie called out to him. "One other thing, Bobby. Make sure everybody doesn't run over to the port side to get away from the waves. That will overload us on that side."

A few minutes later, some of the passengers wondered why the

Pelican seemed stuck where it was. The more experienced ones knew that the currents in The Rip were strong, and most likely Eddie Carroll was having trouble negotiating them during a storm and with just one engine.

But others knew only that the *Pelican* was as motionless as a deer in the headlights. Or maybe the captain couldn't decide what to do, and wasn't going to move until he did. To Angelo Testa Jr. it seemed as though the *Pelican* stayed where it was indefinitely and might never move again. He was afraid for his father, who was clutching the rail and appeared exhausted.

Albert Snyder was getting pretty tired too. Like most of the other passengers lining the deck, he had a tight grip on the rail. People were shoulder to shoulder. There were gaps, though, because some had sought shelter in the wheelhouse or the cabin.

Passengers on the starboard side probably felt the way Snyder did—a little afraid of being washed overboard by the next large wave. There would be more protection from the wind and hurling water on the port side, but Snyder stayed put, along with many others. Letting go of the rail to get to the port side would be risky; getting hit by a wave at the wrong moment could mean a one-way trip into the ocean.

But some of the passengers couldn't think straight or didn't care. Staying on the starboard side and being punished by the relentless waves was too frightening and brutal. Even the smaller waves projected an intense spray when they erupted against the side of the boat. There was at least a little relief to port.

A few people lurched across to the port side and grabbed the rail there. Others kept a loose grip on the rail and slid their way around by way of the stern. This wasn't as safe as they'd hoped, though, because the passengers on the starboard side weren't about to loosen their grip and step aside to allow someone through, so the sliders had to time the waves and move around the obstacles.

Ben Tasman was one of those staying put. He held his breath and braced himself on the rail as another huge green wave thundered against the *Pelican*. He felt helpless, knowing that the boat and the people on it were at the mercy of the sea.

The man next to him shouted, "Nobody would laugh at putting life preservers on now!"

"Who knows where they are!" Tasman shouted back. "Could be more dangerous trying to find them!"

Another wave approached. The men watched it rise up like a huge fish about to crash down and devour them, ten feet, twelve feet, maybe more. Then it descended, staggering the *Pelican* as the passengers tried desperately to keep their grip on the rail and their feet planted on the deck. The receding water took with it cans, bottles, tackle boxes, rods, and net bags of fish torn free of the railing.

"The captain ought to be jailed for taking on so many people!" Tasman yelled.

The man next to him didn't hear; he had slumped to his knees. Tasman thought perhaps he was worn out or figured that this might be his last chance to pray.

"Where's the mate?" someone yelled.

A few people who cared enough to scan the deck between the crashing waves spotted him. Bobby Scanlon stood with his back against the cabin door, as though the wind had pinned him there.

64

Shortly before two o'clock, Les Behan spotted the *Pelican* to the southeast of the *Bingo II*. It was just a glimpse through the rain and mist, but he saw enough to make him worry. It appeared that Eddie's boat was stuck in The Rip and wallowing in the waves

Behan caught another glimpse. Yes, it appeared that the *Pelican* was making no progress at all. He was surprised that Eddie was still out, given that he had likely gone to Frisbie Bank and would have had to cover a shorter distance than Behan to get back to port.

But then he had to return his attention to his own boat. His passengers, already soaked and unhappy, were even more unhappy when they heard thunder. Then they saw a thin, jagged bolt of lightning stab down from the sky. Behan could have sworn the lightning struck the cliff at the point, if not the lighthouse itself. More thunder followed.

He gripped his wheel even tighter. He'd been tired in the morning, but that was nothing compared with the exhaustion he felt now, after a tense three-hour slog from offshore. His responsibility was to get his passengers safely to port. Eddie knew how to captain a boat. His situation probably just looked worse than it was.

65

All Howie Carroll could hear on the radio was someone on a trawler on the other side of Block Island. The storm conditions were lessening there. Maybe another hour, or less, and the weather over Montauk would be easing too.

At a few minutes before two o'clock, Howie tried again to raise his brother. The way this storm was interfering, perhaps none of the lower-power radios were able to get through. He wondered whether Eddie was using his radio at all.

The *Pelican* was in some sort of scrape, there could be no doubt about that now. It was a question of how bad the trouble was. Word had come from Lake Montauk that the *Bingo II* was also missing. Maybe one of the boats had had engine problems and was being helped in by the other. Or maybe the *Pelican* had become unstable in the building seas and needed to off-load passengers, and Les Behan had worked his way close to help out Eddie. It would be tough maneuvering in those seas, but both captains knew their boats.

Then Howie had another thought: maybe one or both boats were even now showing up at Lake Montauk. He hurried to the pay phone outside Goble's office and called his wife.

"Still no word?" she asked right away.

"No. Listen, Rita, call over to the yacht club and Gosman's. See if anyone's seen the *Pelican* or the *Bingo II*."

"Behan is missing too?"

"Yeah, and there's nothing on the radio. I figure they met up and one's helping the other."

Howie gave her the number and hung up. He went out on the dock again. Nothing. He tried the radio again. Nothing. He stared angrily at the dark, roiling sky. No help came from there either, just a faceful of dashing rain.

He heard the phone ringing, and ran to it. "Rita?"

"Yeah, Howie. No sign of Eddie."

"How about Les?"

"*Bingo*'s on the way in. One of the fellas saw it behind him."

"By itself?"

Rita paused, then answered, "Yes."

"Okay," Howie said with a sigh. "I'll keep waiting here."

He stationed himself at the end of the dock. Howie had the crazy thought that enduring the chilling wind and rain out there by himself would somehow bring Eddie back.

66

Some of the *Pelican*'s passengers began to panic.

Maybe it was being stuck in The Rip and losing hope that the *Pelican* could somehow jerk free of the turmoil and make some progress toward shelter. Or maybe, over the last three hours, they had been worn down by the storm's ever-intensifying onslaught, chilled and flailed by the stinging rain and whipping wind.

Eddie was struggling at the wheel—Bobby back at his side now—and most of the passengers were cowering on the port side. Only the few stalwarts to starboard saw the largest wave yet as it came hissing in. Some would later claim that it was a twenty-footer, but exaggerated estimates of wave heights are common in storms at sea. Nevertheless, a one-knot contrary current will double the size of a wave, and a two-knot current will increase it still further, so a twenty-footer was possible. Even a fifteen-footer—with its face steepened to a vertical wall by the contrary tide and its unstable crest spilling forward in a frothy mass of white water—would have been a terrifying sight. When it hit the starboard side, its breaking crest licked at Eddie's shoulder.

The wave knocked the *Pelican* onto its port side. Eddie clung to the wheel to avoid being hurled into the angry water. The port-side passengers held onto the railing and one another as the boat rolled almost on top of them and their feet lost traction. The few who had begun to slide along the deck toward the water were grabbed by family, friends, or strangers.

Tackle boxes, rods, coolers, bags, and other items were hurled off the boat. On the starboard side, as the water receded, heads and bodies and boots emerged, mouths gasping for air, arms numb with the effort of holding on. They were higher up than they had been before, near to lying on their backs, almost ninety degrees above the water. The Testas thought for sure that the *Pelican* was about to go all the way over.

It didn't. With agonizing slowness, and with Eddie and Bobby both wrenching the wheel, the *Pelican* rose back up into the wind, fighting to right itself. It managed to do so, and passengers who still had breath in their lungs shouted and cheered.

But those ragged cheers were shredded in the wilderness of receding waves to leeward, and grim silence returned. There was no chatter, and on many faces no expression. Men turned their gazes inward, as though embarrassed to reveal the fear in their eyes and stitched on their frozen faces.

Wallace Manko might have smiled wryly if he hadn't been picturing the *Pelican* sinking. He had still been a teenager when he went off to war, a marine no less. He had seen his share of action and had weathered a few storms in the Pacific. He'd survived Japanese grenades and dive-bombers and snipers, come home to Queens, gotten married, and had a son, only to find himself six years later facing possible death on a dinky little fishing boat close enough to the Montauk Lighthouse to hit it with his Marine Corps rifle. Was this how it was going to end?

He had to think about something else. There was Joan. His wife was a bit short—she liked to say "petite"—and she kept her dark hair on the short side too, not much below the ears. And Steven, who was one year old now, a beautiful kid with a winning smile. Wallace was still trying to figure out where that bright blond hair came from. His own was dark brown, though not as dark as Joan's.

Then there were his parents. They had sweated bullets the whole time he was overseas.

Thinking of his family helped. He'd been scared before. He had to make sure, whatever happened, that he got out of this. All around him now, the silence was breaking. He heard people coughing, and one or two sounded hysterical. He wanted to be one of the passengers who didn't panic.

67

Harold Bishop couldn't tell whether Jeanne and the others on the *Betty Anne* sighed loudly with relief when they came within sight of the Montauk Light, or whether the sound was coming from inside him. He glanced behind him. Well, whether they had made any sound or not, they all looked relieved.

Harold figured as he turned north that the *Betty Anne* was a mile east of the light, maybe less. The Rip awaited them, but he wasn't too worried about that. His engines were top-notch, there were only five people aboard, and the boat had overcome challenges before.

"How much longer, Harold?" his wife said, stepping up next to him.

"Half hour we'll be tying up. And just as wet as we are now."

"I can't get any wetter."

"Parents okay? Jim?"

"Better now."

"Once we get past the point and through The Rip, the rest will be easy."

Ten minutes later, his wife having gone back down to the others, Harold felt good about their progress through The Rip. He was giving Montauk Point a wide berth, and the lighthouse was falling behind the *Betty Anne*'s port beam, almost a mile to leeward. The rain had eased to a thick, almost suffocating mist whipped about by the wind. The Coast Guard and the press would later estimate the prevailing wind at thirty-five knots, but the thunderstorm cells embedded in the gale were creating stronger squalls; Harold estimated the strongest at more than fifty knots. When mist descended from the close, dark gray sky, the point was rendered visible only by the flashes of white water cascading on its rocky face.

Harold figured they had to be about halfway through The Rip. The smell of salt water was as strong as if he had dipped his nose into a bucket full of it. His ears hurt from the almost incessant buffeting of the wind. Then he heard someone—his father-in-law or Jim—shout, "Hey, look at that boat over there, behind us and to starboard!"

Harold peered through the mist and slashing rain. About 250 yards away was a boat he didn't recognize—probably one of the open boats, not a charter, because there were far too many figures on it—wallowing badly, caught in the middle of The Rip. Why it was caught, Harold couldn't understand. It looked like a good-size boat, at least forty feet. But there it was, and as he watched, it was hit on the starboard side by a wave tall and furious enough to send green water through and over to the vessel's other side. The boarding sea pushed the boat over to at least a forty-five-degree angle. Even when the boat righted, it retained a ten-degree list to port.

Harold hesitated for a moment. He had his own people to think about. Another twenty minutes or so and the entrance to Lake Montauk would be in his sights. A wave hit the *Betty Anne*, and he heard his wife cry out in dismay as she got soaked again. Then he saw the other boat get hit again, and again it tilted over, even more deeply this time. It appeared helpless.

In a lull between seas, he turned the wheel, and the *Betty Anne* answered smartly despite the wild water and cold, gusting winds. Harold didn't want to look behind him, didn't want to see his passengers' faces as he doubled back. He had to do this. That boat was in trouble and not getting out of it soon. The *Betty Anne* might be able to take on a few people or help in some other way. They had to try.

Harold felt as though he was in the navy again. But then as he got closer, staring intently at the other boat, he saw something he'd never seen in the navy or anywhere else.

68

Eddie Carroll didn't see it coming. He was staring at the Montauk Light, willing the reluctant boat to pull past it, even if only an inch at a time. He heard the wave, though, and involuntarily hunched his shoulders. The sound told him that this one was taller and steeper and breaking closer aboard than those that had come before. The *Pelican* was so tantalizingly near home. If The Rip would release its hold, if the storm would grant even a temporary reprieve, if they could find a soft spot in the outgoing tide . . .

The *Pelican*'s starboard side got hit squarely this time, and the wall of foam-crested gray-green water had to top fifteen feet. For a few seconds the *Pelican* disappeared from view. Eddie knew only that he was, incredibly, underwater. The sea cascaded over him, cold and salty and roaring. His ears fizzed with petulant, annoying foam. Then, just as suddenly, he was free of the water, and what had abruptly become an opaque undersea world was replaced by the dark sky and roiling rip, the lighthouse atop the rocky brown bluff, and his passengers huddled or sprawled on the deck below.

But something was terribly wrong, and it took Eddie, still disoriented, a moment to understand what it was: his boat was going over.

He had lost control of the *Pelican*. He, the captain, could no longer direct or even influence his boat. He knew every inch of it, had maintained and repaired it, had made the payments on it, had learned to feel as safe in it as in his bathtub at home. But it was going over—turning, spinning, its stern emerging from the water, the one propeller still gamely grinding, a forlorn and desperate target for the northeast wind.

Even as the wave pounded to leeward, the boat kept rolling. More in wonder than in fear, Eddie estimated that the boat had to have rolled at least sixty degrees to port. If he leaned over the bridge, he thought he could reach out with his left hand and touch the waiting sea.

But he was captain, still. He righted himself, digging his left heel into the unyielding wood of the bridge, and turned the wheel to starboard. His mind raced: could the roll be stopped? It *had* to be.

The *Pelican*, vying to be the most resilient boat in the Montauk fleet, began to roll back, giving its captain a second chance. In a few moments, Eddie's boat was upright and, he thought, ready to take it on the chin as many times as necessary to get back to the barn.

The *Pelican* was still shedding water when Eddie heard shouts from below. One was from Bobby. He saw his mate at the bottom of the ladder, but his words were torn away by the wind. Then a passenger yelled, "That was a pretty close one!"

"Don't worry," Eddie hollered back, "we're over the worst." He hoped the man had heard him. He wanted to let go of the wheel and run down the ladder to comfort his passengers, but that was out of the question. He could only hope that his words of reassurance were true, and that now the *Pelican* might finally break free of The Rip and limp home on its one laboring engine.

But Eddie was wrong. The first wave had been only a mugger's accomplice, knocking the crutches away from a one-legged man. It had left the *Pelican* upright but unsteady, and now came the mugger's blow. As the biggest wave of all crashed down on his boat, Eddie kept his hands on the wheel but turned his head to meet the punch. He had never backed down from a fight.

Eddie felt as though the boat had been hit by a torpedo. The wave slammed the *Pelican* with brutal, disinterested violence. The force of it shouldered the *Pelican* nearly out of the water. Eddie felt himself rising, his shoes almost losing contact with the floor of the bridge as the air itself came alive with motion and pressure.

When Eddie's feet touched the deck again, it was as though his legs weren't there. He felt his torso, arms, and head plunging straight down, with nothing to stop him, as though falling through an endless hole. The *Pelican* was being pushed once more onto its port side, and Eddie knew with sad certainty that this time it was not stopping.

69

Archie Jones had been watching the *Pelican* for some time. He watched all the boats going out and coming in every day. As the keeper of the Montauk Lighthouse, his job was to take care of the lighthouse and everything in it. But you didn't last long as a lighthouse keeper if you didn't like gazing out to sea, and Archie never tired of it. And when storms blew over the sea, Archie kept a particularly close watch.

From his vantage point in the eighty-eight-foot tower atop the eighty-foot bluff, Jones had seen the early indications of the storm to the northeast. He had listened on the radio to the captains' chatter. Then, as dark, angry clouds overwhelmed the sky and the wind buffeted the lighthouse, Jones had observed the fishing boats returning. The pleasure boats, open boats, and charters all came in one by one. The *Pelican* was the straggler.

It was moving with frustrating slowness as it rounded the point, as if in no hurry, as if this were a lovely Saturday afternoon and the captain and all aboard were reluctant to head back in. Jones used his binoculars to identify the *Pelican* and confirm what he'd seen that morning, that it was weighed down with passengers.

Riding so low, the boat's deck seemed constantly awash. Jones could see how, with some desperation, people were clinging to the railing and struggling back up after getting knocked down. Through the rain he could barely make out Eddie Carroll on the bridge with his hat pulled low and forward.

It had to be engine trouble. Jones tried to raise Carroll on the radio but heard nothing but static. He thought about alerting the Coast Guard, but he knew that the Montauk captains didn't like to accept the Coast Guard's help, particularly if they didn't really need it.

Once the *Pelican* was north of the lighthouse and halfway through The Rip, it appeared to come to a stop. Jones knew that the boat hadn't really stopped; if it had, the twisting ebb tide would have begun washing it back out to sea. It was as though Eddie Carroll had hit a wall and couldn't penetrate it.

Jones had been watching for some time when he saw a tall, on-rushing wave strike the *Pelican* and roll it over. No, it was coming back, straightening slowly. Then he saw the second wave strike. He watched the *Pelican* roll over again. This time there was no rolling back. The boat kept going. Then Jones saw only the bottom of the hull.

After a few moments of stunned disbelief, he radioed the Coast Guard. That was the best he could do from where he was, stuck in a tower on a bluff. He wished he was on the water.

Sea Change

Full fathom five thy father lies;
Of his bones are coral made;
Those are pearls that were his eyes;
Nothing of him that doth fade
But doth suffer a sea-change
Into something rich and strange.

The Tempest,
WILLIAM SHAKESPEARE

70

Eddie Carroll was in the water, and next to him was the overturned hull of the *Pelican*. Instead of being dazed, Eddie's mind was sharp, and he immediately swam to the *Pelican*.

But then, with his hand on the sleek, wet hull, he was overtaken by a sickening sense of dismay. This was not how it was supposed to be. How many trips had he taken out of Fishangri-la on the *Pelican*, always with a good crowd on board? Sometimes his boat was full to the brim with anglers, many of whom he knew. The *Pelican* was a party boat all right, and Eddie always felt like the host of the party.

But the party was over. The people who had trusted him were now in the water. Dying in the water, less than a mile from the lighthouse.

Someone climbed atop the hull, gasping for air. It was Bobby Scanlon. Eddie saw how frightened he was. Eddie looked at the faces straining to stay above the water, and they all displayed terror. But why? thought Eddie. We got this far. He hoped they were visible from the lighthouse. If so, with Archie up there, help might be only minutes away. But what if nobody knew they were out there?

Then it would be up to him. He was responsible for everyone on board. He couldn't let them down. He had been taking out some of these people all summer, some even longer. They were folks he saw week after week, had spent time with on the ocean as the *Pelican* drifted and they fished. By September, they were his people; he knew them and they trusted him.

It was bad luck, he thought—this northeast squall coming suddenly out of nowhere and catching them unaware. Bad luck that the engine had quit. Bad luck that the tide should be ebbing through The Rip. Bad luck that this day, of all days, the *Pelican* was so overloaded. But it was his fault too. He shouldn't have taken so many people aboard. He should have heeded the signs of the approaching storm earlier. He shouldn't have let his passengers talk him into staying out longer. He should have brought them in.

"Captain Eddie, what do we do?" Bobby asked. His legs were straddling the hull above the churning gray water.

The mate's voice was like a slap in the face. Eddie climbed on the hull, wiped the water out of his eyes, and looked around. Dozens of passengers were in the water, many of them thrashing about; few could swim. Boots, jackets, and other heavy clothing weighed down many of them. What had become of those in the cabin, and how many had there been? The rollover, occurring so fast, might have trapped whoever was in there.

As Eddie surveyed the scene, people called out, seemingly to him. One voice after another, at times four or five simultaneously, called, "Help! Help me!" "Please . . . I can't swim!" "Captain, help!" "God help me!" To Eddie it was as though he were in hell, with water replacing fire. His passengers were dying, and he could not save them.

A wave washed over him and Bobby. Eddie realized that they couldn't just sit on the hull. They could save *some* people, or at least help as many as they could to keep their head above water until another boat arrived. Somebody had to have seen the *Pelican* capsize. Maybe the Coast Guard would show in another fifteen minutes.

"Bobby, we've got to drag some people back here. This hull is the only thing to hold onto."

Bobby looked terrified. Another wave hit them. Eddie felt himself slip off the hull, and he let himself go. He would rescue these people himself if he had to.

He could see that several people who could swim were staying afloat well enough, keeping an eye on the waves and timing their dives under them, coming up and sucking in air. And others had found a few loose life preservers or other debris to cling to and were trying to stay calm. He thought about the people in the cabin; perhaps they were being kept alive by an air pocket and could last a while. He made up his mind to bring people in the water back to the hull, one by one, getting other swimmers to help out. If he could gather his passengers, they could keep one another afloat until help arrived from the Coast Guard, or maybe a straggler boat still on its way in past the point.

Eddie saw a man moving more and more feebly in the water, trying to stay afloat with one hand and remove his jacket with the other. He shouted, "Hey, buddy, I'm on the way," and began swimming toward him.

71

The *Betty Anne* was drawing closer to the overturned boat, but it seemed to Harold Bishop to be taking forever. Bishop had turned his boat into the teeth of the howling northeast wind. Steep seas were smashing into and over the bow. The boat's engines seemed to roar with frustration.

Only minutes had passed, but the wait was agonizing for those on the *Betty Anne*. Harold, on the flying bridge, had the best view of the overturned vessel and the people struggling in the water. They disappeared repeatedly under the waves, then reappeared, flailing more desperately than before.

Harold estimated that two dozen people were clinging precariously to the upside-down hull and keel, and about as many more were in the water. As he watched, a head submerged by a wave failed to reappear in the next trough. Men and women, old and young, were indistinguishable. After yet another wave swept over the hull, Harold saw two or three fewer people clinging to it.

To make matters worse, the overturned boat appeared to be slowly sinking, offering less to hold onto. As the *Betty Anne* drew closer, the Bishops, the Smiths, and Jim Bolton watched in horror as people drowned before their eyes.

But at least the *Betty Anne*'s struggle to reach the overturned boat had given Jeanne Bishop and Jim time to prepare. They had collected every life jacket and flotation cushion on board and prepared coils of rope for throwing, and now they stood poised for action, holding tightly to rails and bulkheads so that they, too, wouldn't end up in the water.

Harold had radioed the Coast Guard several times but couldn't tell whether his message about a capsized boat and its location had gotten through. He hoped he wasn't making a terrible mistake. He could not possibly turn away from the stricken vessel, yet he was risking four lives in addition to his own. Did he have that right? And it might be a fool's mission. His crew comprised his petite wife—already weary from the pounding of the storm—her elderly parents, and a teenager. Could they hope to rescue anyone?

They were about to find out. Just ahead of the *Betty Anne* now, a man in the water was screaming for help.

72

Angelo Testa Jr. found himself underwater, feeling cold and extraordinarily heavy. He was sinking. He recognized one imperative: to push upward and breathe again.

When he broke the surface at last, his head and shoulders were battered by wind, waves, and driven spray. It was a struggle to fill his mouth and lungs with air. He didn't know what had happened to put him in the water, why he wasn't stuck under the overturned boat. It didn't matter. He could only try his best to survive.

The last thing he remembered was standing just behind his father and Nick Trotta, who were crowded against the port railing, each holding it with both hands. Then the port side of the boat had rolled down into the sea, and Angelo didn't know what had happened after that.

He had one advantage, though—at least he could swim. He'd be better off swimming than staying where he was to be overwhelmed by waves. But swim where? There was no other boat visible, nor could he pick out his father or Trotta from the desperate and terrified faces around him.

The waves washing over his head and the surreal, swirling clouds of mist that enveloped the scene made it difficult to see much of anything. But then Testa caught sight of a large white object, and realized after a moment that it was the bottom of the *Pelican*. About a dozen people were clinging to it, and three figures sat astride it—Captain Carroll, the mate, and a man who looked like his father.

His father was still alive; he had not been trapped under the boat! But as Angelo watched, a big wave hit the overturned hull, and when it passed over it, his father was gone.

Angelo wanted to swim toward the hull, but he hesitated. All around him people in the water were screaming, grabbing, flailing, and pulling one another down in a vain attempt to climb above the sea. Surrounding the hull, which appeared to be sinking, people were fighting one another for what was left to hold onto.

And swimming was hard. The rain suit he had put on earlier felt heavier by the second. His infantry combat boots were like anvils attached to his feet. Struggling to tread water with one hand, Angelo reached down with the other. His fingers found the laces of one boot, and after a lot of twisting and tugging, he felt the laces come loose.

He pulled off the boot. Now the other one. But the laces wouldn't budge, and with every wave that washed over him it became more difficult to keep his head above water with just one arm free.

Angelo had to leave that boot on; he couldn't spare another second. His father was in the water—still somewhere near the hull, he hoped—and if he had to force his way through screaming and thrashing people to get to him, that was what he would do.

Approaching the hull, Angelo looked from face to face, but none belonged to his father. He pulled away to make a wide arc around the *Pelican* to get to its far side. The effort seemed to take forever, and several times he felt hands clutching at his arms or legs. The mere fact of his floating made him a life preserver—indistinguishable from any other flotsam—to those desperate not to drown.

He had almost reached the other side when two people hurled themselves at him simultaneously. Both were heavier than he, and immediately Angelo was underwater again. He fought his way to the surface, and for a moment he heard the harsh wheezing of his irrational assailants—he thought both were men—in his ears. Then a wave broke over them, and all three were underwater.

Angelo knew that if he didn't break free right away, all three of them would drown. He let his arms go limp, and felt the grips on him loosen. Perhaps they thought he had died, and they should look for someone else to keep them afloat. Suddenly, he yanked his arms free.

Instead of heading for the surface right away, Angelo stayed under. His lungs and throat burned with the strain, and there was a deep ache in his chest, but he swam what he thought was a good ten yards before breaking the surface on the other side of the *Pelican.*

A man floated facedown in the water near him, apparently dead. Angelo was about to shove the body away when he noticed something familiar about the hair, ears, and clothing. He reached for the body and turned it over. His father's lifeless eyes stared back at him.

73

The *Bingo II* was heading east, and soon False Point would be to starboard. Behan hoped he wasn't making a really dumb mistake.

The boat had never reached Lake Montauk to drop off its charter passengers. Behan hadn't been able to shake the sight of the *Pelican* out of his head. The more he thought about it, the more he believed Eddie was in genuine trouble. He'd heard nothing on the radio, but that didn't mean much. Eddie's bridge microphone might have shorted out, or the radio itself might have gotten wet or simply chosen that time to stop working. (Durable, dependable, weatherproof radiotelephones were still in the future in 1951.) Possibly the intensity of the storm was disrupting communications.

Of course, the intense storm had been the best reason for continuing on to the safety of the town dock. His passengers were a pretty miserable-looking bunch. But he'd convinced Bill that there was a boat in trouble out there with as many as thirty or forty people on it, and it was captained by one of their own. There was room enough on the *Bingo II* to take at least half those passengers back to Montauk, which in turn would make it easier for the *Pelican* to escape The Rip.

They passed False Point. Les had to fight the wheel because the northeast wind gusts kept trying to force the boat toward the cliffs adjacent to the lighthouse.

Bill climbed up beside him. "I'm thinking engine trouble," he said.

"Wouldn't surprise me," Behan replied. "I can't think of any other good reason to be stuck where he was."

"Think we can tow him in?"

"I don't know. We're not much bigger than the *Pelican.*"

"Bigger engines, though."

"Yeah, but in this sea . . ."

Behan turned the boat southeast to enter The Rip. Rain lashed his face. He heard Bill say something, and wondered whether his mate was cursing the storm or him.

Then Bill shouted, "There's something in the water!"

"What is it?"

"I don't know."

Behan stared through the rain and mist, the driven drops stinging his eyes. Now he could see a lot of objects in the water. A dozen. No, more. Most of them were white. To him it looked as though a flock of seagulls had set down in the turbulence.

"I hear something too," Bill said.

Behan strained his ears, then he heard it too. The sounds were cutting through the noise of the wind and waves and the *Bingo II*'s engines. Shouts. Cries. Pleas for help.

The *Bingo II* pushed closer. "Jesus, Les . . . the *Pelican?*"

Behan saw it too: the overturned hull protruding from the water, and people clinging to it. Those weren't gulls spread out on the water; they were people's heads. And from their mouths were coming those piercing pleas for help.

"Yeah, goddammit. The *Pelican* capsized."

As Behan reached for the radio, he saw a head go under the roiling surface; it didn't come back up.

74

A few fortunate passengers had had the time and presence of mind to act to save themselves. Stanley Olszewski, all three hundred pounds of him, had jumped over the port gunwale as it rolled underneath him. Somehow he managed not to get trapped under the boat when it capsized. Perhaps his girth made him more buoyant, because he remained afloat with a rudimentary dog paddle, and his body fat delayed the onset of hypothermia.

Benjamin Tasman had been gripping the *Pelican*'s port rail alongside his friends Max Stein and Albert Snyder. Fighting seasickness, he was unaware that the boat was turning over. One moment he was standing, the next he was in the water. He couldn't see his friends, or anything else for that matter.

Several moments passed before the disoriented Tasman realized that he was trapped under the boat. He tried to swim clear, praying he wasn't heading into the overturned boat's wheelhouse. It was too dark to know. Then the darkness eased enough to show him that he was free of the boat. As soon as his head emerged from the water, he took a great gulp of air and attacked the onrushing waves with flailing arms. Then his rational mind started posing questions: What am I doing? Where am I swimming to? All around him, stunned and terrified passengers screamed and cried, shouting for friends and family members. They were exhausting themselves with what appeared to be wasteful movements.

An odd sensation of calm overtook Tasman. He couldn't fight the storm and his circumstances. Swimming would get him nowhere but worn out. He turned over on his back and floated, but that didn't work because waves swept down on top of him. He turned on his belly again and spread his arms and legs. Fortunately, he had dressed for a warm day, so he wasn't weighed down by heavy clothes.

Each time a wave passed behind him, Tasman lifted his head and gulped air. He was content to float; it was his only alternative until another boat came by or he finally got waterlogged enough to sink.

Martin and Lawrence Berger had been sitting next to each other on the port side of the deck, with Cynthia Zurendorf to Lawrence's right and Cynthia Chamades on Martin's left. When the first huge wave hit the starboard side, they felt and saw the boat reeling, but when the *Pelican* rolled back, they thought everything would be all right. Martin could only trust that the captain knew what he was doing. Probably Captain Carroll had been in dozens of storms, dealing with a bad engine and worse.

Then the second wave blasted the boat and began rolling it again, only this time nothing felt right. It was as if the entire world were turning upside down, and nothing could make it stop. When Martin looked up and glimpsed the other side of the *Pelican*, he knew that this time the boat wasn't going to right itself.

He grabbed his brother, and each of them grabbed his girlfriend, and they forced themselves to their feet. The *Pelican* continued to roll over. The boat became a large, gaping mouth that was closing on them, and in just seconds they would be swallowed. The port-side rail was disappearing beneath them. With Martin yanking his brother's hand, their fingers linked, they launched themselves off the edge of the deck just before it entered the water. They leaped into the waves.

Then their link broke. Under the tossing water, Martin felt one hand wrenched free, then the other. The impact had torn the four apart. He pushed forward, hoping the others were doing the same.

When the *Pelican*'s starboard side crashed down into the water, Martin had barely escaped being crushed, and the force of the boat's capsizing hurled him farther away from the boat. A wave hit him as he broke the surface, and for a few moments he breathed nothing but water.

When his mouth and eyes were clear, Martin turned completely around, searching for Lawrence. He wanted to locate the two Cynthias too—but, first, where was his little brother?

The *Pelican* was a frightening sight, bottom up and the hull settling deeper in the water. Breaking seas pounded it from above. Soon, only the forward part of the hull and the keel were visible.

People swam or threw themselves at what was left of the *Pelican*'s bottom. But another deadly hazard, something of a cruel joke, added its influence to the tumbling waves and the inexorable weight of sodden clothing: dozens of fishing lines that floated like translucent webs in the water entangled arms and legs. A few passengers—including the oldest, James Hyslop—exhausted by the struggle and ensnared in the lines, surrendered and sank.

Martin couldn't see his brother or the girls. He wondered whether they'd gotten as far from the boat as he had; if not, they might be trapped under it. They might panic and fail to understand that they had to swim down first to slip under the sides of the descending *Pelican*, then head for air.

He had to go down there, and he couldn't waste another second. The hull was still above the roiling surface, so he didn't have far to go. They must be almost out of air by now. He was the best swimmer of the four. He could do it; he *had* to do it.

Martin sucked as much air as he could into his lungs. Just as he was about to plunge under, his arms and legs and neck were grabbed by people trying to stay afloat. Martin was dragged under.

75

Howie Carroll was as wet as he'd ever been. While waiting and watching for most of the last hour, he had tried several spots around Fishangri-la to find shelter from the wind and rain, but there was no complete protection. He refused to go inside. With the thick mist swirling about the docks, it was hard enough to see into Fort Pond Bay, and he wanted to be the first to see the *Pelican* when it appeared.

Something had gone wrong. No way would Eddie have stayed out this long in a squall. Howie had gotten back to Fishangri-la not long after 12:30, and he figured that Eddie would be a half hour to an hour, tops, behind him. Eddie took care of his passengers. Even the diehards would have agreed with Eddie to head for home in this weather.

Howie hadn't heard back from Rita, so maybe Eddie had headed for the first place he could tie up, in Lake Montauk. The way the wind and waves were picking up, half of the folks on the *Pelican* could be as sick as dogs and begging to be off the boat, and wouldn't care where. The docks on Lake Montauk would be very appealing to people seeing their breakfast all over again.

Howie walked down to the *Jigger II* and radioed over to the town dock. No one had seen the *Pelican*. The fellow he spoke to said he'd check with Gosman's and the yacht club too, then radio back if the *Pelican* had been sighted.

Howie was thinking he should find Gene Goble and have him call the Coast Guard. If Eddie was still out there, it had to be because the *Pelican* was in trouble. Howie figured that, since he'd gotten back, the waves in the ocean had gotten bigger and steeper, and the wind could have picked up too. It was miserable here at Fishangri-la, even in the comparative shelter of Fort Pond Bay.

Eddie would be mad as hell if the Coast Guard was called and five minutes later he came chugging into the bay. There would be a "big brother, little brother" argument for sure. But Howie had a bad feeling, and the *Pelican* was the only head boat not back.

Just to be sure, Howie decided to try to raise the *Pelican* one more time. As he began to speak into the radio, a voice interrupted him, a skipper of a boat. "Get off the air!" the voice said loudly.

"Who the hell are you?"

"*Sun Beam*, out of New London."

"What's the matter?" Howie said.

"There's been a Mayday, so keep the channel clear."

The bad feeling got worse. "What happened?"

"A boat called the *Pelican* turned over."

"Where—" Howie began, but the radio crackled, then was silent.

His first impulse was to start up the *Jigger II* and head toward the Montauk Lighthouse. But Howie knew that a single guy on a boat wouldn't do much good. He had to get help. He knew where a few of the other captains liked to ride out a storm. He headed toward the Liar's Lair, wondering who could have placed a Mayday call. If the *Pelican* had capsized, it couldn't have been Eddie. Howie didn't know that Harold Bishop was out there on the *Betty Anne*.

76

Eight men and one woman had been in the forward cabin when the *Pelican* rolled over. It must have been with total disbelief that they found themselves in a heap on the cabin's ceiling.

Then the reality set in: They were in a small cabin underwater. The *Pelican* had capsized. Unless another wave righted the boat, they would die if they didn't get out.

Though the cabin door was closed, water was rushing in underneath it and from several other openings. It was impossible to know whether the cabin would fill with water or an air pocket would form. Even if air remained, it might not last long with nine people drawing from it.

Panic ensued as the trapped passengers tried to disentangle from one another and stand up. Once on their feet, or even on hands and knees, they lurched toward the cabin door. Opening it, of course, would allow the sea to cascade in, but staying inside the closed, claustrophobic space was unthinkable.

Passengers fought one another to reach the door. Those who got there first fought over the doorknob, then they fought one another as they tried to push the door open. Even if they cooperated, they were out of luck, because they were pushing desperately against a heavy wall of water that was much stronger than they.

The cold water spewed into the cabin, and the level rose up to their knees, then their thighs and waists. The horror of their situation became more real with every passing second, and the water kept rising. A couple of the passengers who had been injured when the boat capsized—bones broken when they were flung to the ceiling or by having others land on them—were having trouble standing and staying above the water. Even if an air pocket formed, they might not be able to reach it, and they couldn't depend on the panicked people around them for help.

The door wouldn't open despite the volume of water now in the cabin. Men hollered and grunted at the obstinate door and at one another. Some passengers were wailing and sobbing, shouting prayers or good-byes to loved ones.

Then the door opened, and the horror reached a new level.

As water gushed into the cabin, the passengers battled to get out. The doorway was narrow, and only one person at a time could pass through it.

But panic had chased all rational thoughts from their minds. The water rose to chest level while passengers clawed, grabbed, punched, scratched, tore, and howled at one another. All that mattered was getting through that door and out of the watery tomb, and each one was going to be first.

77

Within fifteen minutes of the capsizing, word of it had spread through Montauk. Betty Edwardes heard about it over the ship-to-shore frequencies on the radio in the back of her shop. David was at the counter with a customer. She told him the news, then started making phone calls, including one to the police. David grabbed his cameras and headed out into the rain, hoping to be the first news photographer at the scene.

Frank Tuma Jr. was in a coffee shop in East Hampton. He was in a lousy mood. First he'd waited half the morning for his charter customers to show up, so he'd gotten a late start, then the squall closed in and he'd had to turn around and come in early. The morning had sure cost him a few bucks. He'd decided to get away from Montauk and treat himself to a second breakfast for lunch.

When he heard an approaching siren, Tuma and the half dozen or so other customers turned on their stools. The siren came loudly through the window, and there was a flash as a town cop car sped by. A couple of people remarked on that, then they heard another siren and saw another police car speeding past the window. Both were heading east.

When the East Hampton ambulance rushed by, following the cops, Tuma stood up. He slapped some money on the counter, gulped the last of his coffee, and strode out into the rain. Something was up, something big. Time to get back to Montauk.

Across Peconic Bay in Greenport, Renee Carey was the first to hear of it. She was the telephone operator that day; all calls had to go through her switchboard. She answered one call the usual way: "Number, please?"

"Renee, it's me." It took a moment to think of the name; she had quite a few friends who identified themselves the same way. "Did you hear? A boat went down off Montauk Point."

"Which one?"

"The *Pelican*."

"Don't know it."

"It's one of the head boats out of Fishangri-la, full of passengers."

"That's horrible. Okay, thanks, got another call."

The next call was someone she knew who was calling a friend in Southold. Before Renee made the connection, she told her about the *Pelican*. And the caller after that . . .

78

Frank Dickinson of the state park police was debating whether or not to call it a day and head home. In addition to Montauk State Park, he had Hither Hills State Park to patrol. But even though Hither Hills was right on the ocean and its campsites had been booked for weeks, there wasn't much to patrol this afternoon. With the squall, even with south-facing Hither Hills not taking the brunt of it, no one was at the beach. Even the tents put up that morning were gone—a few had blown away, but most had been taken down by campers smart and quick enough to understand that all they had might be blown out to sea.

There were still a few cars in the parking lot. Dickinson weaved among them in his state park police car. The vehicles were empty. Most likely the owners had gone back into town with others, riding out the storm in a restaurant. Dickinson parked his car and, braving the wind and rain, walked up over a dune.

If this had been a storm coming up the coast, the green waves would have been throwing themselves against the beach, rushing almost to the dunes. But the northeast wind was actually stopping the waves rolling in from the ocean in their tracks, even trying to push them backward. At the top of each wave, as though a prize being fought for by the water and wind, was a thick crest of foam. Large pieces of it flew off toward the sky, the wind winning, while the rest slid back down to be absorbed by the sea and formed again.

Dickinson knew that this struggle of natural forces might go on for hours. He was tempted to watch it. He appreciated being stationed in Montauk since getting out of the service after the war. As the only patrolman, he had a lot of territory to cover, but it was beautiful, dramatic territory. The salary was barely adequate, but he had the state park police car, and he and his wife had been given a house on a bluff near Montauk Point where they could see the ocean, The Rip, and a bit of Block Island Sound.

With little else to do, he decided to go home. Depending on the damage from the storm, he might get called out tonight. Plus, his friend Lewis Koch and his wife had come out for the weekend. Being stuck inside all afternoon due to the storm put a burden on Frank's wife to entertain them. Well, maybe the view, with boats hurrying home, had kept them interested for a while.

Bending his head against the wind, Dickinson trudged back down the dune to his car. As he opened the driver's door—carefully, so the wind wouldn't wrench it off the hinges—his radio crackled, and he answered it. Lew Koch was calling from his home.

"Frank, I'm looking out your picture window here and I saw a boat turn over."

"You mean turned turtle?"

"Yeah. Thought I was seeing things at first. Right off the point."

"What boat, do you know?"

"No. But I think I see people in the water."

"On my way."

As Frank left the Hither Hills parking lot, he radioed the state park police. If there were people in the water off the point in this weather, one man alone couldn't do much good.

79

William Friedel couldn't keep his head above the water. He would break the surface for only a moment and gasp for air, but most of what he took in was cold seawater. There was nothing nearby to cling to, and the waves swooping down on the people in the water were battering their heads and shoulders and pushing them back under.

Friedel had several disadvantages: He couldn't swim. He had recently been diagnosed with heart trouble, and he could feel his chest aching. He was wearing a thick jacket and heavy boots, and every time a wave came down on him, it felt like his jacket and boots were conspiring with the water to send him to the bottom. He didn't know how long he'd been in the water, but he was exhausted. He was going to drown, he realized. He prayed not for himself but for the safety of his son, then for his brother and his wife.

Richard Friedel was all right for now. The twelve year old had just that summer taken Red Cross swimming lessons, and as the water roiled around him he tried to focus on what he had been taught. He found the best way to move his arms and legs to stay afloat. The next step was to find his father.

Richard didn't recognize most of the people in the water. It was hard to see clearly anyway because of the colliding waves and windblown spray, which stung Richard's eyes like cold, tiny toothpicks. Faces were so contorted by fear and desperation that they looked alike. Richard saw one man about ten feet away whose eyes were open, staring out of a head tilted left, his mouth submerged. The boy realized suddenly that the man was dead.

Richard didn't want to think that the man could have been his father, or his uncle. He didn't want to think that his father was not visible at all, having sunk down, never to surface again. He began swimming, figuring that he would be able to recognize his own father's face, and his aunt's and uncle's if he came to them first.

He found three compact white life preservers bobbing in the water. Apparently, some had been loosened from their storage area when the *Pelican* capsized. Richard grabbed them and moved on. He was determined to find his family.

He saw no sign of John and Helen Friedel. Neither could swim. It's possible that one or both were injured when the *Pelican* capsized, but in any case their heads were not visible above the water. Later it was determined that John Friedel likely drowned within minutes of entering the water. His was one of the bodies found by rescuers.

William Friedel couldn't know that his sister-in-law was on the other side of the *Pelican*. Weighed down by clothing and becoming exhausted within minutes of exposure to the rough water, she was moments away from drowning. She slid under for what would certainly be the last time.

That's when Eddie Carroll grabbed her. He had seen her go under, and he dove off the hull once more, reaching her in what he hoped was enough time. He wrapped one arm under her arms and lifted her head clear of the water. With his other arm and kicking his legs, he swam back to the hull. He couldn't help the way the waves fell over the woman, but at least he had a good hold on her.

William Friedel felt himself plunging down, the weight of a wave ganging up with nature's other bullies to put him under for good. He didn't have the strength to push himself back up. His arms seemed to be made of cold lead. The water parted above him for just a moment and his head was free. He managed to breathe in a little air before the water closed over him again, and he began to swallow some of it.

"Dad!" he heard. "Dad!"

Was Richard alive, or was William just hearing his voice in his mind as he drowned? Then he felt pain at the top of his head. He was being pulled up by the hair. After his head was back in the air and the salt water rinsed off his face, he saw his son and felt Richard's hands holding him at the shoulders.

William was too tired to speak, to say anything at all. He even wondered whether he could keep his eyes open. Richard was having difficulty, too, his mouth open and taking in big gulps of air. His father noted that, in spite of everything, Richard still had his glasses on. That had probably saved his life—at least for now; his son could see well enough to find him, spotting his head just above the surface the last time he had been free of the water.

Richard let go of one shoulder and gave his father one of the life preservers he had slung over one arm. Once his father had it on, Richard intended to continue swimming and find his aunt and uncle. The two remaining life preservers would be for each of them. He could manage without a life preserver. He was tired, but not too much. All those Boy Scout hikes and the Red Cross lessons were paying off.

But his father's face was gray. His lids kept drifting down over his eyes. The life preserver would keep his father afloat, but it couldn't prevent his head from slumping into the water. And he knew that his father had some kind of problem with his heart.

William felt his son propping him up, working with the life preserver. He eyes closed as a wave washed over them. They wouldn't open again. He was just too tired.

For a moment, Richard wondered whether his father had died. No, he could see him breathing. He must have passed out. Richard had no choice now. He prayed for his aunt and uncle, and stayed with his father.

80

All around the *Betty Anne*, people were thrashing in the turbulent water. Some shouted for help, others seemed too frightened to utter a sound, still others looked as though they were in shock and had already given up. A few more seconds to wait, then it would be all over.

Jeanne and Jim had tossed life preservers over the sides, along with everything else they had collected that could float. Hands reached desperately for the objects as they bounced by on the waves, kicked in circles by the water's motion. Harold watched from above. He had to keep the engines going as though the *Betty Anne* were moving forward when in fact it was treading water in a way, not losing ground and not being sent spinning by the fierce action of The Rip.

"The ropes!" he shouted down. "Throw out the ropes!"

Jeanne managed to hear him. She lifted her head to him and seemed to nod. Harold looked past her to the water, where a man was reaching out for one of the *Betty Anne*'s cushions skimming by. Then, as though he had changed his mind, he pulled his arms back and disappeared under the next wave.

Jeanne and Jim took the free end of the two coils of rope, then hurled the coils toward a cluster of people swirling in the frothy water. Immediately, a man took hold of one. Bracing herself against the side of the boat and with Jim recoiling rope behind her, Jeanne began to haul the man in.

It seemed like an impossible feat: the man, especially with all his sodden clothing, had to be at least half again as large and heavy as Jeanne Bishop, and he appeared unable to do anything other than cling to the rope and be dragged. Yet she tugged again and again. A few times when a wave struck, the man was submerged and almost torn away. Jeanne had to let the rope slip through her hands, giving a bit of slack, then looked to see if, like a fish on a hook, the man was still attached to the end of the rope.

Slowly and painfully the man was drawn closer. Jeanne's shoulders felt as though they were being ripped out of their sockets. The salt water on the rope was stinging newly opened cuts in her hands, and every time she paid out a little rope, the friction burned her palms. She was practically sitting on the deck; if she straightened up at all, the weight on the other end of the rope could pull her over the side.

Finally, the man was next to the *Betty Anne*. Jeanne leaned over and grabbed his jacket and tried to haul him in. He was gasping hoarsely and coughing up seawater. She couldn't get him up herself, and he was too weak to help. Then Jim took hold of him under one arm and Jeanne did the same with the other. The wind screamed in her ears and then a wave hit, rolling the *Betty Anne* away and then back, rocking so the deck almost touched the water.

That gave her an idea. "After the next wave!" she called to Jim.

They waited, the man growing heavier by the second. Then they were covered by a new sluice of cold water. When the boat rolled back, they had less distance to cover to haul the man up, and they could lift and slide him onto the deck. All three fell in a heap. Jeanne looked at her hands. Blood seeped from several scrapes and was immediately washed off by the driving rain. Her forearms and wrists felt bruised.

The man might have been whispering something, or perhaps gasping for air. They managed to get him to crawl toward Jeanne's parents, where there was some protection from the wind and water. They wrapped a blanket around him. He sat with his back to the cabin and his head bowed.

Jeanne felt sick from the effort. Then Jim shouted, "We've got another one!"

Looking over the side, she saw that a person had wrapped the second rope around his chest and was waving frantically to them. Jeanne motioned to Jim to get the first rope back in the water. Then she began again the process of bringing in a drowning man.

81

Chief Boatswain's Mate Purnell Curles had called off the search in Napeague Bay at two o'clock. The small outboard boat with three people aboard they had been called out for was nowhere to be seen. That meant either it had gotten back safely, or bodies would be washing ashore in the next two to three days. Either way, there was nothing more to do.

Curles and the other two men had taken the boat in at Promised Land, north of the Napeague Stretch. The docks at Promised Land were used by boats that brought material to and from the canneries there. When Curles and crew arrived and told the men on one dock what they had been doing, they were told that they had been on "a wild-goose chase" because the outboard and the men had gotten back fine.

"Why didn't they let us know?" Curles demanded.

All he received were shrugs and sympathetic nods. He was about to take the boat back into the bay when he decided to try the radiotelephone again. It still wasn't working right. This time, Curles was determined to get it going. After the useless search, it would be just his luck to head back to Lake Montauk, then find out that the boat was needed farther west again.

He couldn't tell whether the problem was the radio or the storm. If it was the storm, then anything he pushed or jiggled or tapped on the radio wouldn't do any good. The two crewmen smoked cigarettes and chatted idly with the men on the dock, seeming oblivious to the wind and rain. The rain was more like a heavy mist here, and the wind was not gusting as high as when they had left the town dock.

Back at the Ditch Plain station, Boatswain's Mate Kenneth Whiting was trying to figure out what to do. Curles and the others had been gone since around noon; now it was almost 2:15, and during that time there had been no radio contact. With this storm, if something happened out on the water, was it up to him to decide what to do? Maybe he should call the Shinnecock station for instructions. But that might make him seem like just a nervous kid, afraid of what might happen, instead of a twenty-year-old Coast Guardsman.

Then the call came from the park police barracks.

That's it, Whiting thought—time to call Shinnecock. Then the radiotelephone squawked to life. It was Curles, finally. He had gotten the radio working and they had left Promised Land. Whiting told him about the capsized boat and lots of people in the water.

Now Curles was furious with the three people who hadn't reported in to the Coast Guard. The lifeboat hadn't even rounded Goff Point yet and headed back into Napeague Bay, so even if he got every ounce of power out of the engines, Curles had to estimate a good forty minutes to get to the Montauk Lighthouse, probably more; his bow was pointing right into the wind, and the water was choppy. It could be as much as an hour before they reached the overturned boat.

Curles explained this to Whiting, and concluded, "By the time we get there, those people in the water will be dead from exposure and exhaustion."

"Should I contact Shinnecock?" Whiting asked.

"No, they're also too far west. Call New London. One of their big cutters can get through the water faster. Then grab whoever's there and get over to the town dock. You'll have to take the picketboat."

"Jesus, the waves are . . ."

"I know. Whiting, right now you're the only chance those people have of being rescued by the Coast Guard."

In other words, Whiting realized, if he didn't get that small boat out there off Montauk Point, everybody would die.

He contacted the New London station to officially request a cutter. He was told that a ship was on its way to Block Island. It would be rerouted for Montauk and placed under the jurisdiction of the New York office. New London would alert the officer in charge there.

When Whiting left the station building, a seaman was just pulling up in a jeep. Whiting jumped in and said they had to cover the four miles to the town dock in Lake Montauk in record time. The ride was harrowing. The rain had flooded the paved roads and turned dirt roads into mud paths. Wind-driven water beat against the windshield. It was 2:30 when they arrived. The people had been in the water just fifteen minutes.

Whiting leaped onto the picketboat and was about to start the engine when a machinist mate suddenly appeared and told him that the engine had been disconnected because he was doing some minor repairs.

Whiting was incredulous. This man was picking the middle of a squall to work on the picketboat? "Look, I need that engine working *now!* We've got a capsized fishing boat out in The Rip."

The machinist was surprised too. "You're going out in *that*," gesturing at the sky, "in *this?*"

"It's all we've got right now. Dozens of people are in the water."

The machinist pulled the engine back together, and Whiting eased the boat out of its berth. The delay had cost ten minutes. Had cost *them* ten minutes. After going through the channel and turning east, Whiting felt the full brunt of the heavy seas and the headwind. He also fully realized the desperate situation the people in the water were in, and knew that he couldn't save them all.

82

Frank Mundus's clothes were drying right on him as he sat at the bar in Fishangri-la with a bowl of soup and a glass of whiskey in front of him He'd had more of the whiskey than the soup, but both were doing a good job of warming his guts.

The boat captains didn't always stop in for a pop after a day out. But in weather like this, Mundus figured that at least some of them would want to get dry on the outside and wet on the inside the way he was doing. He sat chatting with Carl Forsberg and Bill Reichert, and Harry Conklin of the *Arab*, and a couple of others.

Mundus idly wondered where the Carroll brothers and Les Behan were, sure that their boats were in by now. He finished his whiskey and was debating another one when the door flew open. A girl about eight years old came in. "There's a boat turned over!" she shouted, sounding more excited than upset.

"Where?" the bartender asked.

"Right off the point!"

Mundus was at first skeptical. Why were they finding this out from some little girl? And where had she gotten her information? Anyway, if it was some pleasure boat—a sailboat maybe that tipped over in the wind—that wasn't the worry of anyone here.

Still, he asked the girl, "You know what boat?"

"One from here. The *Pelican*."

"Shit," Mundus said, little girl or no. So that's why Eddie Carroll wasn't here. Mundus felt foolish asking the girl for information and was thinking about who to call when Howie rushed in.

"That true, Howie, about your brother?" one of the captains asked.

"Yes," he replied, then paused to catch his breath. "The *Pelican* capsized. It's about a mile off the point. All those people . . ." He took another deep breath. "I'm taking my boat out there."

"I'm with you. Let's go," Mundus said, and he gestured to the others.

There was no reaction. A couple of captains shook their heads. "I'm not going back out in that shit," said one. "We're the farthest away," said the other. "Let the guys in Lake Montauk go out. They'll get there faster."

"We don't know who's doing what or where," Mundus said. "We do know that one of ours is out there."

Forsberg, Conklin, and Reichert put their caps back on, and followed Mundus and Howie Carroll down to the docks. It wasn't just the danger of the storm, Mundus knew; there was also the issue of using up precious fuel on a day that had already cost the skippers plenty.

In ten minutes the *Cricket II* was leading a small flotilla of open boats away from Fishangri-la and toward Culloden Point. Mundus had been on the radio and gotten a better fix on the *Pelican*'s location.

As soon as they passed Culloden and were in more open water, the wind attacked as though it had been crouched behind the point, waiting to spring. It wasn't raining as hard as before, but the wind whipped the mist at the boats. Within minutes, Mundus and the other captains were as wet as they had been before. They knew that, where they were going, conditions would be worse.

Mundus checked his watch: 2:35. He'd been told on the radio that the *Pelican* rolled over at about 2:15. Mundus was at full throttle, but the waves crashing into the bow slowed down the *Cricket II*. Thinking they would get there too late was driving him crazy, so he tried to think about anything else. That didn't work, because he kept thinking about that morning and how he'd let the overloaded *Pelican* go out. He began cursing loudly at the storm, which made him feel better.

83

About twenty people clutched at the *Pelican*'s slippery hull, only about ten feet of which remained above the surface. Did anyone notice the irony—that in the morning the passengers had jostled for room at the railing, and now they fought for room on the overturned bow?

Eddie Carroll had managed to drag and persuade people in the water to make for the hull. A few people had struggled through the water to it anyway, recognizing that it was the only relatively stationary object in the shifting sea. It offered no protection from the waves, though, which washed relentlessly over it as though bent on dislodging those who clung to life.

For Eddie, it became like a cruel game that he and everyone else was losing. Each time he swam to someone and raised his head, he found a dead man. He didn't want to think that those clinging to the hull were the only ones still alive.

The worst was when he pulled a head back or turned someone over and recognized the face. It made him want to stop. Then he thought he heard a woman calling out to him, and with renewed strength and hope he swam toward her.

84

Despite the rain and wind that still scoured the Montauk bluffs and beaches, people who had heard about the capsized boat wanted to catch a glimpse of it and the rescue efforts. Others went to the point in case their help was needed.

Twelve-year-old Stuart Vorpahl climbed into the truck with his father and uncle in East Hampton, and rattled along the bumpy Montauk Highway, rain slashing the windshield. The two men dropped off Stuart to join several other onlookers on the bluff at the lighthouse, then drove down to the beach.

For a few minutes, all the boy could see were wind-driven green waves and swirling white-gray clouds of mist. Suddenly there was a break in the clouds, and for a few seconds Stuart had a clear view of the *Pelican*. He saw its white bottom dotted with dark, moving objects, then realized that the objects were people clinging to the boat and being tossed about by the waves.

He tried to count how many people he saw, but the clouds rushed together again. Stuart stepped gingerly toward the edge of the bluff, willing the clouds to open again. They did. Fascinated, he stared at the overturned boat, and this time he guessed he saw twenty people clutching at it. Near the boat he could barely see other forms. He imagined them stroking to stay afloat, and begging desperately for help.

The clouds closed ranks again. Stuart couldn't risk stepping any closer to the bluff's edge, especially with the grass being wet and slippery. He waited, impatience making his body twitch. Just one more look—he had to see the *Pelican* again.

His wish was granted. The boat, like a mirage, appeared. Something was different—a bit more of the white hull was visible. Stuart stepped back. It hit him abruptly that he had seen something he never had before: people who were alive one minute and could be dead the next, swept away by the disinterested force of the waves.

He left the bluff and began to hike down to the beach below the lighthouse, hoping to find his father.

85

As David Edwardes drove east, he did some fast thinking. It was quite possible that the police and other emergency personnel already had the roads closed off. They might let him through—he knew many of them—but then again, they might not.

Also, he knew those bluffs next to the Montauk Light well. Even if he got to them, given the darkness of the day and the storm conditions, he might not be able to see the capsized boat, let alone get good pictures. Then he had an idea.

Edwardes pulled over, checked behind him, and then made a U-turn, heading west. Cars, some with lights flashing, rushed past him going the other way. Five minutes later, he screeched to a stop at the East Hampton Airport.

Mel Lamb, the airport manager and a good friend, emerged from one of the hangars. After Edwardes explained his dilemma, Lamb said, "Let's go."

Edwardes did turn out to be the first photographer at the scene. He snapped picture after picture as Lamb slowly circled his plane above the *Pelican*.

86

Inger Perrson, the future Mrs. Eddie Carroll, was on her way to the point with the Pilbros. She sat in the backseat. Mr. Pilbro was going to drop off the women, then drive back to the restaurant to make plenty of hot coffee, soup, and sandwiches and wait for information on where the survivors would be brought.

Other than Mrs. Pilbro saying, "I'm sure Eddie's all right," there was no conversation during the trip east. What could be said? The report was that the *Pelican* had rolled over with dozens of people aboard, who were all in the water in the middle of a squall. The Pilbros didn't want to ponder the extent of the disaster. Neither knew of anything like this happening to the Montauk fleet before.

Despite the kindness of the Pilbros, Inger had never felt so alone. If someone had said to her that morning that her fiancé's boat would turn over in a storm, that would have been as believable as blinking her eyes and suddenly being back in Sweden. Eddie was an excellent captain, everyone said so. He was a dashing and energetic man, full of confidence and laughter. How could he now be in the water or under a boat? Were people dying? Was Eddie?

Inger had gotten to know Eddie pretty well in a short amount of time. What worried her most was that if passengers under Eddie's care were dying in these waters, he could well wish he would die too.

87

At the Coast Guard board of investigation hearing, the press had
been waiting anxiously for Howie Carroll to testify. Next to Eddie,
Howie was the best source of knowledge about what happened that
day off Montauk Point. He was blood kin and the closest friend of
the *Pelican*'s skipper.

As Howie stood before the officers and was sworn in, his right
hand trembled. His hands had been trembling for days. Somehow, he
had managed to shave, and his dark brown hair was parted neatly to
the right. He wore a plaid jacket and a tan shirt over a white T-shirt.
He hadn't noticed that it was warm in the room on 80 Lafayette
Street.

He sat down at the table across from the officers. Admiral Olson
began the questioning.

COURT: Mr. Carroll, did you or your brother know anything
about a squall approaching that morning of September 1?
CARROLL: No, sir. In the weather report posted at Fishangri-la, it
looked like a good day if we didn't stay out too long, like into
the later afternoon.
COURT: But there was a squall, and it arrived during the late
morning.
CARROLL: Yes. It came out of nowhere.
COURT: What did you do?
CARROLL: I'd been talking to a few of the captains on the radio ...
COURT: Was one of them your brother?
CARROLL: Yes.
COURT: What was the conversation about?
CARROLL: That there was a storm coming this way. We'd heard
from a ship on the other side of Block Island that it was kick-
ing up pretty good.
COURT: Did you tell your brother to head for port?
CARROLL: No.
COURT: You didn't discuss that at all?

CARROLL: Sure. I told him I was taking the *Jigger II* in. I was to the northeast, near Block Island. It made sense; the storm would hit me first. But I didn't *tell* Eddie anything.

COURT: You brought the *Jigger II* and its passengers in?

CARROLL: Yes.

COURT: Then what did you do?

CARROLL: I waited at the dock. For the *Pelican*.

COURT: It was your brother's decision to keep the *Pelican* out where it was to continue fishing?

CARROLL: Yes. But where he was, it wasn't bad. No captain likes to come in because of a little wind and rain, and his passengers think he's not much of a captain.

COURT: How did you find out that the *Pelican* had capsized?

CARROLL: I was trying again to reach Eddie on my boat's radio. Then someone cut in from New London. Said a boat called the *Pelican* had flipped.

COURT: Let's go back to your radio conversation with your brother. Did you urge him to head for port?

CARROLL: No.

COURT: Why not?

CARROLL: You don't tell other captains what to do. They run their own boats, make their own decisions.

COURT: Even if one captain is your brother?

CARROLL: [Pause.] Especially if he's your brother.

COURT: We're to accept, Mr. Carroll, that you had made the decision to protect your passengers and take your boat in, you knew other captains were doing the same, and the safety of the passengers on the *Pelican* was not a concern of yours as well as your brother's?

Camera bulbs flashed. The photographs caught Howie looking as though he had just received a death sentence. As he continued staring at the officers of the court, there was a tense shifting of feet and crossing of arms by many in the stuffy room.

CARROLL: Let me tell you something, *mister*. Eddie Carroll was one of the finest captains you could get. And it's not just because he was in the navy defending our country during the war and had gotten to know the waters off Montauk like the back of his hand. He was cautious. He would never put anyone in danger. The day the *Jack* sunk last June, that was a day Eddie wouldn't go out even though it cost him because he saw how rough it was out there. He put his passengers first, always. A lot of these people, they weren't just passengers, they were friends now. They went out with Eddie over and over again. They loved jumping on the *Pelican*. It was *their* boat.

Howie began to cry, and couldn't stop. The officers, the witnesses and family members, and the press waited in hushed silence. Howie got up from the witness chair, covered his face with his hands, and started to leave the room. But he ended up by the windows and stood there sobbing. Finally, Joseph Meehan took his elbow and led him out of the room.

Admiral Olson declared a brief recess, but no one got up. The family members tried not to look at one another. They had been prepared to hate the Carroll brothers, and perhaps had expected arrogance from Howie. They had gotten something else—loyalty, love, and anguish.

A few minutes later the door to the room opened and Howie and Meehan returned, Howie in the lead. His normally tan face was splotched with gray and white, as though he had been sick. He pushed past the press, sat back down in the witness chair, and cleared his throat.

COURT: Are you ready to continue, Mr. Carroll?
CARROLL: I'll say one more thing. A lot of people came out there week after week for a special boat. We considered them our friends. It was not just a matter of hustling. Unfortunately, outside of a couple of people, most of Eddie's regulars were aboard the *Pelican* that Saturday.

COURT: Mr. Carroll . . .

CARROLL: That's all I got to say about my brother.

88

Out of the mist the *Bingo II* appeared. Those in the water who saw her immediately began to shout for help, except for those who needed help badly but had lost the ability to make a sound.

Lester Behan and Bill Blindenhofer on the *Bingo II* spotted the *Betty Anne*, and thought they could see someone being hauled aboard. Then, being up on the bridge, they saw what remained above the surface of the *Pelican*'s hull. They estimated about a dozen people were clinging to it.

"I'm going in as tight as I can, and we'll get those people off of there," Behan said. "Whoever's between here and there, let's drag them on board."

"Got to be careful, Les," his mate said. "We hit the *Pelican* under the water, we might need someone to fish us out."

Behan nodded. What choice did they have? There were bodies around the *Bingo II*, those still kept afloat by the air in their lungs. They were probably dead from heart failure, hypothermia, or overwhelming fear. Behan wished he could close his ears to those still alive who were screaming and crying and pleading for their lives.

Behan glanced at Bill. His face was pale. He was horrified by the scene. People were dying and there were just the two of them plus the *Bingo II*'s six passengers, who looked too frightened and ill to be of much help. Les would have to handle the boat against the wind and waves while Bill attempted to pull survivors aboard. It seemed almost hopeless.

"Let's do it," Behan said.

He eased the boat forward. It wasn't just that he had to maneuver around and between people. The fishing lines and other debris in the water could foul the screws and rudder. He positioned the *Bingo II* with its bow against the current on the ocean side of the *Pelican*. That's the way people were being dragged through the water. The dead bodies moved faster than the live ones fighting the current, trying to avoid being pushed far away from what was left of the *Pelican*.

Bill wondered how he could save anyone. The momentum of the water made him realize that he could just as likely get pulled over the side as get a guy on board.

That gave him an idea. He grabbed a rope and tied one end securely around a cleat. The other end he tied around his chest. If he fell overboard, this was his lifeline. He glanced up at Les, who gave him a thumb's-up.

A thump against the side of the *Bingo II* told Bill it was time to get to work. Looking overboard, he saw two figures in the water, both wearing life preservers. One was dead; the other was a kid with glasses who looked close to death.

"Please, take my father," the kid said, his teeth chattering and his lips blue.

How do you make decisions at a time like this? Bill thought of getting the kid first before both of them floated away. But the kid's eyes pleaded through his glasses to take his father, pleaded right through thick glasses like the ones Bill himself wore.

Bill pulled the man up and over the rail, then he grabbed the kid's hands, which had been clutching the side of the *Bingo II*. The waves made the boat rock violently, and Bill wondered whether he could keep the kid's hands from being jerked through his fingers. Then he got a good hold, and his strong shoulders took over. The kid was suddenly in his arms before they were knocked to the deck by a wave.

It took the kid a few moments to shake the water out of his eyes and off his glasses. Then he cried "Dad!" and crawled over to the man who was sprawled on his back on the heaving, sea-washed deck.

Maybe Bill saw it before the kid did—the guy was still breathing. His chest heaved up and down and his throat made a gurgling sound. The kid got to his knees and began artificial respiration. Meanwhile, Bill heard another thump against the *Bingo II*. He tested the rope again and leaned overboard.

Finally, Behan saw what he had been hoping to see: Eddie Carroll alive in the water. His face was as white as the overturned hull. His hair was plastered to his head. With one arm around a woman and his other around a man, he was trying to keep their heads above the surging water. That left only his legs to propel them toward the *Pelican*. They were moving slowly through the waves. It was almost as though the two passengers were keeping Eddie up.

Behan turned the *Bingo II* slightly to move closer to them. Eddie looked up, and Behan tossed him a rope. "Put it around all of you!" he called over the wind.

Eddie didn't hear him, or didn't listen. He fastened the rope around the woman and tugged on it. Behan began to pull her to his boat. She looked dead already. Behan thought of leaving her tied to the boat and throwing another rope to Eddie. Then he saw that Eddie had pushed the man—who also looked dead—against the side of the *Bingo II* and begun to swim away.

"Eddie, goddammit!" Behan shouted. "Get over here! Get on board and help us!"

Eddie kept swimming. Taking a risk with the engines going, Les leaped down from the bridge. He directed Bill toward the man whom Eddie had pushed close, who was already bobbing past the *Bingo II*. Les got a good hold on the woman's heavy clothing and dragged her the rest of the way in.

She was dead, all right, and probably had been the whole time Eddie was trying to keep her afloat, the dead weight exhausting him even more.

Behan yanked the woman to a far corner of the boat and stretched her out on her back. The two other rescued people had to be watching him, but there was nothing he could do. Whatever he tried to cover her with would blow away.

Richard Friedel looked over at the body. That was how he learned the fate of his Aunt Helen.

89

Eddie Carroll was as exhausted as he was desperate. The exhaustion he thought he could deal with. It was the desperation that made him want to simply sink under the next crashing wave.

He couldn't save them all. His passengers were dying too fast—drowning, hearts stopping, succumbing to terror, or just giving up. The last three people he had managed to reach had had to be left in the water. They were already dead and would eventually sink or, with luck, be hauled aboard as other boats showed up.

As much as the cries and screams of the people in the water had squeezed Eddie's heart, what he heard now—or didn't hear—was worse. With the roar of the waves and whining wind, it was anything but silent, but he no longer heard pleas for help. Except for the ten or so men clinging to the bow, he might be the only one alive.

He saw the *Bingo II* trying to work its way closer. It was impossible to tell whether the passengers being taken aboard by Les and Bill were alive. Same for the other boat that was farther away. Where were the other boats from Fishangri-la, even Lake Montauk? Where was the Coast Guard? These thoughts were like anguished shouts in his head.

Eddie was tempted to swim for the *Bingo II* and let himself be hauled aboard. But there was more to be done. He had to make sure that the people holding onto the *Pelican*'s bow didn't give up before one of the boats got to them.

He swam back to the *Pelican*, barely able to fight the current and the incessant waves. Two fewer men were clinging to it. Bobby was still there, and Antonio Borruso. Eddie recognized Wallace Manko, too, and five others. No one spoke. It seemed that no one wanted to look him in the eye.

A wave hit, and one of the men wasn't there when the water subsided. Eddie worked his way to the spot and reached down. He grabbed a hand and yanked upward. The man appeared, sputtering, then vomited seawater. He didn't seem to care that he was alive.

Eddie yelled above the noise, "Keep holding on! See that boat? It's getting closer. I know that captain. He won't leave until he's got us all!"

No one looked impressed. Eddie wanted to work his way around the diminishing circle of survivors on the bow and shout what he'd just said into everyone's ear. He'd keep doing it until Les and Bill were above them, reaching down. When everyone else was on the *Bingo II*, then Eddie would leave the water.

But he realized that he was too weary to last that long. When the next wave pushed him under, for a few seconds his arms refused to work and he couldn't get back up. Then desperation won out and he clawed his way to the surface.

When his eyes cleared, Eddie thought he saw someone, alive, maybe twenty yards away. A hand waving. Eddie waved back and called out. No response, but it was unlikely that his voice had carried that far. The person was moving with the water, away from Eddie and the *Bingo II*. He had to decide: stay here to encourage people to hold on, or go after the person being swept out to sea.

Eddie shouted to those clinging to the *Pelican*, "Keep yourselves up! Look after each other! I'll be right back!"

Seeing the captain setting off again seemed to squeeze out of Wallace Manko the little strength and hope that he had left. "I can't stay up anymore," he gasped to the old man next to him.

Borruso knew what he meant. It took a lot of strength to hold onto the slippery hull, and the waves kept pounding the hull and the men clinging to it. Borruso couldn't begin to estimate how long he had been in the water—ten minutes or two hours.

Worse, the chance of being rescued was diminishing. There were still only the two boats plucking people out of the water. Borruso had given up calling for help. His shouts had been thrown back at him by the wind. And despite what Eddie Carroll said, it didn't look to him like the boats were getting closer. If anything, they were being pushed out to sea faster than what was left of the *Pelican*.

Borruso's only alternative was to leave the hull and swim toward the nearest boat. But he knew that in this storm, and being sixty years old and already feeling the effects of hypothermia, it would be impossible.

Groans from Manko interrupted Borruso's thoughts. "It's no use. I just can't keep from slipping."

"You must keep trying to hold on," Borruso told him. Then, harshly, "You're saying that this old man can outlast you?"

Manko didn't appear to have heard him. His eyes rolled back in his head and he coughed up seawater. His arms flailed as he tried again to get a solid hold on the hull. A wave hit and water burst into his mouth.

"See those boats? They're coming!" Borruso thought this lie was fully justified if it snapped Manko out of his stupor. "One more minute. Stay with me one more minute, you'll see."

"I can't."

"Yes, you can."

Manko's eyes came to rest on Borruso. "Pops, I'm finished. Goodbye."

Borruso watched as he sank under the water. He waited, hoping to see Manko's head bob back above the surface. It did not.

Borruso felt like doing the same, letting the sea swallow him. He shook his head, then knocked it against the hull to gain some clarity. He spotted the captain swimming farther away and decided to pay attention to the rescue effort. That would distract him from thoughts of death.

Eddie was about ten feet from the hand that still seemed to beckon him. The man stared at Eddie, as though willing him to close the gap between them and lead him back to life. Then before Eddie reached him, he knew it was too late.

After confirming that the man was dead—Eddie felt grateful that he didn't recognize him—he swam back toward the hull. It was such a strange object to him now, just a slick white piece of his boat jutting above the turbulent water. How long ago it seemed that he and his passengers had set off from Fishangri-la. It had looked like a good day for fishing. Holiday weekend. A wave to Howie, trading barbs with Mundus, nods to a few other captains. This was their life, and it had been working fine.

Ready to get married, finally. Inger, a Swedish girl. Who would have thought she'd choose a guy from Staten Island? Beautiful woman. And she loved him too. Things could have worked out. Live in Montauk full-time. Have kids. Move up to chartering most days. It could have happened.

Now he knew that it wasn't going to happen. The knowledge was as deep inside Eddie Carroll as the exhaustion and the sense of unfulfilled responsibility. There was nothing he could ever do to make up for this horrible tragedy.

Eddie reached the hull. It was lower in the water than when he'd left it. There was nothing he could do about that either.

"Captain Eddie, you stay here with me," Antonio Borruso said to him. "I don't want to lose anyone else."

"Me too," Eddie said, glancing past the older man. "Look at me!" he shouted to the other men. "Hold on!"

It was a big wave. But every wave had been big. Eddie couldn't tell anymore what wave mattered most. But this was a big wave to him, and it was heading toward the hull of the *Pelican*. Antonio stared at him.

"Here it comes!" Eddie said.

A moment later, they and everyone else still using the hull as a refuge were engulfed by green water and white foam. When his head cleared, Eddie couldn't bear to look around. He focused on Antonio staring back at him. Enough. Eddie pushed away from the *Pelican*.

"Where are you going?" Antonio called.

There was no answer. Eddie kept swimming. It was all up to fate anyway, wasn't it? If he bumped into someone to save, that would be his calling, and he would meet it.

But as he got farther away, carried by the current and wind that seemed to aim him at the vastness and depths of the Atlantic, Eddie Carroll accepted that he couldn't save anyone else and that he was spent. When the next wave overtook him, he embraced it.

Borruso and Bobby Scanlon watched the captain go under.

90

Roland McCann and his staff worked quickly to transform the ball-room of the Montauk Yacht Club into a first-aid station. They pushed tables against the walls and filled the center of the room with cots, blankets, chairs, towels, fresh clothes, and whatever else people thought the storm victims would need.

Captain Harry Steele and members of the East Hampton Town Police Department were on the scene. Steele was coordinating prepa-rations with Billy Ecker, chief of the Montauk Fire Department, and Ted Cook, one of the department's commissioners. State police and more park police were on the way, because the incident was taking place off Montauk Point State Park. They would figure out the juris-dictions and who had authority over what later. For now, one of Cap-tain Steele and Chief Ecker's biggest problems was that neither man knew what to expect.

They did know that the capsized boat was the *Pelican*, skippered by Eddie Carroll, and that two boats were on the scene trying to save those in the water. But how many people were in the water was com-plete guesswork—Eddie could have taken on thirty to fifty passen-gers, maybe even a few more. (Gene Goble had been asked about this, but he claimed not to know and that it wasn't his responsibility.) Of those on board, how many would reach port still breathing? What shape would they be in? The coordination team couldn't get infor-mation from the Coast Guard, because its main rescue boat based in Lake Montauk was nowhere to be found.

Captain Steele had determined that the safest place to off-load the survivors in this weather was Lake Montauk, and the yacht club had offered enough space to house them and dock space to unload them. Local doctors, nurses, and volunteers were arriving and would be on hand to treat the survivors. The more serious cases would be trans-ported in whatever vehicles were available to Southampton Hospital. Much to Chief Ecker's frustration, his fire department did not have an ambulance.

Word about the *Pelican* and the preparations being made spread quickly throughout Montauk. Every few minutes another vehicle crossed the short, narrow causeway to Star Island to bring supplies to the yacht club—dry clothes, blankets, cots, pillows, urns of hot water, coffee, sandwiches, even cigarettes. Captain Steele worried that the supplies and volunteers might fill the yacht club to the bursting point.

Word must have spread well beyond Montauk, too, because the East Hampton police station as well as the fire department head-quarters were getting calls from New York City. Archie Jones, out at the lighthouse, reported a few calls too. That meant that family members and reporters would be showing up soon. Another reason why Captain Steele chose the Montauk Yacht Club was that traffic to it would be limited by the single narrow causeway to and from Star Island.

Chief Ecker's men would take care of the traffic. While a few fire-fighters would join police at the dock to help carry survivors into the yacht club, most of Ecker's men would be on the roadways leading to Star Island and at the base of the causeway itself. Family members would be allowed through, and press people if they had the proper ID, but all others had to be kept away, especially those motivated by nothing other than morbid curiosity.

There was another preparation to make. Just down from the yacht club was the dock owned by the Duryea family, where many of the boats sold what they had caught, much of it to be shipped to New York City. Perry Duryea Sr. gave permission to use the icehouse as a temporary morgue, and company workers began to clear space, wondering just how much would be enough.

Vinnie Grimes was one of those pressed into guard duty. He was a Montauk native whose father had come out in 1926, part of developer Carl Fisher's construction crews. After marrying a Pitts, Vinnie had gone to work for the Duryeas. He was a member of the Montauk Fire Department, but had been away from it for months. He was in the navy, and Labor Day weekend was the first leave he had received.

When the phone rang, his mother answered. Chief Ecker asked for Vinnie.

He got on the phone to learn that he was being recruited. "You sure you need me, Chief?" Vinnie asked. "I've got to report back Monday night." When he was told about the *Pelican*, Vinnie said, "I'll be right there." He hadn't brought a raincoat home, and he hoped there was an old one in a closet somewhere.

Frank Borth, a local cartoonist, was also pressed into service. "We've got to keep a lid on rubberneckers," the chief told him. Frank put on a raincoat and hat, grabbed a flashlight, and set off for Star Island. He had the sense—no, the certainty—that it was going to be a long night.

91

By 2:45 P.M. there were three survivors aboard the *Betty Anne*. Jeanne felt as worn out and battered as if she had just spent an hour in the raging water. Her palms and fingers were like raw meat, and the salt in the air and the water intensified the pain. She knew that, under her long sleeves, her arms were covered with bruises up to her sore shoulders.

She had felt ready to give up after the second survivor was pulled aboard, but then the other boat, *Bingo II*, arrived out of the swirling mist. She hoped that, between it and the *Betty Anne*, they could save most of the passengers. In the gray-shrouded distance, in the direction of the lighthouse, Jeanne could see at least two other boats closing in. She thought they were plucking people out of the water, but she couldn't be sure.

Apparently more people had been on the boat that overturned than she'd expected. She was glad to have saved three lives, but the sea was claiming people fast, and fifteen to twenty people were still in the water.

Jeanne glanced up at her husband. He was guiding the boat forward, very slowly, to approach victim after victim. Jeanne saw him shake his head. Another dead one. She felt as though everyone on the *Betty Anne* had become trapped in a nightmare.

But Jeanne thought she saw someone clinging to the dead body. He suddenly raised his head, and she could see the pale face of a young man. She shouted up to her husband and pointed. Harold adjusted the speed and direction of the boat to draw closer and drift down toward the two forms.

Jeanne tossed the rope, and Angelo Testa Jr. caught it. He wrapped it around his hand, and with his other hand he took as strong a grip as he could on his father's jacket. He felt the tug of the rope on his hand and allowed himself to be pulled, and he pulled his father.

Angelo was surprised that he had managed to catch the rope. Everything was a dream now. Every thought and action and feeling was slow and strange. He felt as though most of him was somewhere else. He had no idea how long he and his father had been in the water. The small, conscious section of his mind wondered whether they were indeed being tugged toward a boat, or was this part of the dream and he was being dragged toward death?

Angelo bumped against the side of the heaving boat, which felt real enough, and he could hear the sound of its engines now above the wind. Hands reached down and grabbed under his shoulders. He was lifted, but only a few inches because he retained the grip on his father.

"Let go," someone said. A female voice.

"My father," Angelo croaked.

"I've got him." A male voice.

Trusting them, if only because he had no other choice, Angelo let go. He heard harsh breathing and grunting against one side of his head as he was hauled aboard and dropped onto the deck. A few moments later, his father's body was placed next to him.

A woman's face appeared above him. She was still breathing hard, yet she managed to say, "I'm sorry."

"Thank you," Angelo said. He wanted to ask whether this was a dream, whether he was really out of the water, when he heard a man shout.

"Another one!" Jim Bolton called out.

A man was at the end of one of the ropes. He had wrapped it around one arm and was attempting to haul himself in with his other hand. Trying not to cry out from the pain, Jeanne wrapped her hands around the rope. She tugged at it repeatedly. Suddenly, it went slack. She looked up, afraid she had lost him, then stared in astonishment. The nightmare was becoming more surreal.

The man appeared to be hovering in the air, higher than the bridge of the *Betty Anne*. He came closer, his legs kicking. Then Jeanne realized that the man had been lifted up and was being carried on the crest of a wave. She thought this was impossible, or possible only well out in the ocean. Yet there he was, gliding in an arc over the boat. The expression on his face matched Jeanne's astonishment.

Stanley McKeegan, the cop from the Bronx, had no control over what was happening. Wasn't it enough that he'd survived the capsizing and a half hour or more in the water? Now, just when he had gotten close to a rescue boat, a wave, as though targeting him, was airlifting him over the boat. For what seemed like an eternity he was suspended in the air, feeling the power of the wave under his body. Then it flung him over the boat, not in a straight line but twisting him toward the stern.

To McKeegan and the Bishops, it looked as though the wave was aiming him at the propellers of the *Betty Anne*.

He landed in the water behind the propellers. At first, that seemed safe enough. But the rope he clung to became fouled in the propeller blades, and began to suck him in. McKeegan didn't have time to think whether he preferred to drown or be chopped to pieces.

Seeing what was happening, Harold Bishop cut the engines. Jim grabbed a knife, and Jeanne regained a good hold on the rope. Jim dove over the side, swam to the stern, and went under. He hadn't paused to say anything to the man in the water, to save time and because he had seen how disoriented the man was.

The rope was wrapped around the stem of one propeller. Jim cut the connection to the man in the water, to free him. He hoped Jeanne was ready to toss a different rope; otherwise, the man might move away, perhaps thinking that the rope around his arm was still attached to the boat.

Jim came up for air, such as it was. He felt the driving rain sting his face, then a wave crashed over him. But the *Betty Anne* sheltered him enough that he could get a lungful of air. Returning to the propeller, he dug the knife in and sawed away, finally cutting the rope pieces free.

With Jeanne hauling from above and Jim pushing from below, McKeegan was pulled onto the boat. Jim had trouble climbing aboard. No wonder it had been impossible for most of the others after being in the turbulent water.

Harold restarted the engines just in time. Dazed and no longer able to fight the current, Ben Tasman was drifting out to sea. Seeing this, Harold moved the *Betty Anne* in front of him. Jeanne called out and threw a fresh rope. Only the desire to survive gave Tasman a last bit of strength to grab hold of the knotted end.

With Jim pulling behind her, Jeanne hauled the man in. Jim held the rope steady as Jeanne leaned down and grabbed the man. Then she heard the wave.

Glancing up, she saw it approaching swiftly. She had maybe five seconds, not enough the get the man all the way on board. If the wave hit while she held him, he might be crushed against the hull. "Let go of the rope!" she shouted to Jim.

He did, and Jeanne pushed the man back into the water. The wave struck the *Betty Anne* and sent Jeanne staggering. As soon as she recovered, she hurried to the side. The man's head was just breaking the surface. She reached down and grabbed him again, and with Jim helping they got him on board.

"I'm glad to be alive," Tasman muttered. Then he passed out.

92

The *Cricket II* was at the head of a phalanx of fishing boats motoring east from Fort Pond Bay. Frank Mundus wasn't necessarily the leader of the rescue flotilla—he had no seniority, since this was his first summer in Montauk and he still depended on open-boat income— but he had been quick to put down his shot glass and vow to face the storm. And he was the first out of his Fishangri-la berth.

The sound of the wind and waves was still so loud that the captains had to communicate with their hands instead of their radios. As they turned south and neared the lighthouse, they gestured and pointed to one another, catching sight of the *Betty Anne*, then the *Bingo II*. They did not yet see the overturned bow of the *Pelican*.

One boat of the flotilla peeled off, then another, and a third. Those captains had spotted bodies in the water. They knew there was little chance that the passengers they saw were alive, because the bodies were up-current of where the *Pelican* probably was now. Any survivors were more likely to have stuck with the overturned boat.

Mundus cursed to himself. Was dragging the dead aboard all that was left to do? He acknowledged that recovering bodies was important for the families, but he held out hope that there was still time to do more. He wanted to find Eddie Carroll and most of the passengers still with him.

By the time they drew abeam of the lighthouse, only Mundus, on the *Cricket II*, and Carl Forsberg, on the *Viking V*, were still steaming forward. When they first glimpsed the *Pelican*'s bow, they thought it was a life preserver.

93

Bill Blindenhofer couldn't keep count, and Les Behan up top was too busy maneuvering the boat to do it for him. There were maybe a dozen people from the *Pelican* on the *Bingo II* now, Bill thought. Nine was a more accurate count, because three of the people he had fished out of the sea were already dead.

Each corpse stared at him with lifeless white eyes. One victim, an old black guy, had his mouth open as though he had died in the middle of a scream. Another victim's shoulder was probably broken; when Bill had hauled him up, it looked as though one arm was coming out of his back. The third victim's fingers on both hands were curled up as though he was going to claw something. Bill tried to drag the dead away from the living, but it was getting harder for him to keep track.

"Bill!" Behan shouted from the bridge. "Bill, you all right?"

Bill nodded and raised his hand, then let it drop. But he was not all right, not at all. He was pretty sure he had missed a couple of people. Because of him, they might die.

The *Pelican* was moving southeast past the point, flushed by the ebb current back toward the Atlantic. Behan kept the *Bingo II* below the *Pelican*. When people clinging to the hull saw Behan's boat, some stopped fighting the waves and let go their precarious hold on the hull, striking out toward rescue.

But without the resistance of the partially submerged fourteen-ton boat, they were thrown and tumbled by the seas, some turning completely around. Even those who still had the strength to swim were too confused and most likely too terrified to fight the waves.

The waves had hidden some of the passengers, too. A person could suddenly appear from behind a wave crest and be swept by before Bill could react. Others were tumbling off the tops of waves as though on a roller coaster.

It was almost miraculous that Bill had managed to pull nine survivors from the water. Behan's maneuvering had made it possible. Despite being lashed by wind and rain as he stood on the bridge, he kept control of the *Bingo II*, moving it carefully with the current and abreast a person in the water. When people came along the side where Bill was crouched and ready, the boat was moving with them enough that Bill could lean over, grab hold of a hand or jacket or hair, and yank them aboard, his strong shoulders and solid body providing enough leverage. Although he had tossed ropes into the water, so far no one had had the strength to grab them.

Bill didn't have time to tend to the people he had hauled aboard alive. Moments spent with them could mean missing a would-be survivor still in the water. He put the victims down as gently as he could on the deck, dropped a thin blanket on them, and got back into position. He couldn't do much for them anyway—a few had immediately passed out, others were vomiting and moaning, still others just lay on the deck staring wide-eyed at the gray-black sky, chests heaving.

"Let's go to the *Pelican!*" Bill shouted up to the bridge. Saying something made him feel less helpless.

Behan shook his head, though Bill couldn't discern the motion. From his lookout, Behan could see people still clinging to the hull, and the *Bingo II* was powerful enough to get to it in just a couple of minutes. But if he did that, Bill wouldn't be able to grab those floating by. On the other hand, getting close to the hull meant plucking people out of the water before they floated away. The other boat was closer to the *Pelican*. Maybe it could take care of them. It was a hell of a decision.

Then the decision was made for him. "Here comes another one!" Behan yelled down to Bill. "And one after that!"

From his vantage point on the bridge, Behan could see what was happening before his mate could. The half dozen or so people who had been clinging to the overturned hull were letting go, one by one, and were being swept away from it.

The victims tried to reach the closest boat—the *Betty Anne*. Behan thought he saw one man grab a rope, but the current pushed the others on. Fortunately, because they had not left the *Pelican* together, they approached the *Bingo II* one by one. It was a stupid thing they had done, Behan thought. If they had just waited it out. . . . But he could understand that they were too scared and weary to keep hanging on.

"Get ready, Bill!" he called.

This was it for the *Bingo II*. Whatever they did here was all they could do. Moving the boat a little faster southwest, and keeping the victims on his mate's side, Behan was giving Bill the best chance he was going to get.

Bill could see them now: five dark, waterlogged, and no doubt exhausted forms in the water, being propelled his way. He felt the motion of the *Bingo II* and knew what Les was doing. It probably wouldn't be enough—the victims were approaching fast, and parts of him had already shut down and were numb from fatigue.

He heard the screaming before he saw the face. Then he saw the man being thrust through the water as though heading for a waterfall, closing in on the *Bingo II*. The mouth moved rapidly but no words came out, only an incoherent screaming plea to be saved.

Bill reached over the side. The rope around his chest went taut again, and he prayed it wouldn't fray or he'd be heading for the Atlantic too. He extended his arms as far as they would go, his hands in the tossing water, and suddenly he felt a shirt and a forearm and latched onto both.

He was able to hold on for only a few seconds, then he felt his grip slipping. Glancing sideways, Bill saw another man in the water coming near. He was going to lose them both. He was going to lose all of them. They were going to die, and on their way to death they would look up at him as they were swept past the *Bingo II*, and Bill would have to live with the knowledge that he hadn't done enough.

The grip on one of his hands loosened completely. Then he had an idea born of desperation. With his free hand, he reached back into the boat and grabbed the handle of the gaff. Just as his other hand came loose, he swung the gaff, digging the blade into the man's shoulder. After that, for Bill it was like bringing in a marlin.

As the man lay gasping on the deck, Bill yanked the gaff out of him. For all he knew, the guy hadn't felt it. Bill turned back to the rail. He was too late: the second person was already past the *Bingo II*. But a third one was approaching. Behan moved the boat in close. Bill wasn't taking any chances this time. As the man came even with him, he swung the gaff again. He got him in the arm and hoisted him aboard.

When Bill turned back to the rail this time, he was faced with another hellish decision. The two people remaining in the water were approaching the *Bingo II* at virtually the same time. At this point, their arms were making only feeble attempts to combat the motion of the water. One of them was going to die.

Les Behan had seen them coming before his mate did. What to do was his decision. He thought of turning the boat so they would both slam into the side of it, and maybe Bill could get to one if not both. But the way they were moving, and considering that they couldn't be in good shape anyway, the impact might kill them. They could bounce off and be swept around the boat. Going between them wouldn't do any good, because Bill could lean over only one side at a time. If Les left the bridge for the deck, the roiling water and wave action could turn the boat any which way, maybe running over both victims.

Behan didn't have a choice. He worked the boat so it was moving in the same direction as the men were, holding back enough that they would catch up while giving Bill some kind of chance. And it would be pure chance—or Bill's choice—that decided which of the victims was plucked from the water.

Bill chose based on common sense. He would go after the first one who got to him. If he got him, he'd haul him aboard and see whether he could get the other guy. If he missed the first one, he had one more chance.

Bill lunged with the gaff, but just as he did, a wave hit the *Bingo II* and the boat lurched away. The gaff missed. The man raced past, giving Bill nothing more than a frozen stare, his arms moving weakly, almost as though he was saying good-bye.

The gaff got the next one, in the side of his right arm. Bill dragged him in. It took every ounce of his strength, because the man was big. Once on board, instead of collapsing the man stood up, the gaff still protruding from his arm. He looked almost a foot taller than Bill. "Thank you, thank you," the man kept gasping.

Unable to speak, Bill pointed at the man's arm. He seemed totally unaware of the gaff. Bill sat down on the deck. He didn't know whether to laugh or cry. He felt like doing both.

94

The New York City newspapers and radio stations were receiving more calls. Not from Montauk necessarily, but from elsewhere on Long Island and from Connecticut and New Jersey. The callers were people who whiled away the time listening to the radio emergency channels, the Coast Guard, and chatter among boat captains.

The callers reported that there had been some kind of big boating accident off Montauk Point. A fishing boat had capsized. Not a commercial boat but a weekend party boat called the *Pelican*. There were people in the water. A lot of them. There were bodies in the water. Might be a lot of them too. The Coast Guard was supposed to be on the way but hadn't shown up yet.

News editors often found out about things when people who knew just bits and pieces contacted them to find out what was really going on. In this instance, that's how a couple of radio stations and the *New York Daily News*, the *New York Herald-Tribune*, the *New York Times*, and the *Daily Mirror* learned about the capsizing. Montauk was a long way to send somebody, and few reporters were available on the Saturday afternoon of Labor Day weekend. So the first thing editors had their newsroom people do was make phone calls to verify that, indeed, a tragedy was in progress.

Phones rang at the fire departments in Montauk, Amagansett, and East Hampton, and at the East Hampton Town and Village police stations, and also at the office of the *East Hampton Star* on Main Street across from Guild Hall, but no one picked up. It's unlikely they would have given away a story to the New York folks anyway. Phones rang even at local businesses, because reporters had dug out a Long Island phone book.

Yes, a fishing boat named *Pelican* had indeed "turned turtle," as one person put it, within sight of the Montauk Light. And there were people dying, and dead already. How many? Estimates ranged from ten to fifty. Even ten was a pretty big story.

Editors ordered reporters and photographers to Montauk. The radio people kept phoning, scratching for information to put on the air. As the afternoon waned, the stations began to issue bulletins about a boat capsized off Montauk Point with rescue efforts under way.

Irene Stein, in Brooklyn, still occupied with her children and the furniture, did not hear the radio reports. Her day continued without much worry as she positioned, then repositioned furniture. Suddenly she heard footsteps pounding up the stairs to the third floor.

Lola, her sister-in-law, burst in, gasping. "Irene, I just heard a report on the radio . . ."

Irene couldn't imagine what was so important. "Lola, sit down," she said. "Catch your breath."

". . . about a fishing boat. One of the fishing boats in Montauk. The radio said a boat capsized."

It was Irene who sat down, and suddenly felt out of breath. John. Her father. Rudolph. The two women stared at each other. It could have been any boat, and not the *Pelican*. But it was also possible that at this moment their lives were irrevocably changing.

95

As Behan's boat drew closer to the *Betty Anne*, the two skippers waved at each other. They didn't need a radio or even words to communicate. Each had come to the same conclusion: there was no one left alive to rescue.

The mostly submerged hull of the *Pelican* was drifting farther southeast. It was well past the lighthouse. It would probably be swallowed by the Atlantic, sucked to the bottom. If there was an air pocket and people were still alive in the overturned cabin, they would then have no chance.

To those on the *Betty Anne* and *Bingo II* who cared or had the strength to stand up and look, the hull looked like nothing more than a piece of white flotsam no bigger than a life preserver tossed about by the waves.

Two decisions had to be made. One was for the *Betty Anne* or the *Bingo II* to go after the *Pelican*. What if it had capsized so quickly that an air pocket was trapped in the cabin and people were alive in there, terrified and rapidly using up the little air that remained? Yet neither boat had the equipment to right the forty-two-foot, fourteen-ton *Pelican*, especially while it was still being battered by waves.

The other decision was whether or not to bring aboard the few bodies that were still in the water. Left out here they would eventually sink or be eaten by sharks, and not having a body to bury would make a family's loss even worse. It could be next week, next year, or never before a body refloated or washed ashore, and in a condition that no one should have to witness.

But without discussion, Behan and Bishop rejected both courses of action. Trying to right the *Pelican* in this sea could kill anyone left alive underneath and possibly capsize one of the rescue boats. The Coast Guard had to show up eventually, or one of the other captains could take a shot. As for bringing the bodies aboard, surveying the people they had rescued made Behan and Bishop realize that if these people didn't get some quick attention on land, there would be a few more bodies to unload at the dock. Bishop looked down and saw his wife sitting on the deck, a blanket wrapped around her. He couldn't see all her bruises and cuts, and especially how wounded and raw her hands were, but he knew she must be in pain.

Almost simultaneously, the skippers called for more power from their engines and turned in the direction of False Point. The first place to put in would be the docks on Lake Montauk. There was nothing more they could do.

Neither of them knew that one more man was clinging to life above the surface. Antonio Borruso peered through the mist and stinging salt water that the waves thrust in his eyes as the boats moved away from what remained of the *Pelican*—and him.

96

Boatswain's Mate Kenneth Whiting ached in every joint from his high-speed charge through the storm. The pounding that the picket-boat was taking on its bow reverberated through the vessel and went right through Whiting and the seaman with him, body blow after body blow.

It was almost 3:15, an hour after the *Pelican* had capsized, yet the first Coast Guard boat on the scene was just drawing even with the Montauk Light. Aside from the resistance offered by the storm, visibility had been so poor that Archie Jones in the lighthouse had to guide Whiting via radio. He sent him east, then south as soon as the picketboat came into view. Whiting was glad for any help he could get, being far from a veteran of the picketboat, or any kind of boat for that matter. The army, even being in Korea, was looking more attractive right now.

Whiting was sore and wet, but he was anxious not to let down the Coast Guard and the survivors. If there were any survivors left. Where was the cutter from New London? It seemed unbelievably unfair that people's lives depended on him, that during this disaster he *was* the Coast Guard.

Whiting knew, at least, that survivors had been rescued. The *Bingo II* and the *Betty Anne* had passed him heading northwest and spoken over the radio. Harold Bishop said he had six survivors; Captain Behan said he had twelve. Eighteen survivors, whatever shape they were in. The question was, of course, out of how many? Maybe that had been all, and no one had died. Whiting doubted that, though. But he'd never been part of a disaster before; maybe people in the water lasted longer than he thought.

It occurred to Whiting suddenly that those boats had been heading to port because no one was left to pull out of the water. And if there were more than eighteen people on the *Pelican*—there had to be, a party boat on a holiday weekend Saturday?—all he would be in time for was the body count. He would be out there by himself, possibly surrounded by drowned men and women.

He received a call from Jones, who told him that there were indeed bodies in the water, no sign of anyone else alive, but that he might want to check the *Pelican*. Who knows, maybe people were alive in an air pocket. Whiting said he would, but that would delay the body retrieval, because there was no way the picketboat could right the fishing boat even if a hundred people were alive in an air pocket.

Past the lighthouse, Whiting spotted the bobbing white hull. The waves were prodding it toward the ocean. Whiting realized that the vessel more likely contained bodies, not passengers clinging desperately to life. Even then, though, it was necessary that he go to it—for the families of the deceased. He hoped there was a way he could put a rope on the *Pelican* and, if nothing else, halt its journey to open water.

As he neared the *Pelican*, Whiting's worst fears were realized. The seaman called out to him, "Port side, other side of the boat, there's someone in the water." He increased speed and rushed past the hull. Then as he slowed and turned, he knew that the person was dead.

He drew the picketboat even with the body, then kept the throttle open just enough to stay abreast of it. The seaman reached down and struggled to draw the body aboard. Whiting couldn't tell whether it was a man or a woman; the body was fully clothed, including a jacket and tall work boots. The weight of the waterlogged clothing had probably slowed the body's drift to the ocean.

Once the body was aboard and covered with a tarp, Whiting pushed through the current back toward the *Pelican*. He was so intently focused on the white hull ahead that when he saw motion coming from it he blinked, then rubbed his eyes, thinking the wind had blown something into them. But, as if appearing by magic, a man was straddling the hull. He was thin and had short white hair. He was waving.

That's how the Coast Guard saved Antonio Borruso, the nineteenth, oldest, and last survivor of the *Pelican*.

97

The *Cricket II* and the *Bingo II* slowed as they neared each other. Carl Forsberg, on the *Viking V*, continued on.

Mundus saw that Behan's mate was sitting on the deck, his head in his hands. Much of the deck was covered with people, close to twenty. Except for two or three who were moving about, he couldn't tell who was alive and who was dead. Maybe the rest were dead.

As if reading his thoughts, Behan called across, "I've got to get these people in or they won't last."

Mundus called back, "I'll go after the *Pelican*. Carl's ahead of me."

Behan nodded. He started to turn his boat away when Mundus gestured and called, "You got Eddie?"

"I don't think he made it, Frank."

We'll see about that, Mundus thought as he pushed ahead. At the least his body would not go unburied.

Mundus followed in Forsberg's path. It already seemed like a long time ago that he had had a bowl of hot soup in front of him and a shot of whiskey in his hand. Now he was as wet and miserable as he'd ever been this day.

With luck, he and Eddie would both be getting dry on the outside and wet on the inside before the day was done.

98

Despite the local cops and firefighters standing watch on the Lake Montauk dock next to the yacht club, the crowd was growing.

Curious locals in slickers had slipped through, most likely because they were related to as many as half of the cops and firemen. David Edwardes, who had been dropped off at the small airport in Montauk, had arrived, and he was usually waved through at crime scenes, which this resembled in a few ways. And since he had gotten a free pass, it didn't seem right to say no to the reporters and photographers from the nearby papers, such as the *Southampton Press* and *Sag Harbor Express* and the county seat paper, the *Riverhead News-Review*. And people from *Newsday* showed up too. This new daily was based on Long Island, so it made sense that their people had gotten here before the big New York papers.

The tough part was, people were arriving already who claimed to be relatives of the *Pelican* passengers. No one—not Captain Steele, not Chief Ecker, not anyone—was quite prepared for that. On the one hand, since most of the *Pelican* passengers were from the five boroughs, how could any of the relatives have heard about the event and gotten out to Montauk so fast? But then, these could be brothers and sisters, aunts and uncles, cousins, whatever, who were less than an hour away. How could they turn them away? Most of those people were let onto Star Island too.

And of course there were the cops, firemen, Dickinson and others of the state park police, the first arrivals of the state police, the captains and mates who berthed their boats on Lake Montauk, the dock rats, idled employees of the yacht club, firemen from Amagansett and East Hampton, various local officials, and several charter boat passengers who had never left the docks because they could see that something was up.

It was as though they were all gathering for a show. And that show was seeing what the boats would bring back from the sea.

99

As Coast Guardsmen on Long Island learned more about the *Pelican* situation, they fed information to Third District headquarters in New York. Going through proper channels—and losing precious minutes in the process—New York officials discussed with officials at Second District headquarters in Boston which district had jurisdiction to supervise the rescue operations. The *Pelican* had capsized in Third District waters, but the larger and better-equipped vessels that had the personnel and power for a storm rescue were based in New London.

It was finally determined that the eighty-three-foot *Tamaroa* would be ordered to set off from New London and dock in Lake Montauk. There, it would request instructions from Third District command—a curious order given that any chance of rescuing whoever remained in the water might well depend on heading directly to The Rip off Montauk Point.

But even if the *Tamaroa* had gone to that spot at top speed, it would have arrived far too late, although Coast Guard officials could not have known that.

Following orders, the *Tamaroa* left New London, headed across Long Island Sound, then swung around the North Fork into Block Island Sound and west into Lake Montauk. There, inexplicably, it remained docked until evening.

There had been a previous Coast Guard boat dispatched, but it would be of no help. That morning a patrol boat had left New London for Block Island to conduct boarding exercises. One of the young men aboard was Howard Barnes. He was not scheduled for patrol duty that day, but because the weather was so nice and a third hand would be useful in the exercises, he volunteered to go. This was the boat rerouted by New London when Whiting had called earlier.

The timely arrival of this patrol boat may well have meant a few more survivors. But according to Barnes, his boat was battered by the storm while crossing the Sound and began to take on water. The crew could not risk trying to return to New London, nor were they confident of reaching Montauk. Instead, they put in at Plum Island to pump the bilges. That done, and with the worst of the storm having been weathered, Barnes and his two companions left Plum Island and headed once more for Montauk Point.

There was also the boat that had taken Curles and his crew on a wild-goose chase to Napeague Bay. It would be the second Coast Guard boat to arrive off the Montauk Light. During its search, it located two bodies, then after an hour turned back toward Lake Montauk.

That the *Tamaroa* remained tied to the dock in Lake Montauk while local boats were going out in the storm angered many of the onlookers. Paul Forsberg, the seventh-grade son of Carl, and a group of friends were part of the crowd waiting for the other boats to come in. They thought the *Tamaroa* was immobile because the water was too rough, and they gave the Coast Guard a hard time, throwing rocks at the *Tamaroa* and taunting the sailors, who tried to explain their predicament.

"People are drowning out there and you're waiting for orders?" Paul recalls people yelling from the dock. Later he recounted, "There were thousands of stones in Gosman's parking lot, and me and other kids took turns getting resupplied. The adults kept shouting at the *Tamaroa*, 'You bastards, get out there!' "

The Coast Guard boat stayed put, paralyzed by confused communications.

100

Carl Forsberg, on the *Viking V*, got to the *Pelican* first. It had drifted more than a half mile from where it had capsized, and the overturned boat—or the few remaining square feet of the bow to be seen—appeared to have little time left above the surface. Any passengers still alive inside were about to go down with the boat.

And there could indeed be people in there. Forsberg noted that the bow was bobbing up and down, sometimes independent of the motion of the water. To him, that kind of flotation meant that air was trapped somewhere inside.

Forsberg eased his boat against the bow. The storm was past its peak, and the seas were decreasing along with the wind and the ebb current, but still he knew he was taking a huge risk. A wave big and strong and mean enough could pick up part of the *Pelican* and slam it against his side. His own boat could be crippled in the ocean. Or his propellers could strike the overturned bottom of the *Pelican* and break or become embedded in the hull. Even if he could get a line on the *Pelican*, there were two additional risks: He had to swing the *Pelican* around to his port side to tow it north without it crashing against him. If that worked, he had to hope that the *Pelican* wasn't pulling him hard to port while he took a wave on the starboard side, or he might capsize.

Where was Mundus? Forsberg wondered. Where was one of those big Coast Guard boats? Forsberg suddenly felt like the only boat left on the water.

Repeated tossing of a line toward the *Pelican* did no good, but then the line caught something under the bow—Forsberg didn't know what. He tugged as hard as he could, and the line held. He gently worked the throttle, and his boat moved forward. He would let the waves bring the *Pelican* around behind him.

At his stern the line came loose, and immediately the *Pelican* drifted away. As Forsberg was circling around, the *Cricket II* arrived. After the delay of talking to Behan, Frank Mundus had searched among the debris still visible in the water, hoping to find Eddie Carroll alive—or even dead. But there weren't any bodies left. Those not picked up early on, or later by Whiting and Curles, had drifted into the Atlantic or sunk out of sight.

Mundus also saw the bobbing action of the *Pelican*'s hull. "What do you think?" he called.

"We got to try it," Forsberg replied.

Nodding, Mundus said, "Maybe Eddie's in there."

They didn't need to go further with that. Nothing was impossible, but both knew that with his boat in trouble, the last place Eddie Carroll would be was in the cabin.

They carefully guided the two boats on either side of the *Pelican*'s bow. They tossed lines, but the lines didn't hold. It was like trying to catch a fish without a hook. But that gave Mundus an idea. He shouted it over to Forsberg, who tossed him his line.

Mundus took the line and threaded it through a couple of links of his anchor chain, then knotted it. He would "fish" for the *Pelican* with his anchor as the hook; if he caught onto something, the boats could share the burden of the tow. This would be a necessity before reaching False Point, because they would be going against the wind and the waves, dragging a boat almost as big as each of theirs.

101

The *Betty Anne* and the *Bingo II* appeared in Lake Montauk and headed for the Montauk Yacht Club dock as fast as the wind and water allowed. As each tied up, a priest went aboard to administer last rites. This ritual would be repeated over the next couple of hours as other boats returned carrying bodies.

Police, firemen, and volunteers immediately formed a line from the boats to the dock to unload the survivors. Each was covered with a blanket, then gently handed over the side of the boat and placed on a stretcher. They were offered water and more blankets, then two men carried each stretcher up to the club's ballroom.

It was a heart-wrenching job. As the *Daily Mirror* reported, "Nearly all of those rescued were suffering from severe cases of shock, sobbing and moaning as they were carried on land."

Once the survivors were taken care of, it was time to remove the bodies. To preserve some sense of dignity, each body was wrapped in a white sheet before being lowered to the dock. Then they were taken to the temporary morgue that had been set up in the Duryea icehouse.

More boats left port to head for the capsize area. It would not be impossible to find a survivor clinging to something floating in the storm-tossed water, although the captains who went out were fairly certain that their mission now was retrieval of bodies that hadn't already been carried out to sea.

Bob Conklin was on the *Arab*, captained by his father. The storm was still strong enough that it had the boat "rolling all over the place," Bob remembered. "We saw a body off Shagwong Point. Another guy on the *Arab* hauled it in, then I went below and got a blanket and tried to cover the body of the man without touching it." The thirteen-year-old Conklin would have nightmares for months of being trapped and dying in water over his head.

Only minutes after the *Kingfisher* tied up at the town dock after searching for bodies, a small dragger from Block Island arrived. The captain asked where the wreck was; Jim Miller, the mate on the *Kingfisher*, volunteered to guide him to it, and climbed aboard the dragger. When they got out there, they saw the *Cricket II* and the *Viking V* slowly towing the *Pelican* past the lighthouse.

When the dragger radioed that the two fishing boats were towing the *Pelican* in, the state police called for a couple of divers. As soon as the *Pelican* was at the town dock, it would be searched for bodies—and, just maybe, a survivor or two.

For a moment, Miller thought he saw something red under the

overturned bow of the *Pelican*. A wave had lifted it up, then released it, and just before the bow plunged back into the water, Miller caught a glimpse of something stuck to the handrail. This was only the beginning of the longest night of the sixteen-year-old's life.

102

It wasn't long before Frank Mundus saw the red object too. Between the wave action and the momentum of two boats steadily pulling the *Pelican*, the bow rose a little bit higher, maybe just an inch.

What Frank saw was red hair waving to and fro like seaweed, barely beneath the surface of the roiling water. Then he saw the dead boy's eyes; they were wide open in a horrified stare, and his hands were locked in a death grip on the rail as he disappeared one more time.

"Goddammit!" Mundus shouted. That was all he could do for John Furness—keep shouting angrily into the mocking wind.

103

The survivors were placed on cots in the yacht club's ballroom, and moments later they were surrounded by volunteers. One, perhaps too much in the spirit of things, offered Stanley McKeegan whiskey from a flask, but McKeegan responded that he was "on a strict water diet." The Bronx police sergeant had retained his sense of humor throughout the ordeal.

The *New York Herald-Tribune* reported: "The Montauk Yacht Club, a 22-room structure, was quickly converted into an aid station. Mrs. Martin R. Evans, a nurse's aide who had been vacationing here with her husband, took charge of the emergency service in the club's small ballroom. Mrs. Evans commandeered blankets and mattresses from neighboring homes."

The survivors' conditions varied. Some were so exhausted that they feel asleep immediately in their still-wet clothes. A few, including Antonio Borruso, responded to all the attention being given to them—more blankets, dry clothes, coffee or tea, offers of food that had been intended for that night's banquet—and to the growing realization that they were indeed alive. They were almost jovial, already recounting their adventure to the volunteers. But there were also those who remained frightened, their minds tortured by images of the last couple of hours. They continued to cry and moan no matter how kind the volunteers were to them.

The *East Hampton Star* ran this account of the evening:

> Several members of the East Hampton Chapter, American Red Cross disaster committee assisted with the patients, helping doctors, getting clothes for victims and giving out information to friends and relatives about survivors. Members of the disaster committee helping were Mrs. Charles Peele, Mrs. Stephen L. Marley, Mrs. James H. Mulford, Mrs. Andrew A. Carson, Mrs. S. Gardner Osborn, James H. Mulford, George B. Hand, and Charles R. Mansir. Members of the committee had gone to the Montauk Manor and announced the need for dry clothes. Guests at the Manor left the dining room and donated all kinds of clothes for the needy. Donations of money were also received. Mr. McCann kept some of his staff on duty to supply hot coffee and food for survivors and workers.

The weekly also noted that "the New York Telephone Company set up four emergency telephones, two at the Yacht Club and two at Duryea's dock, for use of the relatives, friends, police and newsmen."

Station wagons were loaned to transport people to Southampton Hospital. The volunteer physicians and nurses in the aid station in the yacht club determined who could recuperate there and who should be hospitalized.

Eventually, eleven people were carried from the yacht club and put into the station wagons. Onlookers watched silently. A few survivors appeared more dead than alive. Volunteer firefighters and policemen were there to keep the crowd away.

Among those placed in station wagons were Richard Friedel and his father. Richard had kept his father afloat for almost an hour before both of them were hauled aboard the *Bingo II*. Ben Tasman was going to Southampton Hospital too, alive thanks to the *Betty Anne*, as was Costas Candalanos. Albert Snyder had also been picked up by the *Bingo II*.

Cynthia Dunwell, the student nurse at Southampton Hospital, was the only staffer on the 2:30 to 11 P.M. shift that day. But that changed less than an hour into her shift. Calls from police and firemen in Montauk emptied the next-door nurses' residence. Dunwell recalled that her supervisor gathered the nurses together to say there had been a boat accident and the hospital might be getting a couple of patients.

"Suddenly, cars and pickups arrived one after another," Dunwell remembered. "All the patients were cold, suffering from exposure, but the initial observation was that none of them were in a life-threatening way. Their clothing was still wet. We did chest X-rays for all of them to see if their lungs were congested with salt water. Then we put them to bed and kept them warm. Most of them still wore expressions of shock. After a while, all there was to do was make them tea and maybe hold a hand or two."

Richard Friedel didn't want to be put in a bed. He had held onto his father for so long—he said it seemed like years—that he didn't want to be separated from him. Anyway, he said he was okay, and not that tired.

But he was exhausted. Half asleep, he heard his father muttering, between deep breaths, to a nurse. He was asking what had happened. The last he knew he was in the water and about to die. Then he asked about Richard, who was pointed out to him. Richard couldn't even lift his head off the hospital bed.

He heard his father say, "My son, he saved my life, that's what happened." His father wondered how he would find out about his brother and sister-in-law. Richard couldn't tell him. He fell into a deep sleep, and didn't wake up until noon the following day.

104

Kathryn Rauscher and others at the Guild Hall theater had hopes of fame for appearing in *Life* magazine. But their hopes were dashed when the magazine editors, after hearing about the *Pelican*, shifted the photo assignment from the theater party to the disaster.

Actually, the bevy of photographers with camera equipment hanging around their necks had already taken plenty of pictures at Guild Hall. Rauscher, her best friend Patty Osborne, and four other young women looked lovely, and posing for the magazine was one of the most exciting experiences of their lives, even though the photographers had to leave in haste, and even though the feature never appeared. The story that replaced it was titled "The 'Pelican's' Final Cruise."

105

A crowd wasn't wanted in the icehouse. On the other hand, there had to be some contingent of local cops, state police, state park police, and anyone else who could help to identify bodies, then track down and phone the families. The easy IDs, of course, were those with wallets. But not everyone had a wallet.

For those not yet identified, the officers and volunteers in the icehouse had the grisly chore of examining the bodies for distinctive marks such as tattoos and scars. The grim silence of the icehouse was broken only by the sound of pencils scratching notes on paper.

What had startled onlookers at the docks more than the sight of the bodies was that there were so few of them, even after the boats had brought back their cargo. Everyone knew by now that nineteen people had been brought back alive. No one knew how many passengers had been on the *Pelican*, but from accounts of how crowded the boat had been that morning, the general opinion was at least fifty, probably closer to fifty-five.

With the tragic day's light waning, seven more bodies had been deposited on the dock. As many as two dozen could still be missing.

By this point, four hours after the capsizing, the missing equaled the dead. Yes, there was the slender hope that because of an air pocket there were survivors in the overturned cabin, but no one knew whether there might be three people or a dozen.

The Coast Guard boats and planes that had been requested might locate more bodies, or they might not. Those on the dock recognized the growing possibility that those who hadn't been found would never be found. There could be twenty to twenty-five or more people who would never return to their loved ones, who—over time—would be nibbled on by fish or gradually decompose. It would be hard for anyone in Montauk to look out from the point and not think of the water housing a boneyard.

An Associated Press photo published in the *New York Daily News* was callously captioned, "Their holiday ended, bodies of fishermen lie in temporary morgue at Montauk." The photo showed several rescue workers and a policeman standing in the icehouse; at their feet are fully clothed bodies, some in contorted rigor-mortis positions, hands raised as though asking for one more chance to be rescued.

106

After dark, the storm weakened. The wind out of the northeast lost its brutality, and the waves, which had dropped substantially with the change of tide, lost half their remaining height.

By 10 P.M., Frank Mundus on the *Cricket II* and Carl Forsberg on the *Viking V* had been towing the *Pelican* for more than six hours. No Coast Guard vessel had intercepted them to offer assistance, which was fine with them. This was their tow, the least they could do for Eddie Carroll and the diminishing chance that anyone was still alive inside the boat. After they rounded Shagwong Point, the wind and waves and tide helped them make some progress west.

Even so, the tow had been agonizingly slow. Combined, the *Viking V* and the *Cricket II* were almost outmatched by the submerged weight of the *Pelican*. And Forsberg and Mundus feared that at any moment one of their lines would tear free.

Shortly after ten o'clock, the *Tamaroa* received orders to leave the dock at Lake Montauk, proceed with any other Coast Guard vessels available, and rendezvous with the fishing boats towing the *Pelican*. The Coast Guard was to assume control of the tow. With the tide about to start ebbing again, and the captains of the Montauk boats most likely on the verge of exhaustion, Coast Guard intervention would make the difference.

These orders were both right and wrong.

107

The dragger that Jim Miller was on had stayed out on the water, at first searching for bodies, then slowly following the overturned *Pelican* as it was towed toward the entrance to Lake Montauk. Midnight was approaching.

As Miller recalled, "We made it all the way around to False Point and were just off the lake when the eighty-three-foot Coast Guard boat came out. We closed ranks and all started yelling, 'Where the hell were you guys all this time? We've been busting our ass out here!'"

Mundus and Forsberg shouted over to the Coast Guard boats that they didn't want to give up the tow. They would wait until the tide turned, then bring the *Pelican* the rest of the way in. Unspoken was the sentiment that this was one of their own, and they would finish the job.

"We're the Coast Guard. You have to give us your lines," was the response. "We'll take it from here."

Carl and Frank continued to argue, and the Coast Guard continued to insist. The Coast Guard had the law backing it up in situations like this. Finally, with curses echoing through the misty night, the two captains relented.

For whatever reason—perhaps still hoping against all odds to find a survivor inside the boat—the Coast Guard wanted to commence the tow into Lake Montauk right away rather than wait for the tide to change.

Mundus recalled, "They threw us a heaving line over, but one of my crew, cold, tired and wet, cut my towline and tied the Coast Guard's heaving line on it and threw it in the water for them to pull up. Instead, the Coast Guard cutter backed down and got my towline tangled up in both his propellers. When I saw this, I went over to Carl, told him what had happened and suggested he go home because he couldn't tow the *Pelican* by himself. He tried, broke his line and went home."

Eventually, the only way to get the *Pelican* into Lake Montauk was for all three Coast Guard boats to attach lines to it. Still, the doomed boat resisted. At one point, something gave way—the railing. There was one last glimpse of red hair before John Furness sank out of sight forever.

As though housing a great burden, or protesting the end of her last voyage, the *Pelican* pulled against those who tried to bring her the last few hundred feet to the town dock. One could almost imagine the boat being embarrassed at having succumbed to wind and wave, or reluctant to give up her remaining passengers, or miffed at not having been courted enough by her exhausted suitors. During the last hours of Saturday and the early hours of Sunday, the *Pelican* inched toward the berth that had been cleared for it on Lake Montauk.

Then it resisted once more. The Coast Guard towlines snapped, and the force flung the lines into the shallow water. Everything came to a stop. There was silence on the dock. The scene was especially eerie because of the number of hastily assembled lights and the directions they were aiming. There was a collective sense that nothing more could be done, that the *Pelican* would not leave the water. Indeed, as if to taunt the Coast Guard and onlookers on the dock, the boat started to sink.

Lenny Riley found a life vest and put it on. Originally from New Bedford, Massachusetts, he was the nineteen-year-old mate on the charter boat *Marie II*. He grabbed a three-inch hawser off the *Marie II* and coiled the rope around his waist, then jumped in and began swimming to the *Pelican*.

The nearby boats in the harbor trained their lights on the *Pelican*, further illuminating what was left of her. By the time Riley arrived at the hull, only five feet of the bow remained above the water. Despite water slapping his face and the motion of the *Pelican* bumping him, he managed to secure his line to a windlass on the bow. He swam back and handed the line to the Coast Guard.

The reluctant *Pelican* was finally dragged to the dock and snubbed in next to the fishing trawler *Mary Ogden* at 2:45 on Sunday morning. The *East Hampton Star* reported, "In the grim aftermath of yesterday's tragic wreck of the fishing launch *Pelican*, Coast Guard personnel, state troopers and local fishermen labored through the night to bring the hapless craft ashore."

Observed the *Herald-Tribune*, "Listing steeply to starboard, with her bow barely above the water, the boat was brought alongside the *Mary Ogden*, a commercial fishing dragger at the dock, which was equipped with hoisting gear. The *Pelican*'s stern immediately slid under the *Mary Ogden*, and it took more than an hour to extricate her."

A rope sling was finally rigged around the submerged stern. As the boat was raised and righted, spectators saw the door of an outside locker aft of the pilothouse swing open. A stack of unused life preservers fell out.

Despite the hour, eleven-year-old Jimmy Hewitt was awake, wondering why his father wasn't home. When he asked his mother, she told him that his father was down at the town dock, but she wouldn't tell him why. That left him curious, and as the hours passed he became increasingly worried.

Jimmy sneaked out and made his way to the town dock. He couldn't find his father in the crowd of people and the glaring lights. From what he could see, there had been some kind of shipwreck. His father must be helping out. Relieved, Jimmy proceeded to wander around.

He saw the open door to the Duryea icehouse and thought it strange, because he knew that the ice would melt. He went inside and found himself in the midst of bodies, faces frozen in horrible expressions, arms and legs twisted. A few of the blocks of ice near the door were steaming from the warm air coming through the opening.

For the boy, it was as though he had found himself in hell.

108

Wind still gusted around the docks, though the gusts came at longer intervals and with much less force. Emergency floodlights penetrated the thick black-gray mist, their glare augmented by the lights that a few captains were training on the scene from their boats. Some of the cops and volunteers, never expecting to be here so long into Sunday morning, were not dressed for the night's damp chill, and were shivering. Hundreds of individual spirals of cigarette smoke rose up to be swallowed by the mist.

Reported the *Herald-Tribune*, "Most of the [recovery] work was performed on a wind-swept pier, against a background of desolate darkness pierced by the eerie illumination of boat lights and emergency flood-lamps focused on the rescue operations.

"Perspiring volunteers shivered in the night chill. The shouts of seamen, mates and captains from other fishing boats—it was they who carried out most of the task of raising the *Pelican*—resounded across the water. Generators from local fire equipment supplying emergency power added to the din."

Few believed that by this hour there were survivors in the overturned cabin, but some of the people who lined the dock knew from experience or had heard tales during the war and after of overturned boats yielding survivors thanks to air pockets or some other miracle. Some onlookers felt that the tragedy of the *Pelican* could not be worse, that there had to be a reprieve. The cynics in the press conceded that "Miracle in Montauk!" would make a catchy headline.

Sergeant Tom Innes of the state police, wearing white long johns and a mask supplied with air through a hose by a compressor, pushed himself under the water and down to the cabin. After less than a minute, he backed out of the *Pelican*'s insides and stood up.

Water drained off his head as he removed the oxygen mask from his face. "Jesus Christ," he muttered.

Those around him were surprised by what he said, but not in the way they had hoped. Innes shook his head. "It looks as if they were tearing each other apart trying to get out," he said. He shook his head again. "They never had a chance."

Only seconds after he said this, word spread across the dock area. When it reached the victims' family members, sounds of weeping intensified. For a few moments, that was the only sound to be heard other than the hissing and sputtering of the lights.

If Innes was going to pull rank and have the other diver, Trooper Thomas Denlea, retrieve the bodies, now was the time to do it. But he couldn't. Innes was the experienced man; this was his job. "I'm going to get them out," he told Frank Dickinson, Jim Miller, and the others standing on the dock. "You guys get them off here."

Then Innes strapped the mask back on and reentered the water.

The bodies he could see were pressed against the doorway. The door was half open. It was clear to Innes that whatever chance these passengers had of survival was lost when everyone had tried to squeeze out of the cabin at the same time. He figured that all had drowned, but he wouldn't be surprised if the autopsies showed that one or two had been crushed to death.

There was a chorus of gasping and cursing as the first body was extracted from the cabin. This indeed was confirmation of their worst fears.

An informal body brigade was arranged. Innes would pull out a body and hoist it above water. Miller was closest to the dock. Standing in cold, oily water up to his chest, he shoved the body upward, and two men on the dock took it. Volunteers would wrap it in a white sheet and pass it from one hand to another.

A former navy diver, Innes had seen a lot, but this case was the worst. After handing off a body, he had to rest and recover before he could bear to go back down again. He shook the seawater off like a dog, and asked for drinking water and a cigarette each time.

At one point, talking to anyone who would listen, he said, "It looks like they ran for the door and then started clawing at each other. They're jammed together, locked together like a bunch of wrestlers. Jesus Christ, one man still has his fishing rod clutched in his hands." One of the bodies brought up had an ear clutched in his fist.

Recalled Vinnie Grimes, "When we got enough water pumped out [of the hull] and we were down in the cabin, you could see where fingernails scratched in there, and you could see that these people evidently had an air pocket for a short period of time. They thought they could scratch right through, but hell, there was one-inch planking on the other side."

But there was one more grisly discovery to make as the night wore on—a tenth body, this one under the main deck, wedged between the two engines. It was Swede, the would-be mechanic who had passed out on the *Pelican*'s deck. Maybe the engine hatch had sprung open as the *Pelican* capsized, and Swede had tumbled in. Or maybe, regaining consciousness to find himself trapped beneath the overturned hull, he had forced his way up into the engine space seeking an air pocket. He may even have found one, but if so it hadn't lasted. Gus Pitts had to chop Swede's big, rigid body free with an ax.

109

Of the several hundred people who now crowded the dock area, a few were simply curious; most felt helpless as they gazed at the bodies lining the outer section of the dock. Those who had the grim task of moving the bodies to the icehouse at least felt as though they were doing something.

This was not like seeing dead people in newsreels of the war or in photographs in books. These were people who the day before had gotten out of cars or jumped off the Fisherman's Special to get on their favorite open boat for a fine day of fishing. That they now looked so undignified only added to the horror and sadness.

Rigor mortis had set in. The bodies were contorted the way they had died or, with a few of them, they way their limbs had been moved to untangle interlocked bodies. A foot stuck out here, a fist was raised there, a mouth frozen in mid-scream. Most were fully clothed, even down to their shoes. It looked as though they had gone to sleep, then died in the midst of a nightmare.

Two at a time, the bodies were put into the back of pickup trucks. Like packing fish, the volunteers put one body in head first, then one next to it feet first. Each truck made the short drive to the icehouse, traveling slowly to move carefully through the crowd and, it seemed, out of respect for the cargo. No one wanted to make the victims' indignity any worse.

Frank Borth recalled, "There were some people who came peeking in the icehouse and there was this vat of lobsters right there crawling around and there were these bodies on the floor not far from it. This lady looked at the lobsters and said, 'I'll never eat one of those things again.' "

110

Dawn arrived slowly, a subtle lightening through shades of gray. There was no sun to see rising above the Atlantic horizon. It would be two more hours before Sergeant Innes extricated the last body from the submerged cabin.

Jim Miller had never been so exhausted. He hadn't slept for more than twenty-four hours, and for the last several hours he had been standing in water, waiting for the next body to come out. The first body had been one more than he'd seen in a lifetime, and by now his mind was full of bodies—the lifelessness, the horrible expressions, the torn clothing, the contorted arms and legs. He wanted to be home, up-island, dry and in bed, with his biggest burden being going back to school.

The only break had occurred right before dawn. Jim had been pushing a body ahead of him up a short ladder to the dock where hands waited to take it from him. Suddenly, a photographer appeared and yelled, "Step aside, let me get a picture, let me get a picture! Hold there!"

He kept shouting, and Jim didn't know what to do, other than feeling protective toward the body and the man's family. What am I doing here? he thought.

As Miller remembered: "Then the two biggest state troopers I ever saw in my life, wearing knee-high leather boots, appeared and grabbed this guy. 'You ain't doin' nothin', fella,' one said to the photographer. Next thing you know, the guy's in the water, hollering and cursing. To me, those troopers were instantly big heroes."

After the last body was removed, the lights were shut off and people drifted away from the dock. The *Pelican* bobbed forlornly in the still-choppy water.

The reporter for the *News-Review* from Riverhead observed, "A torn piece of a woman's percale dress, colored in soft shades of red and green, had become caught in a part of the *Pelican*'s superstructure and flapped mournfully in the breeze. Rescue workers had seen the bright bit of cloth during the night and at first thought it was a distress flag."

Jim Miller's ordeal was not yet done. "I was cold and miserable and pretty upset. I stopped by the fish house and saw the corpses all lined up with their hands up in the air. Somebody took me to a bar and said, 'Give this kid a drink. He's really cold and he needs a shot.' That was my first drink. Other people gathered around, talking about the *Pelican*. I couldn't think straight. Maybe I was in shock. Somebody bought me another drink."

Miller woke up in a Montauk motel room on Wednesday morning, with no recollection of the previous three days. (The blackout remains to this day.) He went out to get breakfast and discovered that he had no money. The cafe let him eat for free.

111

The open boats didn't go out of Fishangri-la on Sunday, even though anglers showed up on the dock. The reason given was the remnants of the rogue storm. The drizzle and clouds lingered, visibility was poor, and the water was still choppy, although the wind had dropped. Unofficially, none of the captains wanted to go out after losing one of their own and those who went down with him.

The story in the *Herald-Tribune* read:

> None of the party boats docked here ventured out to sea today, although no small-craft warnings were posted, as had been the case yesterday. The reason given for today's inactivity was not the *Pelican* disaster, but poor fishing weather, due to choppy waters and low visibility. Although the fishing was considered too poor to venture out today, about 400 persons arrived this morning in hopes the weather might improve. Most of these disappointed fishermen later strolled down by the yacht club where the *Pelican* was now empty and unguarded.

Soon after dawn on that Sunday morning, a wide-ranging search was undertaken for what was believed to be fifteen to eighteen missing *Pelican* passengers. The search was hampered by lingering rainstorms that, throughout the day, intensified across Long Island Sound to the Connecticut shoreline and over Montauk. Southern Connecticut received more than two inches of rain, and in Salisbury, in northern Connecticut, the tally was 2.57 inches.

Coast Guard planes and surface craft patrolled the ocean and Block Island Sound. The army sent troops from Battery A, 703rd Anti-Aircraft Battalion, stationed at Camp Hero in Montauk, to the beaches to search for washed-up bodies or, by some miracle, someone who had survived the past fifteen or so hours. At 5 A.M., a mobile communications truck arrived from an army base in Brooklyn, and throughout the day it coordinated radio reports from the search parties. No one was found during this search, but one passenger, Charles Drew, fifty, of Brooklyn, who had been brought in as "unidentified," was found by his family in a funeral home in Riverhead.

Recalled Howard Barnes, on a Coast Guard vessel: "Instead of going back to New London, they kept us in Montauk to do search and rescue. Best I remember we were out there for three days. We were out there long enough that the skipper kept wanting to go in. He told them we needed food and supplies. We were told that as long as we had fuel, we should stay out there."

Investigators from the Suffolk County District Attorney's office and the Coast Guard arrived in Montauk to interview survivors, Gene Goble, and some of the captains who had gone out of Fishangri-la. The Coast Guard and state police compiled a list of those missing and presumed dead. The list was repeatedly revised as new information came in. For example, three men from New York City believed to have been on the *Pelican* turned up in Manhattan, the Bronx, and Brooklyn.

Lindsay Henry, the county district attorney, announced his own investigation, saying that someone in his office, Henry Tasker, who lived in Greenport on the North Fork, would be in charge of it. Lindsay told reporters: "After all, party fishing boats are a big business. Every summer, thousands of persons entrust their lives to the operators of these boats. Most of the people think the government makes a rigid inspection of such boats, as they do of other common carriers. Such is not the case."

Coast Guard commander Joseph De Carlo, who had been put in charge of the search, arrived early Sunday morning. After conferring with other Coast Guard personnel and the state police, he told the press that panic had been responsible for most of the fatalities and that some of the trapped fishermen "looked like they had been tearing each other to pieces."

Reporters and photographers from a half-dozen newspapers roamed the beaches, the Montauk Light, and Fort Pond Bay, gathering anecdotes and taking pictures. Bobby Scanlon was nowhere to be found, but during the afternoon Goble issued a statement to the press that he said was based on Scanlon's account of the disaster (much of which was repeated during his court of inquiry testimony). Goble told the reporters: "My feeling in the matter is that I hope we won't have to wait for another tragedy to bring about the rules and regulations for the protection on the waters for the hundred to two hundred private yachts and fishing boats that use Montauk waters every weekend."

112

More family members arrived in Montauk throughout Sunday morning, from before dawn until well after daybreak, depending on when they heard about the *Pelican* and how far they had to travel. Some of the families, including those of Grover Menton, Harold Pinckney, and John Carlson, had been contacted by the state police, because the victims carried wallets and were quickly identified. But some victims had yet to be identified, and several were still missing. Many family members made the long trip east not knowing what they would find.

Paul Manko made the journey from Queens hoping to find his son Wallace alive, or not to find him there at all. Paul had been getting ready for bed Saturday night when he heard a report on the radio about a fishing boat going down off Montauk. He remembered his son mentioning going fishing this weekend. Or was it next weekend? Maybe with the weather, Wallace hadn't gone at all.

Paul called his daughter-in-law, Joan, waking her up. She was pretty tired after taking care of one-year-old Steven all day and night. Yes, Wallace had gone fishing, but no, he wasn't home yet. Maybe he had stopped off at a friend's place to grill the fish and have a couple of drinks.

Paul arrived in Montauk well before dawn, and found his way to the docks at Lake Montauk. It took some persuading to get past the firefighters and across to Star Island, but they could see that Paul was trembling with worry, so they let him through.

Paul found Wallace just as volunteers were carrying his body from the dock to the icehouse. "That's my son!" Paul shouted, pointing, his finger shaking. "That's Wallace, my boy!"

The men carrying the body stopped, unsure what to do. Paul stared down at his son's face and clasped his cold hand. As hard as he rubbed, he couldn't warm it up. "He was such a good boy," Paul whispered. "I told him always to be careful."

State troopers arrived just in time to catch the grief-stricken father as he collapsed.

Irene Stein did not go to Montauk. She had gotten a phone call late Saturday night from Rudy. It was not the first call Rudy made, however. The first was to his wife, Lola, to let her know he was all right. The second was to Adolph, his brother. He told him about their brother John, and they cried. Then he told Adolph about Mr. Kolesar. They cried for Irene, and Adolph offered to go see her.

Irene thought it was strange that Adolph would show up at the door after nine o'clock at night. The children were in bed, fast asleep, and she was about to turn on the radio and read, waiting for John. Adolph looked upset, and seemed reluctant to reveal the reason for his visit. She offered him coffee. He declined, but said yes when she offered him a beer. Well, it was a Saturday night.

Then the phone rang. She thought that was strange, too, at this hour. On the other end, waiting for the call to be answered, Rudy wondered whether he should tell his sister-in-law about her husband or her father first.

Alexander Finkelberg went to Montauk from Flushing, Queens. His brothers Solomon and Victor were missing. Maybe that was good—against the odds, yes, but still a chance. The original plan had been that all three brothers would go fishing together on Saturday on Sheepshead Bay. Then a neighbor, Frank Laurenzana, was going too, and overnight the plans changed to fish out of Montauk. But Alex couldn't do that; he had other engagements. So he didn't go with his brothers.

At the Montauk Yacht Club, Alex was told that Laurenzana was one of the bodies in the icehouse. There was no information about his brothers.

Weldon Furness, of the Bronx, was a bus driver, the kind that Jackie Gleason would portray a few years later in *The Honeymooners*. When he got home from work late Saturday night, his wife was already asleep. He wondered why his son and father-in-law weren't back yet, but he wasn't worried. It was entirely possible that John had stayed with his grandparents.

He was reading the late edition of the *Daily News* and listening to the radio, letting the stress of the job leak out of him, when he heard a report about the *Pelican*. He dropped the tabloid and, without waking his wife and still in his uniform, started driving east.

The wife of Alvin Brown, of Brooklyn, walked up and down the dock on Lake Montauk, shaking as though she had palsy. She had been told that her husband was one of those extricated from the cabin. "My Al!" she cried repeatedly, like a mantra. By coincidence, matching her steps was the wife of Armas Dolk, of East 63rd Street in Manhattan, who asked everyone she encountered, "Where is my husband? Have you seen my husband?"

There were some joyful reunions on Sunday. Amado De Jesus and his sons Juan and Braulio drove from the Bronx to Montauk. The men found the third son, Antonio, recovering on a cot at the Montauk Yacht Club. Tony was still too stunned to provide much information about his experience, but otherwise he was doing well, his head on a mound of pillows and the rest of him covered by blankets.

Reina Borruso also found her husband, Antonio, at the yacht club. They returned together to their home in Queens, where neighbors were waiting. That evening, Borruso, wearing a suit, sat at his table in the crowded kitchen, and as everyone drank coffee he told them all about the *Pelican* incident.

The weather finally began to improve in Montauk late Sunday afternoon. More people than before arrived to stand on the dock and other vantage points and gaze at the *Pelican*. News photographers came and went too. David Edwardes had gotten all the photos he needed, but the city shooters needed to return with lots of film to compensate for not being there on Saturday.

Reporters milled about until dark. They drank coffee and smoked cigarettes, scratched occasional observations on notepads, and searched in vain for anyone other than a cop or Coast Guard seaman to interview. Then they hit paydirt.

Howie Carroll came down to the dock. He had a dazed look on his face, almost as though he didn't know where he was, or at least why he was there. He wore a dark sweater, and his regular white cap was tilted back on his head. The press left him alone at first. He slowly approached the *Pelican*, as though sleepwalking. He stared at the battered hull for a few minutes, then turned away.

The reporters and photographers closed in. They weren't merciless, they weren't rude, but they had to have something for the next day's editions. Howie was stunned, but able to speak, recounting Saturday's events and how he had tried to raise his brother on the radio when he thought that big trouble might be on the way.

He emphasized what a cautious captain Eddie was and how so many of his passengers were his friends. Then Howie silenced the group of newsmen when he said softly, "I hate to say it, but maybe Eddie's better off where he is."

113

Before closing its investigation, the court of inquiry called Bobby Scanlon a third time. The members of the panel, all professional mariners, couldn't make the connection between the rigorous practices of Coast Guard training and service and the apparent nonchalance of the Montauk fishing fleet.

When the reluctant mate of the *Pelican* was questioned again, he spoke even more quietly and haltingly than before. In every response, though, he defended Captain Eddie. One of the officers asked, "If it was not the captain's fault, what caused the accident?"

"The terrible, rough sea." As though Bobby had startled himself by that response, he fell silent for a few moments. Then he repeated, "The terrible, rough sea. That's what it was."

EPILOGUE

By Monday morning, the death toll had risen in published reports but still was not accurate. "Thirty-eight lives were lost in the wreck of the fishing-party boat *Pelican* off Montauk Point, L.I., on Saturday afternoon," reported the *New York Times*. "Only nineteen of the vessel's fifty-five passengers and two crew members survived the disaster."

The bodies in the Duryea icehouse had been identified and transported to funeral homes. Because the nearest facilities were immediately filled to capacity, some of the dead were taken the twenty-five miles west to Riverhead or even to the boroughs.

All the survivors were home by Monday morning. The last two, Costas Candalanos and Ben Tasman, had been kept at Southampton Hospital Sunday night because they hadn't recovered enough from their ordeal in the water. The following morning, though, they were on their way back to Queens and Huntington.

Official information was provided periodically by the Coast Guard, which still had no firm figures. With Eddie Carroll missing, Scanlon keeping his mouth shut, Gene Goble and the Fishangri-la captains and mates protecting their own, and survivors dazed and confused, the number of people on the *Pelican* remained no more than an estimate. This frustrated the Coast Guard, because the searchers could not know how many victims might still be out there, or whether they were searching for bodies in vain.

The Montauk fishing captains were keeping their mouths shut, their normal reaction to any event. Never fond of questions from outsiders about how they conducted their business, they especially didn't care to volunteer information or theories about why they had made it back to port and the *Pelican* hadn't. Let the Coast Guard handle it. Plus, Eddie Carroll had been one of the best of them, and no one wanted to risk dishonoring his memory.

The boat captains figured it might be a different story if Eddie had survived. He'd be dealing with the Coast Guard and everyone else directly, and fellow captains would support him but keep some distance. Even if none of what happened was his fault, he would be coping with his bad luck and his anguish over the victims and their families. But he was dead, no doubt about it. Howie was devastated. Eddie's fiancée was in shock. Every time they turned around, there were more questions from state police, local cops, Coast Guard, family members of victims, investigators from the Suffolk County District Attorney's office, guys from the newspapers, and people hanging around the dock taking pictures and hoping to see one more body brought in.

The captains figured it was best to say nothing. Maybe it wouldn't be so bad for Eddie's memory. And maybe it wouldn't be so bad for the late-summer fishing season—though as Bob Tuma muttered, gesturing at the *Pelican* and the picture takers, "This isn't very good advertising."

People came by the hundreds across Long Island, from New York City, and even from New England, to see the *Pelican* where it rested cockeyed in its berth in Lake Montauk. The survivors and their families, and family members of the victims, had left; none of them wanted anything more to do with Montauk fishing.

For a few hours Sunday morning, the firefighters who didn't have to be on a job elsewhere had stayed at their posts bordering Star Island. Frank Borth hadn't had much food or sleep since Saturday evening, but he remained polite as he and the others turned away the rubberneckers. Every so often he let someone through, after checking with the local police chief or the state police.

Finally, the firefighters were told that it was all right to go home. Vinnie Grimes could report back to the navy. There were no more bodies to gawk at, so there was no need to stop folks from coming and going.

The *Pelican* disaster boosted the nation's holiday weekend death toll. The Associated Press reported on Monday that from Friday through midnight on Monday, 389 people died—283 in traffic accidents, 52 drownings, and 54 in "miscellaneous accidents." The *Pelican* accounted for 38 deaths.

Monday was a nice day, the way travel brochures portray late summer. For the holiday day-trippers and those who had made the trip to Montauk solely to look at the *Pelican*, it was hard to believe that two days earlier a violent storm had capsized a boat and caused one of the worst peacetime losses of life on the water in U.S. history.

"The narrow causeway leading to the capsized *Pelican* is crowded with very busy tourists," observed Stan Smith in his "Woods and Waters" column in the September 4 issue of the *Daily News*. "Each has a camera and each is taking pictures which doubtless will be viewed on some cold rainy night next Winter. . . . There's a strange feeling when you watch all this. It seems indecent. . . . I mean the sunny day and the *Pelican* out there. I wish they'd take the *Pelican* away."

Funerals were held on Long Island and in New York City. Perhaps the biggest was the one for Captain John W. Carlson on Tuesday at the Walter B. Cooke Funeral Home on West 190th Street in the Bronx. Reverend Elmer Dressel, pastor of the Saint Paul Evangelical Lutheran Church in Parkchester, conducted the service. In addition to Carlson's wife and children, extended family, and neighbors, the service was attended by David Monaghan, brother of the police commissioner; James Kennedy, head of the Confidential Squad; and Sergeant Stanley McKeegan. Carlson, with a New York City Police

Department tribute, was buried the following day in the Ferncliff Cemetery in Hartsdale.

On Monday, several of the New York City dailies published photographs of survivors. A story in the *Daily News* was accompanied by three photos. One showed Cynthia Zurendorf "comforted by her mother, Mrs. Raye Zurendorf." Cynthia looks chastised, as though realizing how right her father had been about a nonswimmer venturing into the deep waters off Montauk Point.

The second photo was of a broadly grinning John Griffin displaying his bandaged thumb at his Brooklyn home. And the third showed Renee Sherr being tucked into bed by her sister-in-law, Carol. Both are flashing big smiles. Antonio De Jesus is shown lying on a cot in the Montauk Yacht Club surrounded by his relieved father, Amado, and two brothers, Juan and Braulio.

A photo of the wife and children of Sisinio Salvaterra, taken in their Bronx home, formed a stark contrast. The widow's son, four-year-old Richard, sits on her lap, and her nine-year-old daughter, Florence, sits next to her on the couch. As the caption states, they "stare in wide-eyed bewilderment" after hearing about Sisinio's death.

Despite the attention devoted to the *Pelican* disaster, activity didn't cease completely for Montauk head boats as September wore on. The September 12 issue of the *East Hampton Star* reported, "From the Fishangri-la dock eight open party boats sailed on Saturday, with 110 passengers from the LIRR, and on Sunday the train brought 128 fishermen. Half the party boats sailed that day but all the charter boats did. Sea Bass are very plentiful though the Porgies are dropping out and Cod are now putting in a good showing."

There was much fanfare during the last week of the month when a new Montauk record was established by a New Jersey man who, on board the *Scamp II* out of Fishangri-la captained by Buster Raynor, hauled in a tuna weighing 961.5 pounds.

Before long, though, fewer people boarded the Fisherman's Special to Fishangri-la's head boats. Business for these boats waned—anglers seemed to think that spending more money on a charter better ensured their getting back to port alive.

Brad Glass, son of George Glass and a boat captain in Connecticut, remembers: "After the *Pelican*, business was so bad, the only way to survive was to shoot deer, and it was illegal to shoot deer on Long Island. It was open season and they were running rampant. [The captains] had to poach deer to feed their families, and they all did it. And the cops knew it. That was the immediate legacy of [the *Pelican* incident]. When you couldn't get the people on the boat to pay for the groceries, you had to go out and shoot your own."

Though at a more subdued, post-season level, the social scene continued in East Hampton Town. General George Marshall and his wife flew into East Hampton to be hosted by Mrs. Howard B. Dean, whose 2004 presidential candidate son was a toddler at the time. The wedding of Betty Trippe, daughter of Juan Trippe, CEO of Pan Am Airways, attracted a huge crowd to Saint Luke's Church on Main Street and an even bigger one to the reception at the oceanfront mansion of the bride's parents.

Bodies kept turning up, which at least provided closure for bereft families. One of those initially listed as missing was William Mellardo, thirty-four, of the Bronx. At noon on September 5, his body surfaced near the Sagawam buoy. Montauk captains were on the lookout for such occurrences, and when the captain of the fishing boat *Sally Ann* saw something in the water, he retrieved the body and brought it to Duryea's dock.

Two days later the Coast Guard revised its list once again, estimating the number of missing at twenty-four, with twenty-two bodies found. Two had turned up the day before, on September 6, near Montauk Point. The one found by the Coast Guard was that of seventeen-year-old Lawrence Berger. The other, fished out by the *Ace II* and as yet unidentified, and was brought to the Leonard & Rogers Funeral Home in Riverhead. He turned out to be Solomon Finkelberg of Queens. His brother Alexander made the identification. His brother Victor was never found.

On September 8, the Saturday after the disaster, there were two grisly discoveries. According to an account in the *New York Times*, during the annual Atlantic Tuna Tournament one of the participating boats, the *Kuno*, "discovered the body of a Negro man floating one mile north of Montauk Light. The body, clad in black shoes, white socks and woolen Army-type trousers, was transferred to a Coast Guard picket boat" and taken into Montauk. "The picket boat then set out to sea again after receiving a message from the *Mary F.*, which had picked up part of a body of a white man fifteen miles south of Montauk Light. The man was five feet, seven inches tall and had brown hair. On the left forearm was a tattoo of a lighthouse, with American and French flags." The bodies were later identified by family members as Constantin Acevedo of Manhattan and George Wallace of Brooklyn.

The next day, the body of Frank Marino of Queens washed up near the Ditch Plain Coast Guard station, three miles west of the lighthouse. It was found on the beach by passersby. Also on Sunday, a Coast Guard boat found a torso off a Bridgehampton beach, more than thirty miles west of the lighthouse. It was identified by his wife as Armas Dolk of Manhattan.

On September 10, the remains of Raymond Lewis, forty-seven, of Brooklyn were picked up by the *Sea Leopard*, a navy submarine on its way back to Norfolk, Virginia, from the North Atlantic. Because of extreme deterioration coupled with the work of sharks, the body was buried at sea after a short service.

The next day, an oil tanker found a body floating four miles off Water Mill, twenty-five miles west of Montauk Point. The victim was found wearing dungarees but was too decomposed for identification. There were no papers in the dungarees, only a fish hook.

In the months following the *Pelican* tragedy, a dozen women who said their husbands had been on the *Pelican* filed life insurance claims. A few managed to collect, because their husbands couldn't be found, and insurance investigators couldn't prove that the men were not on the boat.

When the Coast Guard court of inquiry concluded after ten days, there was no immediate official report. That would take several weeks. But apparently Admiral Olson had heard enough.

After the final session, Olson met with the press outside 80 Lafayette Street and agreed to answer questions. It didn't take much prompting to warm him to the subject.

He acknowledged that the suddenness and ferocity of the storm had been big factors in the *Pelican*'s capsizing. But he noted that "a lot of boats went out that same day, many of them smaller than the *Pelican*. They got back."

Olson didn't specifically criticize Captain Eddie Carroll for his seamanship, and cited the failure of one engine as one of the reasons why the *Pelican* had been at the storm's mercy. Aware that the official report was yet to be issued, Olson hedged a bit but obviously wanted to have his say during what the *Daily News* labeled "a precedent-shattering interview." Said Olson: "The fact that the boat was not handled properly by her skipper may have been due to the failure of one engine. But the boat definitely capsized, and in my opinion, the deciding factor was the overloading."

The admiral concluded that he had never discussed his views on any investigation until a full report had been compiled, but he was "making this exception because I feel so strongly on the matter—that no other boat should be overloaded and that such a thing should not happen again."

The final report of the court of inquiry was issued on October 8, 1951. It blamed Eddie Carroll for the overcrowding and operating the *Pelican* "in a reckless or negligent manner so as to endanger the life, limb or property of any person." The report recommended that "Coast Guard operating facilities on the eastern part of Long Island be modernized and improved to afford more efficient Search and Rescue facilities in the light of increased boating and fishing activities carried on from that vicinity."

It also said: "Because there appears that criminal negligence was involved on the part of an offender who is missing and presumed dead, it is recommended that the record of proceedings of this board be forwarded to the Department of Justice for information." After calling for legislative changes to reduce the risk of a similar tragedy, the report concluded: "It is recommended that no further action be taken and that the case be closed."

On November 28, Suffolk County coroner John Nugent closed his investigation into the *Pelican* disaster, which the *New York Times* declared "the worst of its kind in the New York area." Nugent held that the eighteen passengers still missing were presumed dead, which would allow for the settling of estates.

There was one more passenger missing, the youngest of the victims. Nine years later, on October 29, 1960, a human skull was found near Orient Point on the North Fork of Long Island. It was eventually identified as belonging to John Furness, the fourteen year old with red hair who had been secured to the *Pelican*'s railing by his grandfather.

In January 1956, a lawsuit went to trial in Suffolk County Supreme Court in Riverhead, with Judge L. Barron Hill presiding. The jury consisted of twelve men. Watching the proceedings day after day were some of the widows and children of the forty-five victims. Eleven lawsuits had been filed by relatives of the *Pelican* victims and one survivor, John Griffin, against the estate of Edward Carroll and Gene Gobel and his company, which owned Fishangri-la. The plaintiffs' fourteen attorneys decided to go to trial with one case as a test. If it was successful, they would pursue the other cases. Combined, the eleven lawsuits demanded more than $1.7 million in damages.

The plaintiff in the test case was Rose Trotta of Brooklyn, formerly of Patchogue, widow of Nicholas, whose body was never recovered. But just before the trial began, Trotta's lawsuit was replaced by one brought by Florence Testa of Patchogue. Because her husband's body had been found, and her son Angelo Jr. could give eyewitness testimony, it was determined that this case had a better chance in court.

The six-day trial featured testimony from state police, Coast Guard authorities, and the few captains who could be found in Montauk in the middle of winter. Among the witnesses for the plaintiffs was William Friedel, whose son, Richard, accompanied him to the courtroom. William testified that he had lost his brother and sister-in-law in the capsizing, and would certainly have lost his own life if not for his rescue by Richard. A photograph of father and son published in *Newsday* showed Richard, now eighteen, with a slight mustache and taller than William, looking smart in a jacket, tie, and raincoat with the collar up.

Angelo Testa Jr. did testify, wiping away tears the entire time. Responding to a question by James McKeon, an attorney for the plaintiffs, Angelo said: "On the trip back, I was standing next to my father. We were wet from the spray. The second wave, about fifteen feet high, hit and spilled everybody into the water.

"I landed in the water. I was down somewhere and I came up. I saw my father in the water. The people were screaming and grabbing at each other and pulling each other down. The next time I saw my father in the water he was dead."

John Lyle Wilson was another witness for the plaintiffs. Now living in Nebraska, he had spent thirty-three years as a naval architect and engineer for the American Bureau of Shipping and had investigated such disasters as the burning of the liner *Morro Castle* in 1935. He testified that, given the dimensions and weight of the *Pelican*, it should have carried no more than twenty passengers "to ensure proper and safe handling," and that ten square feet of clear deck space should have been provided for each passenger. That day on the *Pelican*, each passenger had only 3.17 square feet.

"When that many people shifted to the port side, they created a load of ninety-six hundred pounds, six feet off center," Wilson testified. "As a result they canceled out the stability of the vessel beyond the point of no return, with the inevitable result that the *Pelican* could not right herself when the second [fifteen-foot] wave hit broadside." (The defense later countered with its own naval architect, Langdon Pickering of Rye, New York, who disputed Wilson's calculations and said that the fifteen-foot wave that struck the *Pelican* "hit at the right time, in the right place, to upset the boat's stability.")

After the plaintiffs rested their case, McKeon moved that the estate of Eddie Carroll be excluded as a defendant in present and future lawsuits. Judge Hill granted the motion. Perhaps McKeon was being kind. More likely, with the Carroll estate having consisted of little more than the *Pelican* and the engagement ring that went down with Eddie, naming him as a defendant would only have elicited sympathy from a jury. Ironically, this bolstered the defense's strategy, which was to put the entire blame for the tragedy on Eddie Carroll.

"It was his engine that failed, his decision to take the boat out," said William Connor, an attorney for Gene Goble, in his summation. "He allowed the boat to become in the position it did, he failed to issue a radio call for help, or for passengers to don life preservers, or for a hand from passing boats. And no one made the passengers stay on the boat."

Connor continued: "The *Pelican* didn't come back because of the engine that failed. I think you'll search in vain to find a case against us. We're here to serve justice, not sympathy."

On the night of January 23, 1956, the jury deliberated for ninety minutes after the judge delivered his charge. Gene Goble and Fishangri-la, Inc., were cleared. McKeon asked Judge Hill to set aside the decision as "contrary to the weight of evidence." The judge refused. The test case that could have resulted in eleven lawsuits totaling $1.7 million in damages was over. No further lawsuits were filed.

Goble later moved to Escondido, California, where he owned a firm that manufactured life preservers.

In August of that year, almost five years to the day after the *Pelican* disaster, the Coast Guard proposed to Congress new safety measures that would regulate the party fishing boat industry throughout the United States, especially boats not weighing enough to have been subject to strict regulations before.

Coast Guard officials said that the proposed regulations were a direct result of the loss of life on the *Pelican*. They did not explain why the new rules had taken five years to develop, but the delay had more to do with Congress than the Coast Guard. The Merchant Marine Council of the Coast Guard had first made recommendations to Congress in October 1951 to change the Motorboat Act of 1940, but the recommendations went nowhere. *Newsday* reported in August 1956 that the move for legislation "gained impetus when the *Levin J. Marvel* foundered and broke up in Chesapeake Bay last year with a loss of 14 lives."

Among the proposed regulations were (1) a maximum number of passengers allowed, (2) a requirement for all boats to carry life-saving and firefighting equipment, and (3) mandatory qualifications for crew members on party boats. The Coast Guard had created a first draft of the legislation with an organization formed after the *Pelican* tragedy, the National Party Boat Owners Alliance (NPBOA). Active to this day, it is headed by Brad Glass of Connecticut, son of Montauk captain George Glass and an open-boat operator himself. George Glass was awarded a distinguished service medal posthumously by the Coast Guard for his part in developing the industry-changing regulations.

Congress enacted the legislation and President Dwight Eisenhower signed it into law before 1956 ended. At the same time, more than 8,000 boats nationwide less than sixty-five feet long and fifteen gross tons were affected. As tragic as the *Pelican* capsizing was, it was the catalyst for the regulations that govern the recreational boating industry to this day and have saved hundreds if not thousands of lives.

There was also a local benefit from the disaster. The *ad hoc* transporting of survivors to Southampton Hospital the night of September 1 further emphasized the need for a Montauk-based ambulance. The Montauk Fire Department had been trying for years to raise funds for one. A few months after the *Pelican* incident, the owner of a Chevrolet dealership in Flushing, Queens, who had known one of the victims, donated a used station wagon to the Montauk Fire Department. That was the beginning of the Montauk Ambulance Squad, which is still active.

On May 24, 1952, at the forty-second annual meeting of the National Council of the Boy Scouts of America in New York City,

Richard Friedel of Troop 29 was awarded the Gold Medal with Crossed Palms for saving the lives of his father and another man on the *Pelican*. Richard was chosen out of ninety other Boy Scouts across the United States who saved lives in 1951.

The Montauk fishing industry survived, but it had to change to do so. Charter boats became the preferred option for fishermen. And spurred by Frank Mundus, the rage became shark hunting.

"Had a day off, looking for a party at the dock," Frank recalled in his memoir, *In the Slick of the Cricket*, written (in Mundus's distinctive dialect) with Russell Drumm of the *East Hampton Star*. "You couldn't say shahk fishin', we needed a fancy name. Three idiots come walkin' down the dock, and I tell 'em we're goin' monster fishin'. They said 'okay,' just like that. They was shahk fishin' and didn't know it. It woiked. The only thing we caught was shahks. The next time they said, 'Let's go shahk fishin'. We'd get back and cut up the steaks, 'cause back then these guys came out to Montauk for meat. I was chummin' people with the twist of a woid, from sport fishin' to monster fishin'."

Mundus and Donnie Braddock, another captain, caught a 3,450-pound, sixteen-foot eight-inch great white shark forty miles off Montauk in 1986. Nicknamed "Big Guy," it reportedly remains the biggest fish ever caught with a rod and reel. This broke Mundus's own record for a great white that he harpooned off Amagansett in 1964. The head of that fish hangs above the bar at Salivar's on Lake Montauk.

Robert Boggs wrote another book about Mundus, *Monster Man*, and Mundas has participated in shark-hunting documentaries on the Discovery Channel. (His website, which emphasizes that the role of Quint in *Jaws* was based on him—and laments that he didn't receive a penny for it—is fmundus.com.) He left Montauk in the early 1990s after selling off his possessions in a sort of yard sale held on the town dock in Lake Montauk. When not on the water, he lives on a macadamia nut farm in Hawaii. [*]

One captain from 1951 is still active in Montauk. At eighty-one, Bob Tuma is the oldest charter-boat captain on Long Island still going out into the Atlantic. He still rises at 5 A.M. every day and has no lack of customers. One of his daughters, Debbie, is a reporter for the *New York Daily News*. His cousin, Frank, left the fishing business and now operates a real estate company.

Paul Forsberg, Carl's son, now runs the Viking Fleet, which operates ferries in Montauk, Block Island, southern New England, and Florida.

In November 1951 a dinner was given in Lester Behan's honor by the Coast Guard Auxiliary of the Third District. At the dinner, Admiral Louis Olson awarded Behan a citation for rescuing twelve of the nineteen *Pelican* survivors. Behan's former mate, Bill Blindenhofer, did not attend.

At least one of Les's children, John Jr., was fascinated by fishing too, although he first enlisted in the Marine Corps. He was sent to Vietnam and won several medals, including a Purple Heart—while out on patrol, John stepped on a land mine, which blew off both his legs.

Back in Montauk, John became politically active and was eventually elected to the New York State Assembly. He represented the 2nd Assembly District in Albany for sixteen years, then in 1996 was appointed by Governor George Pataki as the state commissioner of Veterans Affairs. When he retired, he returned to live in Montauk.

Bill Blindenhofer continued to be troubled by what happened on the *Bingo II* on September 1, especially his self-perceived failure to rescue more passengers from the water. According to his son, Bill regularly woke up with middle-of-the-night sweats and heart palpitations, or sobbing and yelling. He once broke the bed table with his fist in a rage of remembered frustration. Essentially, Bill was suffering a nervous breakdown. He finally went to a doctor who prescribed sleeping pills. Eventually, Bill recovered. He earned his own captain's license in 1953. He bought the *Bingo II* from Les Behan and fished out of the Shinnecock Inlet. Bill and his wife also opened a small restaurant there; they had four children.

Harold and Jeanne Bishop and Jim Bolton were recognized in the press for their heroic rescue efforts, but they avoided the limelight.

A heartbroken Inger Perrson remained in Montauk and continued waitressing at the restaurant owned by the Pilbros, who were very kind to her. Eventually, she married the Pilbros' son, and the newlyweds moved to Texas. When last heard from by Montauk acquaintances, she was still there.

Howie Carroll also stayed in the fishing business, and shifted to being a charter-boat captain. He would not discuss his brother's death. When he died suddenly at age fifty-seven, his son, Howie Jr., took over the business and was a much-recognized figure in Montauk. A few years ago, he died of a heart attack, also at age fifty-seven. Rita Carroll resides in Montauk and remains an active volunteer in local history projects.

Angelo Testa Jr., age seventy-five when interviewed, has not set foot on a boat since September 1, 1951. "I still have nightmares," he says.

Martin Berger got married several years later. He named his son Lawrence.

Dozens of families lost children, parents, brothers, sisters, and other relatives who went out on the *Pelican* that Labor Day Saturday in 1951. Irene Stein lost her father and her husband, John. For days after the *Pelican* capsized, Irene scanned the daily newspapers and waited for the phone to ring, expecting to learn that John had been picked up by a commercial fishing boat that had finally returned to Montauk. It was painful that when she spotted the name Stein in newspaper accounts of the accident; it belonged to Max, another passenger who was no relation.

"Each time," she recalled, "I knew they found him. But they never did."

On the eighth day after the capsizing, Irene attempted to commit suicide with an overdose of sleeping pills. She felt there was "no way out" for her. Her mother had died when Irene was nine. Her sister lived in Florida, and she and her brother, who lived in New Jersey, had never been close. At only twenty-five and with two young children, she felt overwhelmed.

Irene was found unconscious in her apartment that night by her brother-in-law Adolph Stein. He cared for her during her recovery, and eventually they married. They had a child, and the five of them moved to Long Island. Adolph died in 1973. Now in her late seventies, Irene continues to work as a monitor in the Shoreham-Wading River school district and enjoys visits with her eleven grandchildren.

One day a class from the school returned from a daylong field trip to the Montauk Lighthouse. The children excitedly reported to Irene that they had "seen her there," referring to a posted *Newsday* article about the *Pelican* tragedy that included a photograph of her. She has visited Montauk several times since.

A few items from the *Pelican* can be found at the marine museum in Amagansett, operated by the East Hampton Historical Society. A porthole and a banner with the word *Pelican* were donated years ago by those who found the items washed up on a beach in Montauk.

Several days after the disaster, the *Pelican* was towed around Montauk Point and across Block Island Sound to Greenport, on the North Fork of Long Island. There the boat was put in dry dock at Sweet's Shipyard.

The *Pelican* remained there for decades. As memories of the incident faded, the boat became little more than a curiosity. Wind, rain, and other elements stripped away its paint and eroded its wood and metal. Pieces of it separated from each other, and it looked ready to fall over. Young children threw rocks at it and tore off protruding pieces of wood, and teenagers used it at night for drinking or making out.

As part of coming to terms with his father's death, John Stein Jr., who became a public school teacher and lived on Long Island in the late 1970s, went in search of the *Pelican*. After visiting numerous shipyards, he was told about the old rotting boat in Greenport. He found the *Pelican*, the name on the hull faded but still legible. He climbed aboard and ripped out an eight-foot section of planking, which is still at his house in New Jersey.

Seeing the *Pelican* that day in Greenport brought back memories.

"I actually have two memories of my father," Stein says. "We used to play with little lead army World War II soldiers on the bed. The other [memory] was a certain kind of candy, little raspberry candies that were wrapped up. And I remember him not coming home, and me wondering, What's going on? I remember that feeling, and my mother was gone for a while too, and [I was] feeling abandoned. That was something that didn't leave for a long time.

"My uncle Rudolph, who was on the boat and survived, and I were never really close. But he was a very nice guy and very family oriented. When I was eighteen he asked me to forgive him. I couldn't think of why. So he told me about when the boat capsized and he found himself in the water, and he tried to get away from the boat. People were pulling on him, dragging him under, and he was beating them with his hands and he couldn't see and he said to me, 'One of them could've been your father.' He wanted to be forgiven for that. I couldn't imagine a man carrying this guilt inside him for that many years. And of course I did forgive him."

Forty years after the capsizing, a developer intent on building waterfront condominiums purchased Sweet's Shipyard in Greenport. Sweet's was shut down, and the owner suggested to the Greenport Fire Department that it burn the shipyard as part of a fire drill. That is exactly what happened.

Renee Carey, the telephone operator who first fielded calls about the *Pelican* disaster, was married to the Greenport fire chief when the fire drill took place. When her husband came home that day after the drill, he said, "God bless those people. And now it's gone."

IN MEMORIAM—THE VICTIMS

Constantin Acevedo
Isaac Beja
Lawrence Berger
Alvin Brown
John Carlson
Edward Carroll
Cynthia Chamades
Armas Dolk
Charles Drew
Solomon Finkelberg
Victor Finkelberg
Harold Fried
Helen Friedel
John Friedel
John Furness
George Hermanns
Harold Hertzberg
William Hoak
James Hyslop
Charles Knight
Andrew Kolesar
Robert Lawrence
Frank Laurenzana

Raymond Lewis
Harold Lolli
Wallace Manko
Frank Marino
William Mellardo
Grover Menton
Cornelius Norrington
Patrick O'Brien
Theodore Ogburn
Harold Pinckney
Manuel Ramirez
Frank Rubano
Sisinio Salvaterra
Gordon Sellons
George Short
Louis Sigal
John Stein
Joseph Stern
Angelo Testa Sr.
Nicholas Trotta
George Wallace
Edmund Charles White

THE SURVIVORS

Martin Berger
Antonio Borruso
Costas Candalanos
Antonio De Jesus
Richard Friedel
William Friedel
Seymour Gabbin
John Griffin
Stanley McKeegan
Stanley Olszewski
Robert Scanlon
Renee Sherr
Albert Snyder
Max Stein
Rudolph Stein
Ben Tasman
Angelo Testa Jr.
John Vallone
Cynthia Zurendorf